PRAYING | PRAYING
ON PURPOSE | FOR RESULTS

How Men Prevail With God

KEN RAGGIO

Praying On Purpose – Praying For Results
How Men Prevail With God

By Ken Raggio

ISBN-13: 978-1475262179
ISBN-10: 1475262175

Edited by Pam Eddings

All scripture quotations in this book are from the Authorized King James Version of the Bible unless otherwise noted. Emphases on quotes in this book are mine.

For Information, Contact:
Ken Raggio, 3312 Hwy 365, #219, Nederland, Texas 77627

VISIT my major WEBSITE at: http://kenraggio.com
Read my BLOG at: http://kenraggio.blogspot.com
FOLLOW ME on TWITTER: http://twitter.com/kenraggiocom
FRIEND ME on FACEBOOK: https://facebook.com/ken.raggio.9
LIKE my FACEBOOK FanPage: Ken Raggio Bible Resources

Dedication

I dedicate this book to anyone who will have it.

The fact that you have taken this book in hand gives me hope that you may become one of the desperately-needed prayer intercessors for this last generation. I pray that you will be.

Most of us living today are likely to see the Lord Jesus coming in the clouds to harvest His Saints and reclaim the kingdoms of men.

Paul warned that "in the last days perilous times shall come." The days ahead are sure to be days in which prayer may actually become a nearly sole means of survival.

There will be days when you will certainly not want to be inept in prayer.

If you have not yet joined the army of God's prayer warriors, consider this your draft notice.

In Jesus' name, I call you to a life of prayer and intercession.

I call you into the company of the greatest praying men and women of all the ages.

If you will answer the call, I pledge to give you my very best efforts in the pages that follow, to inspire you, motivate you and teach you how to pray.

Ken Raggio
November 13, 2012

Contents

"The Church is looking for better methods;
God is looking for better **men**.

The Holy Ghost does not flow through methods,
but through **men**.

He does not come on machinery,
but on **men**.

He does not anoint plans,
but **men**;

...**men of prayer**."

E. M. Bounds
1835-1913

"While others still slept, He went away to pray
and to renew His strength in communion with His Father.

He had need of this, otherwise
He would not have been ready for the new day.

The holy work of delivering souls demands
constant renewal through fellowship with God."

Andrew Murray
1828-1917

"What, could ye not watch with me one hour?"
Jesus

I Give Myself Unto Prayer

The Psalmist David was deeply distressed because some of the people he loved more than anyone else in the world had become vicious enemies. His heart was crushed.

In his anguish, he exclaimed, "But I give myself unto prayer," Psalm 109:4.

Praying was David's way of handling the enormous difficulties of life that weighed so heavily on his heart.

PRAYER.

For every crisis, prayer is the God-ordained remediation tool. Prayer alone gives us access to every divine remedy.

I do not speak of prayer as a monotonous pouring forth of verbiage - worthless!

Prayer is a profound, sacred act that articulates to our holy God the great desires of our hearts.

We think that prayer is an opportunity to tell God about our NEEDS. But His Word says that **He already knows what we have need of**.

> "Your Father knoweth what things ye have need of,
> before ye ask him."
> *Matthew 6:8*

So the greater value of prayer is NOT the articulation of NEEDS, but rather, the articulation of our DESIRES.

Prayer formally expresses our DESIRES to God, and anticipates that He will intervene miraculously and supernaturally because we have asked.

Praying on Purpose

Prayer is in itself an act of faith. If you did not believe that God would hear, you would not pray.

Nothing on earth has more potential than prayer. The timeless adage says, "Prayer changes things." Well, it does. And here is why:

Prayer takes us immediately from our mortal environs into the Presence of our infinite, eternal God. Prayer engages the omnipotent God in our need. Prayer knocks on Heaven's door, and it opens every time.

> "I say unto You, Though he will not rise and give him,
> because he is his friend, yet **because of his importunity**
> he will rise and give him as many as he needeth.
> And I say unto You, **Ask, and it shall be given You**;
> seek, and ye shall find; knock, and it shall be opened unto You.
> For every one that asketh receiveth; and he that seeketh findeth;
> and to him that knocketh it shall be opened."
> *Luke 11:8-10*

When we pray, we engage infinite divine power. That does not imply that God is ignorant, or is not already moving in our behalf, because **He has always known** exactly how He would answer your problem.

> "Known unto God are all his works from the beginning of the world."
> *Acts 15:18.*

But when we present our supplications directly to God, we precipitate - set into motion - all the same miracle-working power that created the universe in the very Beginning.

What God has done with WORDS alone throughout the ages can be done again and again just as easily. Even things that have never been done can be done by the mere Word of our God. There is nothing He cannot do.

And what He has done for others, He will do for you.

If you walk through a grand hotel lobby and step into the revolving door at the entrance, you set into motion something that forces you to follow through. As you push your way into a revolving door, you must carefully move forward with the flow of the motion, or you may be struck by the door. Anyone who attempts to pass through the revolving door at the same time must conform to the same momentum that you have initiated.

When you begin to pray, you are pushing against a revolving door. You are setting something into motion that takes on a momentum of its own. You are saying to God, "I want or I need something to be done from Your world. I am stepping out of my world into Your world, in search of a miracle."

From that moment, the door is in motion. You are now entering into His Holy Presence. It is impossible for Him not to notice your approach or register your request, because He is omniscient - all knowing. He SEES you, and He HEARS you. Never doubt that.

Your prayer forces a divine response. By the many promises that He has made throughout history, God has forever obligated Himself to respond to any man or woman who diligently seeks Him in faith, in Spirit and in truth.

"Ye shall seek me, and find me,
when ye shall search for me with all your heart."
Jeremiah 29:13

You may think that God does not hear you when you pray, but nothing could be further from the truth. Oh, He hears you. Someone has already said that God hears every prayer, and His answer will be one of the following: "Yes." "No." "Wait." or "Do it yourself."

Perhaps there are even more possibilities. Maybe God is willing to do one thing you ask, but He disapproves of something else. Maybe the answer will be a negotiated settlement, or a compromise. Who can know what will happen until you press against the door and set something into motion?

Once you have prayed in faith, something HAS to happen. ALL PRAYER gets God's attention. Now, I didn't say that all prayer gets exactly what you wanted. Anybody knows that you don't always get everything you ask for in prayer. **God knows best.** But that is no excuse for not asking.

Praying on Purpose

In this book, we will look at prayer from just about every conceivable angle - forward, backward, right-side-up, upside-down, inside and out. There are countless dimensions of prayer, and even an astute, seasoned prayer-warrior should be able to find something here to benefit from. At the least, you should discover things that you may have never considered before.

I want to tell you from my own personal experience that I would prefer to give up anything I can think of ahead of giving up prayer. Prayer has been my consolation of last resort more times than I can name. Don't take away my ability to pray. Actually, you cannot.

Even a disabled man confined to his bed can still pray. Even an incarcerated criminal can pray. Rich and poor can pray. Healthy or handicapped can pray. Young or old can pray. Red, yellow, black or white can pray. American, African, Hispanic, European, Asian, or any other can pray.

If you can think, you can pray. You can pray standing up or kneeling down. You can pray in the kitchen, the bedroom, the bathroom, the shower, in the car, in the office, or outdoors.

You can pray out loud. You can scream a prayer. You can whisper a prayer. You can pray without moving your lips.

You can pray in English, Chinese, Spanish, Russian, Arabic, Bengali, Portuguese, Malay, Japanese, German, Korean, French, Dutch, Swahili, Yiddish, Hebrew, or any language known to man. You can write a prayer, or type a prayer. You can scribble a prayer in the sand.

You can pray at breakfast, lunch or dinner. You can pray at 3:00 PM or at 3:00 AM. You can pray in the dark. You can pray in private. You can pray in a crowd. **The most important thing is that you CAN pray.** When you pray, you will never be the same again.

Prayers never die. In Heaven, the smoke from the Golden Altar of Incense, accompanying and symbolically representing the prayers of all the saints, ascends before the Throne of God forever and ever.

Praying for Results

"Another **angel** came and **stood at the altar**, having a golden censer;
and **there was given unto him much incense,**
that **he should offer it with the prayers of all saints**
upon the golden altar which was **before the throne.**
And the smoke of the **incense,**
which came with the prayers of the saints,
ascended up before God out of the angel's hand."
Revelation 8:3-4

Your prayers are among these prayers mentioned in the Bible. Your mother's prayers, your father's prayers, your grandmother's prayers, even those who are now deceased - their prayers still ring in the ears of God.

I am of the opinion that the reason God has ordained incense to accompany our prayers is because **our prayers are not always pleasant. Sometimes our prayers are unsavory**.

Our prayers deal with the most unpleasant stenches of our lives. Sometimes our prayers are about the nastiest, ugliest, most offensive problems we have to face. Sometimes we are literally humiliated to have to bring our problems to God because they stink!

But in Heaven, the angels of God offer Heavenly incenses – sweet fragrances before the Throne – so that Almighty God will be enticed to hear and answer even our ugliest, most nauseous prayers.

What on earth can you do that has more eternal value than prayer?

What can you do for your spouse or your children that will benefit them more than prayer?

You may bequeath a fortune to your descendants, if you can, but you cannot give them a more valuable gift than prayer. Even if you are poor, you can give a priceless gift to your loved ones by praying for them.

I've seen prayer touch the heart of God to heal just about any sickness or malady you can imagine.

After praying, I've seen chronic skin diseases healed overnight. I've seen tonsillitis healed on the spot, and high fevers broken instantly. I've seen heart attack victims healed, and heart damage and brain damage reversed. I've watched comatose victims wake up, cancer victims cured instantly, blind eyes see, deaf ears opened, and cripples walk. **Yes, I really have**!

I have seen prayer bring miraculous sums of money in the mail. Prayer can save a house from foreclosure. Prayer can prevent a bankruptcy. Prayer can save a marriage. Prayer can bring a wandering child back home.

Prayer can deliver an alcoholic or a drug addict or a prostitute. Prayer can move a rebel to contrition. Prayer can save an endangered flight, prevent a crash landing, or make an engine run without gas. Prayer can stop bullets, prevent a bomb from going off, or stop a wild animal from attacking.

Prayer can change the mind of a judge, or a jury, or make a plaintiff drop the charges. Prayer can silence a maniac, cheer the depressed, or comfort the grieving. Prayer can call down an army of angels.

Why pray? **Why NOT pray?**

What can you do that is a better investment of your time? What can you do that can work in any kind of weather, in any season, under any circumstances, like prayer?

"God doesn't answer my prayers!" you may object. Well, I've got news for you. God most certainly does answer your prayers. Look backwards, right this moment at one of your recent prayer requests. So you say that you prayed and nothing happened.

Let's analyze that for a moment. Nothing happened? God didn't hear? Sure He did. THAT happened. But you didn't get what you asked for.

Then what did happen? God may have decided not to respond to you at that particular time. That doesn't mean that He is not going to give you what you ask. It may mean that He is going to put some time between your request and His response.

Praying for Results

Haven't you ever heard of **delayed gratification**? It is one of the greatest human lessons.

Almost nothing in life gives consistently immediate results.

Most things take time.

- **Plant a garden.** Does it come up overnight? No.
- **Go to college.** Do you get your degree overnight? No.
- **Court a lover.** Will he or she marry you on the first date? No.

What do you know of in life that gives consistently immediate answers? Not the government. Not the school system. Not the doctor or the hospital. Not the bank. Not the insurance company.

Everybody puts you off. Everybody takes their time.

Why? Because **work takes time**. Tests have to go to the lab. The papers have to be filed. Reports have to be generated. Checks have to be written and mailed. Everything takes time.

Just because you prayed and didn't get exactly what you wanted as soon as you got up off your knees, don't think that God isn't working.

> He may not come when you want Him,
> but He will ALWAYS come on time.
> He knows the best time to show up.

Meanwhile, God may be answering your prayer, and you don't even realize it. Maybe He is working on somebody you don't even know to bring the results to you. Maybe He is healing something quietly, and you may not know the results until later. Maybe He is turning the world upside-down, but you can't see what He is doing, so you don't think He's doing it. Just wait and see.

Just don't EVER stop praying. The one prayer you fail to pray may be the prayer that would have turned your world around. Maybe YOUR prayer would have saved that loved one. Maybe YOUR prayer would have prevented that crime down the street. Maybe YOUR prayer would have prevented that car crash.

How can you get results if you never set them into motion? Prayer sets things into motion. Prayer is like lighting the fuse on a firecracker. Sooner or later, it has to go off.

In this book, I want to show you how to be a powerful prayer warrior. I will show you a variety of ways to pray. I will suggest whole lists of things for you to pray for. I will show you how to plan your prayers for maximum effectiveness. I will even provide some "prayer starters" to help you get started.

If you will be sure to finish this whole book, I promise that you won't be the same by the time you have read the last page. Just don't lay it down unless you have to. Read this book until you are finished with it, and you won't regret the time you have taken. That's my promise to you. I believe that there are several things in this book that will help you.

As you read it, underline statements that speak to you. Write your own thoughts in the margins. Make notes of important points in the front or the back of the book, and include the page numbers so you can go back and read them again later.

You are going to be different after you have read this book. You are going to be a prayer warrior. In Jesus' name.

"All true religion beginneth with fervent prayer:
Or thus, That when men begin to be servants to God,
they begin it with calling upon Him.
Thus did Saul [who became Paul,
for Ananias was to "inquire at the house of Judas
for a man from Tarsus named Saul, at which he observed],
'Behold he prayeth' (Acts 9:11).
And, 'Lord have mercy upon me.'
is the first of the groans of a sanctified heart."
John Bunyan
1628-1688

Chapter 1

Daily Intercession

You have to PLAN to pray every day of your life. It's not good enough to tell yourself that you will pray when you get a chance or an impulse. You must not let yourself off the hook like that. Real prayer warriors **pray on purpose** and they **pray for results**. Prayer warriors are both deliberate and intentional. Praying is very serious business to them.

Every one of us gets busy, and when we get busy we don't pray. Prayer is far too important to be relegated to such lackadaisical treatment, or such low priority. If the only time you pray is when you get some high-quality free time, you are going to die prayerless.

You have to get it in your heart that IT IS A SIN NOT TO PRAY.

> "Prayerlessness is a sin."
> *Corrie Ten Boom*
> *1892-1983*

You cannot convince me otherwise. Here is why.

Samuel was one of the best role models in the Bible. He was a real man of God from start to finish. He guided Israel from their tribal, nomadic way of life to become a divinely-ordered nation-kingdom; not by his political or social skills, but **by his praying**.

Samuel said,

> "God forbid that I should **sin against the LORD in ceasing to pray**
> for you: but I will teach you the good and the right way."
> *1 Samuel 12:23*

Did you get that? Samuel believed that if he ceased to pray for the people, he would be committing a sin against God!

Maybe you don't want to believe that prayer is that essential in the will of God, but I am telling you now that it is.

If you have children, and you don't pray for them, you are sinning against God. If you have any kind of Christian background, you probably had your babies dedicated to the Lord while they were still infants. But that isn't good enough. You have to take it upon yourself to be a life-long intercessor for those children.

I am not talking about taking their hands and saying a sweet, poetic prayer around the dinner table. That's good and OK, but that is NOT the kind of prayer they need. Your kids are going to need a lot more prayer than your saying grace over the dinner.

A bloodthirsty horde of Hell's angels are going to try to destroy your children before they are grown and living for God. Satan is going to test them, try them, and tempt them with every conceivable type of evil.

Somebody must take the responsibility of putting a prayer covering over those children.

If YOU don't do it, who will? If YOU don't do it, it's not going to get done!

You are their Daddy. You are their Mother. You are the one who has the highest responsibility on earth for those precious little humans, and YOU are the one who will answer to God for their souls if for any reason they are taken early in life. You are responsible for their souls until they become old enough to give account for themselves.

Don't risk a tragedy or calamity coming into your life without knowing far in advance that you have committed everything to God in prayer. Your prayers cannot guarantee you that there will never be a calamity or a tragedy in your life, but they will guarantee that God will be right there on the scene, working miraculously in your behalf through every test and trial. People who don't pray are heavily exposed to life's hazards.

Prayer is something like wearing seatbelts. Maybe you don't like to wear seatbelts. But if you ever see someone who has been maimed or killed because they flew through an automobile windshield like a two-hundred pound projectile - only because they didn't have their seatbelts fastened - then you will quickly understand why you should always wear a seatbelt, and you will sense the urgency to do so.

By the same kind of logic, if you ever compare the lives of families who are constantly under an effective prayer covering to the lives of families who never pray - there simply is no comparison.

A prayerless home is so heavily exposed to the forces of Hell and is at such an extremely high risk to complete devastation that it is frightening. It is far worse than seeing an F-5 tornado utterly destroy your house and suddenly realizing that your insurance policy was not in force. A prayer covering is like an insurance policy. It warrants that you have maintained open and honest lines of communication with God, and He is looking out on your behalf.

**GOD FORBID that I should sin against the LORD
by ceasing to pray for those God has given to me**.

My prayers warrant that intercession has already been made for those I love in the event of hard times that are certain to come. My prayer premiums are paid up.

"You can do more than pray after you have prayed,
but you cannot do more than pray until you have prayed."
John Bunyan
1628-1688

"If parents should thus make themselves advocates
and intercessors with God for their children,
constantly applying to Heaven in behalf of them,
nothing would be more likely not only to bless their children,
but also to form and dispose their own minds to the performance
of everything that was excellent and praiseworthy."

"If a father were daily making particular prayers to God,
that He would please to inspire his children with true piety,
great humility, and strict temperance,
what could be more likely to make the father himself
become exemplary in these virtues?
How naturally would he grow ashamed of [lacking] such virtues,
as he thought necessary for his children!
So that his prayers for their piety would be a certain means
of exalting his own to its greatest height."
William Law
1686-1761

Chapter 2

No Time to Pray

Don't say that you don't have time to pray.

You have time to watch television. You have time to watch movies. You have time to surf the Internet by the hours. You have time for football. You have time for Little League baseball, soccer, Scouts. You have time for tinkering in the garage. You have time to bake cookies and cakes and enormously fattening things that you don't need to eat. You have time to fish, hunt, four-wheel, and vacation.

You most certainly do have time to pray. You have the same twenty-four hours a day that every great prayer warrior in history had. If you don't have time to pray because you are going to the gym three times a week, then stop going to the gym. I'm dead serious. You don't have your priorities right.

Prayer deserves your best time.

The eternal significance of prayer more than justifies cancelling or lowering other "priorities" that may not be legitimate priorities at all.

Why do you invest more in your mortal body than in your eternal soul?

Your body is going to die someday, and all those well-toned muscles are going to rot in a grave. But your soul is going to spend eternity either in Heaven or in Hell. That is an infinitely higher priority that only a fool would ignore or neglect.

On the other hand, if you really do put prayer in its right priority, you may or may not find the time to go to the gym. That will really reveal what your priorities are. Don't use the gym as an excuse not to pray. If you don't set that priority, God may have to mess with your gym thing to get your attention. I know what I'm talking about. I have seen it happen.

Praying on Purpose

You have to PLAN to pray every single day of your life. You have to get it in your head. You have to burn those circuits into your brain cells that the day is not going to end without your praying.

You must be predisposed - pre-programmed - to pray consistently.

I am sure that somebody reading this will probably start squirming right now and feel the urge to throw this book on the floor, but don't do it. Stay with me. I will show you exactly how you CAN pray every single day. It is NOT going to kill you. It's not even going to hurt you. It is going to bless and revolutionize your whole life, because as you give yourself to prayer, your relationship with God is going to flourish and enter a new dimension.

I pray every day. Only very rarely do I miss a day, and when I do, I try to make up by spending more time in prayer the following day. That is not a facetious or silly notion. It is a pact I have made with myself. I have certain demands that I make of myself in prayer, and that is one requirement.

I refuse to let myself off the hook. If I did not pray like I know I should have prayed yesterday, then I demand more of myself today. That self-imposed requirement helps persuade me not to miss a day.

Somebody says, "That is just legalism!" Well, I absolutely, emphatically deny AND denounce that charge. It is not legalism to make extraordinary demands of yourself to pray.

In EVERY area of life, secular **people make demands of themselves**. In sports, in fitness, in diet, in money management, in career paths, in education, in the corporate environment, people make demands of themselves. They establish quotas for themselves. They raise the bar. They stretch. They set goals. They max themselves out to achieve and accomplish more. It is downright amazing how people will **stretch** themselves, even **exhaust** themselves, for a pay raise or special recognition.

It is a cheap and devious insult - even an assault - to accuse a child of God of being legalistic when he or she makes serious or uncommon demands of themselves when it comes to prayer, or godly living. If he RUNS an hour every day, he is praised, but if he PRAYS an hour a day, he is a radical, extreme legalist? Something about that value system is seriously flawed.

Praying for Results

Why is it commendable when athletes or business executives show over-the-top commitment, but when Christians show over-the-top commitment, they are "legalistic!"? **Somebody tell me!**

Why do we bestow awards, outrageous wealth, and celebrity status to people who sell their souls to achieve worldly accomplishments, but speak disparagingly of Christians who sell their souls to do the will of God?

At the least, a Christian has a divine mandate for his commitment. A Christian has a Heavenly edict, not to mention a promise of eternal rewards. Jesus said,

"Whosoever will come after me, **let him deny himself**,
and take up his cross, and follow me.
For **whosoever will save his life shall lose it**;
but whosoever shall lose his life for my sake and the gospel's,
the same shall save it.
For **what shall it profit a man, if he shall gain the whole world,
and lose his own soul?**
…Whosoever therefore shall be ashamed of me
and of my words in this adulterous and sinful generation;
of him also shall the Son of man be ashamed,
when he cometh in the glory of his Father with the holy angels."
Mark 8:34-38

"Every one that hath forsaken houses, or brethren, or sisters,
or father, or mother, or wife, or children, or lands, for my name's sake,
shall receive an hundredfold, and shall inherit everlasting life."
Matthew 19:29

Too many people do what they do for fleeting fame and perishable rewards, so I refuse to apologize or make excuses for setting the highest standards for myself to pray and live godly. There is nothing wrong with setting prayer quotas for myself. It is not wrong to do right.

I must not neglect to pray as I should.

The people that I pray for NEED those prayers. Of all the people I pray for again and again, a huge percentage of them have NO ONE ELSE praying for them. If I stop praying for many of the people on my list, they will have NO INTERCESSOR on earth pleading for their souls to be saved. When I remember that fact, I am persuaded again to pray on.

I don't want anybody I know to go to Hell - not even my worst enemy.

Hell is a horrifying place. More and more Christians and Churches are evading the subject of Hell. Surveys have shown that many professing Christians say they don't believe that Hell is a real place. But if you don't believe in Hell, you don't believe in Jesus Christ, because Jesus taught more about Hell than any other person in the Bible.

For the record, I believe every Word in the Book, and I believe that there is a real, eternal, burning Hell where there will be sorrow, and weeping, and gnashing of teeth.

God never intended for men and women to go to Hell. Hell was prepared for the Devil and his angels (Matthew 25:41). Rebellious angels were the first to provoke God's wrath. Since then, men have followed Satan's lures.

God looked for judgment and righteousness among men, but found instead oppressions, drunkenness, and so many vices.

> "Therefore **hell hath enlarged herself**,
> and opened her mouth without measure:
> and their glory, and their multitude, and their pomp,
> and he that rejoiceth, shall descend into it."
> *Isaiah 5:14*

The fact that men and women will be sentenced to Hell is an utterly terrifying reality. It is far and away the greatest tragedy in all of Creation.

How can you be at peace knowing that someone you dearly love may be destined for Hell? Are you in denial? Nobody wants their loved ones to go to Hell. But you had better get started praying for them now, because if you don't, a lot of the people who are near and dear to you are going to spend eternity in sorrow, pain and torment. How can you sit by prayerlessly, day after day, knowing that unless some of your loved ones have a big miracle, they will be tragically condemned?

Is it really more important to you, to be entertained by a television three or four hours every night, than to **get up and go into a spare room and pray** that God will save the people you love from an eternal damnation in Hell? Will your spouse or children think that you are losing your mind if you tell them you are going to the back room to pray for a couple of hours?

Well? Answer that to yourself right now.

Are you one of the people who complain day and night about the pathetic state of affairs in our nation and in our society? Are you sick of the moral depravity and the tragic absence of godly values among the younger people in our society? Then **YOU are the person** who must take it upon yourself to pray that God will CHANGE the state our world is in.

Read the vision that God gave the prophet in the ninth chapter of Ezekiel. It was about six men God sent to judge backslidden Jerusalem.

The Word of the Lord told one of them who had an **inkhorn** at his side to

"Go through the midst of the city, through the midst of Jerusalem, and **set a mark** upon the foreheads of the **men that sigh and that cry for all the abominations** that be done in the midst thereof," (9:4).

God wanted a mark set on the few **people who sincerely mourned** over the abominations that they saw being committed in their society. After **those who sighed and cried were marked on their foreheads**, God told the men to slay all those who did NOT have that mark. So **the people who were NOT IN SORROW** about the abominations of their city were judged. God instructed that they should be slain. They were destroyed because they were not as concerned about their loved ones as God wanted them to be.

What if God looked upon YOU and ME and said to an angel,

"**Set a mark** on them that sigh and that cry for the abominations."

Would you get a mark? Do you **sigh** and **cry** for the lost people in your city, or even those in your social circle? **Do you sigh and cry for your family, your loved ones?**

Praying on Purpose

The Bible clearly shows that God looks favorably upon men or women who carry the godly burden of intercession for a people, and He frowns upon those who do not.

If you want to shine in the eyes of God, then **take up the burden of the Lord.** Start caring about the things that God cares about, and stop caring so much about the trivial things of life.

> "The prayer that prevails is not the work of lips and fingertips.
> **It is the cry of a broken heart and the travail of a stricken soul.**"
> *Samuel Chadwick*
> *1860-1932*

Eternity will be horrific without God. I do not think that most people ever contemplate the unspeakable dread of being eternally separated from Him.

When I was twenty years old, I began praying that God would help me take the Gospel into every nation on earth. I have prayed that prayer literally thousands of times in my lifetime. As of this very day, my **"Today's Bible Study"** goes by email into 215 nations around the world. I have multitudes of readers in 236 nations. The total number of people who receive my Gospel writings every day are in the hundreds of thousands.

What if I had never prayed?

I'm still talking about "no time to pray." You DO have time to pray; you just have to admit it. **Admit it right now.**

"I DO HAVE TIME TO PRAY!"

"I WILL PRAY!"

> "In fact, I have so much [work] to do that
> I shall have to spend the first three hours in prayer."
> *Martin Luther*
> *1483-1546*

Chapter 3

Making a Prayer List

I've already told you that I plan to pray every single day. There are plenty of times when I wish I could opt out of my commitment because I have been so busy.

I have not made a vow to God that I will pray X number of hours each day.

The Bible says that it's better not to vow than to vow and not pay (Ecclesiastes 5:5). So I don't vow to God about how much or how often I am going to pray. But I set daily minimums for myself. I try earnestly to hold myself accountable for my prayer responsibilities and commitments.

I have always believed that if a man isn't accountable to himself, nobody else can force him to be accountable. If I can't make myself pray, you can't make me pray. But if I do make myself pray, you needn't worry about motivating me. I'm self-motivated to pray.

Every prayer warrior must be self-motivated. You must be a self-starter.

Can you find it in yourself to become self-motivated? You may not be able to get self-motivated to pray without some serious self-talk.

You are going to have to take a brutally honest look at your own life and your own priorities, and consider all the people who are important to you, and all the situations that you care about.

Get a writing pad, a tablet, a composition notebook, or anything to write or type on (or use your computer, iPad, or whatever you prefer).

Sit down somewhere alone, and begin to make a list of people and things that you know in your heart you should be praying for. As you write, tell yourself that **this is a very important list** you are making and that you are going to keep this list indefinitely and review it regularly. You have to convince yourself that this is not a game of trivial pursuit, but **this is very serious business before the living God.**

Either you believe you are going to make a difference by your praying or you don't. If you do believe, there is no better time to get started on a lifetime of genuine intercessory prayer than right here and right now.

As you make your first prayer list, you probably won't see very clearly how all the priorities are going to sort out.

Just **make the biggest, most general prayer list you can for starters**.

List everybody and everything that is important to you. Even if the list gets very, very long (and it probably will), don't hesitate or balk at it. **Just do it.** You won't be sorry.

I have many hundreds of people on my prayer list because I have been adding to that prayer list for many years. It has changed a lot over the years, but I have almost never removed anybody's name from my prayer list unless they passed away. I figure that if they are important enough to pray for one time, I should always pray for them, at least occasionally.

Oh, I know, this already sounds like it's going to be far too cumbersome.

You may think that this is way too radical, and if that's the way it's going to be, you'll go to the Christian bookstore and get somebody else's book about prayer. Go ahead, if you want to.

But if you will stay with me, with God's help, I'll teach you to become a powerful and more effective prayer warrior. And **if you EVER get to be a true prayer warrior**, believe me – it will be very transformational.

I resolved long ago, that no matter what life may dish out to me, no matter what trials and tribulations, no matter what deprivations or reversals -- I MUST continue praying. A lot of things in my life may change, but not my prayer life. That's one thing I don't ever want to lose. I might have to quit preaching, or quit singing, or even quit writing, but **I must never quit praying.**

Praying for Results

There is no discharge from this army.

> "[Jesus] spake a parable unto them to this end,
> that **men ought always to pray, and not to faint**."
> *Luke 18:1*

> "**Pray without ceasing.**"
> *1 Thessalonians 5:17*

Why? I've already said it once, but "prayer changes things."

Is there anything in your life right now that needs to be changed? **Pray about it.** Is there trouble with your job? **Pray about it.** Is there trouble with your family? **Pray about it.** Is there trouble with your financial status? **Pray about it.** Is there trouble with your marriage? **Pray about it.**

Whatever needs to be changed in your life, **that is your reason to pray.** Do your kids need God? Pray. Do your grandkids need God? Pray. Does your Church need a revival? Pray. Does your school or community need a spiritual awakening? Pray.

Make your list. Now. At least start it right now.

If you are faithful to the task, you will be adding to your list until Jesus comes. Get a good notebook that you will be happy to continue using for months and years to come. Spend some money if you have to. This prayer notebook is going to be one of your most important possessions.

You may want to make your prayer list in your computer. That is where I keep my prayer lists. You can put them in a Word Document, in a Task in Outlook, or use whatever software you choose (I recommend Evernote). If you carry an iPad, Smartphone, or a laptop, that will work wonderfully.

I often pray with my laptop in front of me. Maybe you think that doesn't sound very spiritual, but you would just have to hang around me during the days or nights when I am engaged in prayer.

Your computer is an excellent tool for creating prayer notes. You can print your notes periodically and use paper notes to pray with if you prefer.

Keep a separate list of miracles and answers to prayers that come as you pray. Believe me, they WILL come. God keeps His promises.

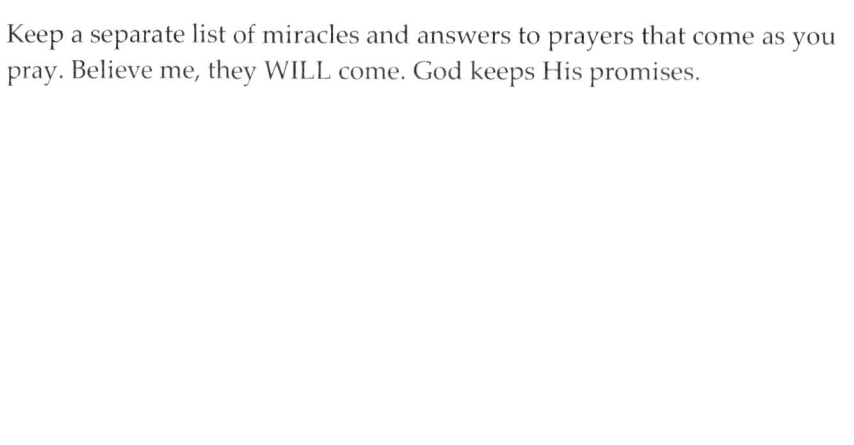

"The effectual, fervent prayer of a righteous man availeth much."
James 5:16

- *John Wesley was known to spend **two hours** in prayer every day.*
- *Martin Luther was known to pray **three hours** every day.*
- *When asked, **George Mueller** admitted to praying "**hours every day**."*

All three men profoundly influenced their generations and subsequent generations around the world to seek after the God of the Bible.

Chapter 4

Praying by Notes

This may seem controversial to some people. Maybe it doesn't sound spiritual enough to suggest that you pray with notes in front of you.

Well, consider this. The preacher preaches from his notes. The Sunday School teacher teaches from a book or from notes. School teachers and college professors teach from notes. Every student prepares for exams using notes. If your company sends you off to a seminar to get valuable training, you come home with a stack of notes that you refer to. Are those enough examples? Even the President of the United States delivers the State of the Union address reading WORD-FOR-WORD from notes!

Now, contrast that to the way that most people actually pray.

Let me qualify myself just a tad bit here. I've spent nearly my whole life in Church, around Bible-believing people, and I reluctantly confide to you that I have NOT been very impressed by the majority of prayer practices I have observed. Too many people really do not have good prayer habits.

I could give you a long list of ways NOT to pray! But I won't, at least not right here. I will give you a couple of examples, however.

Moaning, groaning, and saying "Hallelujah" 40 times, non-stop, is NOT effectual praying. In fact, it just might be an absolute waste of time.

If all you do when you pray is whine about how awful your life is, and you wear out the grace of God with your self-pity, you are not going to be very happy with the results you get, because that kind of praying is not likely to have any results at all.

Real prayer can be just as conversational as any conversation you have with your friends and acquaintances. But it must be FAR more than conversational.

Praying on Purpose

"You must pray with all your might.
That does not mean saying your prayers,
or sitting gazing about in Church or chapel with eyes wide open
while someone else says them for you.
It means fervent, effectual, untiring wrestling with God...
This kind of prayer, be sure the devil and the world
and your own indolent, unbelieving nature will oppose.
They will pour water on this flame."
General William Booth
1829-1912

Powerful praying must be focused, prioritized and specific.

If you typically spend an hour praying for only one or two things, you are probably missing the mark. I'm not saying that should never happen, because in some cases, you really SHOULD spend an hour praying about a great need. I'm only telling you that is not the most effective way to pray.

When you pray, believe that you will have what you ask, and expect that God is hearing and is going to answer your prayers. You don't have to have a nervous breakdown to pray an effectual prayer. You don't have to stress yourself into a digestive disorder or palpitations of the heart.

But you do have to pray earnestly, sincerely, and diligently.

Pray! Believe that your prayers are going to touch God's heart. They will, if you do it right.

The reason I argue in favor of praying by notes is because it helps me to pray for a LOT more of what I want to pray for. Maybe you have a photographic memory, but I don't. If I don't keep a list of names in front of me, I cannot possibly remember all the people I wanted to pray for. If your praying is always over the same little short list of things, you are missing the mark - big time.

When my wife, Dixie, died in 2003, I had something of an epiphany about prayer. I had observed her praying for years for people that she loved. She wanted God to save and help all of them. I knew that the people she was praying for were very dear to her. I also realized that when she died, many of those people no longer had any intercessor. The reason I know that is true is because there are so many people who have no association with or real link to a Bible-believing Christian. I am sure that many of the people on Dixie's prayer list had NO other intercessor beside her.

So, I vowed to myself that I would make a list of everybody I could remember her praying for. Many of those people were already on my prayer list, but several of them were not. Dixie's prayer list caused my list to be even longer than it was. I hesitated at first when I realized how much time it would take me to keep all those people in my prayers. But I made the commitment to myself, and after several years, I still pray for every one of those people over and over again.

Maybe you think that is a wasteful or unnecessary exercise. Well, I can think of a lot of things far more wasteful than prayer. I'd rather "waste" my time praying, than watching 200 TV episodes of "Wheel of Fortune," or spend hours listening to talk radio, or mindlessly surfing the Internet.

If I have said all my prayers for the day, there will still be time for other things. Just don't make excuses. Praying for people is not a waste of time. I can think of a zillion things that are less important than praying, and nothing more important.

"A most beneficial exercise in secret prayer
before the Father is to write things down exactly
so I see exactly what I think and want to say.
Only those who have tried these ways know
the ineffable benefit of such strenuous times in secret."
Oswald Chambers
1874-1917

"Why is there so little anxiety to get time to pray?

Why is there so little forethought
in the laying out of time and employments,
so as to secure a large portion of each day for prayer?

Why is there so much speaking yet so little prayer?
Why is there so much running to and fro, yet so little prayer?
Why so much bustle and business, yet so little prayer?

Why so many meetings with our fellow men,
yet so few meetings with God?

Why so little being alone, so little thirsting of the soul
for the calm, sweet hours of unbroken solitude,
when God and his child hold fellowship together,
as if they could never part?

It is this want that not only injures our own growth in grace,
but **makes us such unprofitable servants of Christ**."
William Reid
1888-1950

Chapter 5

Why People Do Not Pray

I am convinced that one of the primary reasons that well-meaning people fail to pray is because they get bogged down mentally when they try to pray. They try to pray, but the thoughts just won't come. They cannot think of what they need to be praying about. They just give up, and then afterward they feel really dissatisfied because they think they have failed.

Has this ever happened to you?

You should not have to feel like a failure after you have prayed. You should not have to get bogged down in prayer. The solution to that dilemma is to make notes ahead of time that will help you pray. You will eventually realize that praying by notes is NOT a crazy idea, but it is actually a very positive, helpful, and productive idea.

Our modern society is plagued by distractions that rob us of our focus. We must struggle to keep our focus in prayer and Christian living. That is one of the reasons I believe that every praying person should have a prayer list of all the people and things they are praying for.

Keep your prayer list available, and you will never run out of motivation to pray. You will discover that you are able to pray effectively again and again and again. Praying with notes will relieve the frustrations that you sometimes feel when you start to pray.

A written prayer list will help take you into a new dimension in prayer.

You WILL begin to see results immediately. I am telling you as forcefully as I know how -- you will be amazed at what God will do whenever you start taking this business of prayer seriously, and spend major, quality time with Jesus on a daily basis, talking to Him about the great needs in your life, and in the lives of others who are near and dear to you.

Praying on Purpose

Another major reason people don't pray is because they don't have real discipline anywhere else in their lives. Some people live by the seat of their pants. They never know from one day to the next what they are going to be doing with their lives. They live in endless chaos.

Most people do not pray 30 minutes about decisions that will affect them for 50 years.

That is all the more reason why you should pray. Getting your act together in prayer can be the beginning of a dramatic change in every other area of your life as well. I am convinced that praying people are better people. Praying makes you a better person, and for many, many reasons. Here are just a few:

- Praying people have a keener sense of priority.

- Praying people are more mindful of God's will about the details in their lives.

- Praying people are more aware of God's presence and how He is working in their behalf.

- Praying people are more sensitive to the needs of the people that are near and dear to them.

- Praying people are intercessory. They intend to make a difference, and they do.

- Praying people are more caring. They contemplate the needs of their loved ones and make supplication to God in their behalf.

- Praying people have more character. If you don't believe that, line up a thousand people who never pray beside a thousand people who pray daily (if you can find them) and just judge for yourself.

- Praying people are critical components in the home, in the family, in the Church, and in the community. They are the spiritual movers and shakers in the spiritual world – the Kingdom of God.

Praying for Results

Let me stop here and tell you a brief story relating to that last statement.

When I was just a kid in high school, back in Neanderthal times, all the kids called me "Preacher." I carried my Thompson Chain Reference Bible in the same stack with all my school books. Everybody knew I was a Christian. I wasn't a nag. I didn't make a big noise about being a Christian. I just was one. I believed in the Bible, and I prayed, and all those things. I had a few Christian friends that I stayed around.

I did not hang out with the popular crowd. They did their thing, and I did mine. But one day, there was a tragedy in the school. One of the most popular guys, a football player, was killed in an automobile accident. He and his girlfriend lost control and ran off the road into a roadside canal, and both of them drowned.

My phone started ringing. I couldn't believe my ears. It was several guys on the football team. They wanted me to accompany them to the funeral home. They were really upset about their friend being killed. I cannot explain how it happened, but those guys knew that I believed in God and that I prayed, and they wanted somebody like that to help them during their tragic time. I ended up chauffeuring four of them to the funeral. I was fortunate and privileged to be able to talk to all of them about God and give them some spiritual guidance - something that none of them were getting anywhere else.

You know exactly what I am talking about. You may not feel that you have any significance to some of your family or members of your community. BUT... have you ever noticed that when they need somebody to PRAY - you are the one they call? If not, it would do you good to bear down on your prayer life, so that others will come to believe that they can depend on you for your prayers.

I can't think of anything I would rather have than a reputation for being a prayer warrior. In these dark times of social and moral disintegration, the world desperately needs men, women and young people who do not find it uncomfortable to get alone with God for an hour or two each day and bombard Heaven in behalf of the endless list of needs that surround them on every hand.

Nothing could be more valuable to your family and friends than for them to know assuredly that you are their intercessor before God in prayer. You may not have money or means to help them in any other way, but if they know that you are actively and sincerely praying for them, you have done the biggest favor for them that anybody can do.

"If sinners be damned, at least let them leap to Hell over our bodies.
If they will perish, let them perish with our arms about their knees.
Let no one go there unwarned and unprayed for."
Charles H. Spurgeon
1834-1892

"Men may spurn our appeals, reject our message, oppose our arguments,
despise our persons, but they are helpless against our prayers."
J. Sidlow Baxter
1903-1999

Chapter 6

Priorities in Prayer

It's OK to have priorities in prayer. Obviously, you cannot pray about everything in the world every time you pray. You have to decide what things deserve to be prayed about every single day, and what things you will pray for less frequently -- maybe once each week, or once each month.

After a while, you will identify things that should go at the top of your prayer list, and things that have lower priority. Arrange your notes so that if your time is limited, you will at least pray for the people and things that are most important *every single day*.

Then, as often as you possibly can, pray for EVERYTHING in your notes, even the lowest priority things. You should be able to do that at least a few times each week.

When I do not have enough time to pray all my prayers, I pray for those that have highest priority first. I will never stop praying as diligently as I am able. I am absolutely committed to make intercession for everyone who is near and dear to me.

Remember Samuel. His conviction about his responsibility as an intercessor ran deep in his soul, and as a result, he changed his world.

I think I feel Samuel's sentiments exactly. God forbid that I should sin against Him by failing to pray for those that I am responsible to pray for, or who need my prayers the most!

I want to – and I must -- faithfully fulfill this sacred responsibility. I want to daily, faithfully, present these people to Him in earnest and expectant prayer.

Your prayer life will go through seasons. Things that you feel great urgency for today will eventually be relieved. Some things will cease to be a prayer priority after a while. God will answer many of your prayers, and you will no longer need to pray about them. Other situations will change, and you will no longer want to pray as you did about them.

Meanwhile, some of your lowest priorities will move up the list and become more important, possibly urgent. This is a natural course. Respect it. Adjust your prayers, your prayer notes and prayer time accordingly.

From time to time, reorganize your notes. You may have to rewrite them or at least edit them, if they are in a computer document.

Maintaining your prayer notes is a most WORTHWHILE expenditure of time. **Don't consider this a drudgery** or try to avoid it. If you want to maintain your effectiveness as an intercessor, you have to continually evaluate and adjust your priorities. If you are still praying with a three-month-old prayer list, you are probably not being most effective.

I am expecting to see Jesus face-to-face some day, and when I do, I want everyone I love to be right there with me. I already know that if I don't earnestly pray for them between now and then, that just isn't going to happen.

Your loved ones aren't going to be saved without a battle.

The adversaries of their souls never take a vacation.

I have heard a lot of people say that there will be no tears in Heaven. They console themselves by believing that they won't even remember all the loved ones who didn't make it. Surely, Heaven would not be so free of sorrow if we were mindful of all our loved ones who went to Hell.

But, I am not so sure that there won't be any tears in Heaven. I've looked pretty diligently through the scriptures, and I don't find that statement in the Bible. What I have found is that **God will** *wipe all tears from our eyes* (Revelation 7:17; 21:4).

That is a big difference. There WILL be tears in Heaven, but **God will wipe them from our eyes**. So, why will there be tears in Heaven? Maybe, just maybe, that half-hour of silence in Heaven (mentioned in Revelation 8:1) will be that unimaginably sobering moment when all the saints of God suddenly realize **how many of their precious loved ones did not make it into the Kingdom**, but foolishly squandered their opportunity to be saved.

I don't want you to fall out with me if you don't agree with that statement, but my point is that I feel very strongly that **we are not concerned enough** about making intercessory prayers for our loved ones.

I know this for a fact. I don't want ANY of my friends or loved ones to go to Hell. I especially don't want any of my children in Hell. I don't want any of my grandchildren in Hell. I don't know how I could bear the thought that I brought somebody into this world and then didn't give them all of the prayer and spiritual support that I could have given to see to it that they made Heaven their eternal home.

If you have children who have lost their way, I don't want you to feel that I am being harsh. God knows you are probably suffering enough to see them neglecting God. And I do realize that ultimately, every man is going to have to give account for himself before God. The sad reality is that we can't MAKE anybody get saved, including our own children.

But we can surely pray our hearts out for them in the hopes that God will find a way to talk sense to them before it's too late.

If I didn't think God could do miracles like that, I WOULDN'T PRAY! The very fact that I do pray for people is a vote of confidence that God is not only able, but also willing to do what I ask of Him.

So set your priorities. Organize all your prayer notes according to their priorities. You should have one group of things on your prayer list that you pray for every single day.

You can do a LOT of praying in 30-60 minutes if you pray with notes. It is NOT impossible or even impractical to pray for hundreds of people every single day, if you set your mind to it. I have done it for many years. Somewhere along the line, you just have to get it into your belief system that you really are capable of becoming a major intercessor and a true prayer warrior -- the kind that gets things done with God! **Never say never. You can do it.**

You may have three, four, five or more categories of priorities. You may have five or ten pages of notes that you pray through every day. You may have another five or ten pages that you pray through every other day. Then you may have another group of notes that you pray through once a week, or even once a month.

No matter how you organize your prayers, you will become a much more effective prayer warrior just because of the effort. You don't have to do it my way. I don't have to do it somebody else's way. Just make up your mind you are going to the next level with your praying, and you will.

"It is possible to move men, through God, by prayer alone."
Hudson Taylor
1832-1905

"Thus saith the LORD, the Holy One of Israel, and his Maker,
Ask me of things to come concerning my sons,
and concerning the work of my hands command ye me."
Isaiah 45:11

Chapter 7

Track Your Results

As time goes by, you will believe more and more in the power of prayer.

You will do good to keep an entirely separate set of notes just to record the miracles and answers to prayer that you receive.

I have a long list of miracles and things God has done for me and for those I love after praying for the needs. Sometimes, if I begin to feel like I'm wasting my time, it is a rich source of inspiration to re-read that list of miracles and answered prayers. It forces me to acknowledge again that God does hear and answer me when I pray.

Forgetfulness is usually the culprit. Most of us, if we took the time to really count our blessings, could sit for hours thinking of things that God has done for us, or blessed us with. But we neglect to recall all those wonderful blessings.

Whenever I begin to write out a list of all God's blessings to me, I just have to abandon it after a while, because I could continue writing all night long.

Did you sleep in a comfortable bed last night? Thank God.

Did you eat a good meal today? Thank God.

Has anyone you love shown their love for you lately? Thank God.

Has anyone called to see how you were doing? Thank God.

Does your car run well? Thank God.

Can you see? Can you hear? Can you read and write? Thank God!

Remember, one of the Bible prophecies of the spiritual decline in the last days warned that men would be unthankful (2 Timothy 3:2).

Unthankfulness is an ominous precursor to apostasy. When we forget what God has done, we tend to discount Him, and we gradually phase Him out of our lives.

I will guarantee you one thing. If you faithfully keep track of the good things God is doing in your life, of the prayers He has answered, and the miracles He is doing in your life -- you are not likely to backslide. But more than that, you will be more and more inspired to stay before the Throne of God with your prayers and supplications.

If it ever really gets into your heart just how many wonderful things God has done in your life as you have prayed and sought for His blessings, you will want to pray more and more as you get older.

I can't think of anything that motivates me to prayer better than the good results I have had through the years as I have prayed. If you ever pray for God to heal someone of shingles, and He does heal them, then you will be emboldened to pray for someone else who is suffering with shingles. It's almost a syndrome that we fall into.

Successful prayers are the greatest motivators for future prayers. You probably already know what I'm talking about.

I heard N.A. Urshan tell of how he got a reputation for praying for couples who could not have children. He said that he prayed for a young couple many, many years ago, and miraculously, they had a new baby the next year. He began to testify to others about that miracle, and other young couples came to him asking for prayer. Miraculously, many more couples began to have children. As the years went by, he was able to report many, many children had been born after he prayed. That is the kind of reputation I want. Not for the sake of reputation, but for the sake of those who have needs.

I can honestly say that I have seen an above-average number of skin diseases healed through the years. In 1979, I was pastoring a Church in a suburb of Atlanta, Georgia. I was called to pray for a lady at her home. She had been bedfast with shingles for weeks. From her waist to her feet, she was covered in painful scabs. Her two sisters were taking care of her, and they were the ones who asked for me to come and pray. When I walked into the room, I felt the presence of God. I did not make any small talk. I went directly into prayer.

These ladies were all Baptists, and didn't know much about the baptism of the Holy Ghost and speaking in other tongues. But wonder of wonders, I could not pray in English. As soon as I began to pray, the Spirit of God began to move me, and all I could do was pray in another tongue.

For several minutes, I stood by that lady's bed and softly prayed in tongues. I couldn't stop. I knew in my soul that a miracle was in the making. I just knew it. When I got through praying, I politely dismissed myself and left.

Early the next morning, the phone rang at the parsonage. It was one of the sisters. She was beside herself with excitement. She said, "We have been up all night long watching the scabs fall off her legs! Her legs are completely healed!" I was delighted, but I wasn't surprised. I could tell, even as I was praying, that God was going to do that miracle.

Since that miracle in 1979, I have seen as many skin diseases healed as any other kind of miracle. Several chronic cases where the doctors were frustrated and puzzled about what to do next were healed overnight after we prayed. Don't ask me why certain trends like this occur. I can only speculate that when you have seen God do a certain kind of a miracle, it emboldens you to believe for it the next time you see a similar problem.

That is one of the reasons why you should track your results. Write them down. Keep a record. Review your list of miracles from time to time. It will encourage you and renew your faith. It is the best thing I can think of for treating a bout of discouragement.

Recently, I remembered another amazing miracle that I had almost forgotten because I never wrote it down. In the early 1990s, I was pastoring in Birmingham, Alabama. I received a call one day from a lady in Florida. She told me that she had been searching diligently to find a Pentecostal minister who would help her. Her father had been sent to a hospital in Birmingham because it was the only place where they could find a surgeon willing to do a complex surgery on his spine. The man had a massive malignant tumor (about the size of a grapefruit) enveloping his spine in the lower back. The doctor planned to do major, but extremely delicate and dangerous surgery to remove as much of the tumor as possible.

I promised the lady that I would visit her father and pray with him. That evening, I drove across town to Medical Center East hospital and found the man alone in his private room. He had no family in town to attend him through the surgery. We talked for a while, and I told him that I would like to pray for him and ask God for a miracle. He welcomed my prayer enthusiastically. I laid my hand on his shoulder and asked God to do a miracle of healing for him, in Jesus' name.

His surgery was scheduled for the following morning. Early the next afternoon, I received another call from Florida. It was the man's daughter calling again. This time, she was utterly beside herself. She told me that just before surgery that morning, the surgeon had ordered another last-minute body scan to ascertain the size and position of the tumor before he opened him.

But the tumor was gone. Overnight, that giant tumor had completely disappeared. Not a trace. There was simply no possible explanation for its disappearance except that Almighty God had done a miracle for that man. They never performed the surgery, and he went back to Florida and lived many more years. Several years later, that same lady called me again because she wanted me to know that her Dad was still completely healed of that cancer, and she was still thanking God for it.

God has been exceedingly good to us, but we tend to forget it. If we don't write it down, many of the amazing things that God does for us will soon be forgotten.

Keep track of the miracles that God does for you as you pray. In years to come, your "Diary of Miracles" will be a great source of inspiration.

> "I live in the spirit of prayer. I pray as I walk, when I lie down
> and when I rise, and the answers are always coming."
> *George Mueller*
> *1805-1898*

Chapter 8

About Intercession

God said,

> "I sought for a man among them, that should make up the hedge,
> and stand in the gap before me for the land,
> that I should not destroy it: but I found none.
> Therefore have I poured out mine indignation upon them;
> I have consumed them with the fire of my wrath."
> *Ezekiel 22:31*

God consumed an entire generation of backsliders because nobody made the effort to turn them back to God. The only thing that troubles me more than the wrath of God demonstrated in those verses is the possibility that I might be the man who fails to stand in the gap for MY generation.

I don't think it's impossible for one man to make a huge difference. I can't think of a clearer example of that than **Moses' mother, Jochebed.**

If Jochebed had not made the effort to weave the little basket she placed baby Moses in; if she had not waterproofed it with pitch; if she had not risked her own life by attempting to save the male child alive in the first place (against Pharaoh's orders); then Moses would have never lived to become an adult.

Think about it.

No Moses. No Exodus. No burning bush. No rod turned into a snake. No confrontation with Pharaoh. No plagues upon Egypt. No Passover sacrifice. No Red Sea crossing. No fire on Mt. Sinai. No tablets with the Ten Commandments. No Tabernacle. No Promised Land. No Nation of Israel. No Christ.

Jochebed. One intercessor. One tiny thread.

An entire nation's survival hung on that tiny thread called Jochebed. The whole Bible came from a tiny thread called Jochebed. The entire Judeo-Christian civilization that we live in came from a tiny thread called Jochebed. Our modern rule of law came from that thread called Jochebed.

Don't EVER think that you don't count.

You count FAR more than you could ever possibly imagine. And the reality of it is that you will probably NEVER know how important your intercession is until you stand in the presence of Jesus Christ one day and hear Him say, "Well done!"

Then you will be able to look around the Heavenly multitudes and recognize all the people whose lives were clearly impacted by your godly role in this life.

By the same logic, your failure is just as profound. If you backslide, or neglect the purpose of God in your life, countless miracles that MIGHT have emanated from your life will never be done, including countless men and women whose lives might have been positively impacted, even saved for eternity. But if you fail, they may also be lost forever.

You must not fail.

Many years ago, I began an Internet ministry, long before most folks got involved in the Internet. In those days, you could find my articles on the first page of Yahoo's search results on just about any Bible subject. Over those years, countless millions of people from 236 nations - every nation in the world - have visited my website and read my articles on a wide variety of Bible subjects. I have tens of thousands of emails from people I have never met who have thanked me for writing them.

I can't wait to get to Heaven and discover what came out of all those efforts. Right now, because so many of my readers are in far-reaching places, distant from where I am physically, I can hardly lay a finger on many of the long-term results. But I still get a never-ending stream of letters every single day from around the world from people who read those articles and are blessed.

Praying for Results

I have prayed countless prayers for people who sent me their prayer requests, and I have received countless "Thank You!" letters and other testimonials when God heard those prayers and granted those requests. By now, I receive more letters than I can respond to.

But, do you know what? I believe I am going to be wonderfully surprised when I get to Heaven to see how many people were changed by the articles I have written, and the efforts I have made. And I don't think it will be limited to the people who emailed me. I expect that there will be multi-generational results from those efforts.

Many of those articles were translated into other languages and published in newspapers, magazines, Church bulletins, and taught in Bible Classes, Bible Colleges, Ladies Prayer Groups, preached as sermons and on and on. I have seen those articles appearing in French, Portuguese, Spanish, Filipino, Vietnamese, even Chinese. I cannot possibly imagine how many people have seen and read them.

That is what I mean by the power of ONE. So many men and women of God have made their mark without ever receiving recognition in this world, but don't ever think that God loses track of those efforts. God is not unrighteous, and He will not forget your labor of love in His service (Hebrews 6:10).

You may not be a preacher, a teacher, a singer, or a public figure of any kind. But you can pray. So help me God, **I don't believe ANYBODY holds a more important office in the work of God than a true intercessor.**

Eternity will be full of multitudes of people who came into the Kingdom of God because someone carefully interceded for their souls.

I must add one more observation on this subject, perhaps more important than the ones I have already made:

NOBODY GETS SAVED WITHOUT AN INTERCESSOR!

If you can prove me wrong on that statement, I challenge you to. If you can find one person who was ever saved without the influence of an intercessor, I'd like to know who it was and how it happened. That's like saying you were born without a mother! That just can't happen! SOMEBODY played a role in every single conversion, even if it was a distant influence.

So ask yourself this question: "For all the people I love and hold so dear - will I be their intercessor?" If you can't identify an intercessor for someone you love, then YOU may be their only intercessor! The extension of that logic says that if YOU don't do it, it won't get done.

So, it's up to you. Is your mother-in-law going to be saved? **It's up to you.** Is your boss going to be saved? **It's up to you.** Is your nephew going to be saved? **It's up to you.**

On one hand, it's a daunting task and an awesome responsibility. On the other hand, it's one of the most exciting privileges you will ever have! Just the possibility that YOU and you alone can stand before God's Throne and call that person's name in believing prayer, and touch the heart of God -- that is exciting! And when the results come in, that is the most joyous and gratifying experience on earth!

What is the price of a soul? The Bible said that **if a man gains the ENTIRE WORLD, but loses his soul**, he has not profited.

That tells me that **ONE SOUL is worth MORE than all the wealth in the entire earth**! One soul is worth more than all the diamonds, rubies, oil, uranium, minerals, cattle, livestock, all the harvests of all the crops on earth, and all the profits of all the stock markets, banking conglomerates, industries and corporations.

Just one soul. Your mother-in-law. Your nephew. Your boss. Worth more than three worlds just like this one.

So, are you going to try to intercede for them, or are you just going to sit there and watch some ridiculous, insulting, mind-numbing, immoral situation comedy on television tonight instead of praying?

"There is nothing that makes us love a man so much as praying for him."
William Law
1686-1761

Chapter 9

How to Intercede

I am going to do my best to help you become an intercessor. I have already tried to plow a furrow in your soul in an attempt to make you sensitive about your sacred responsibility to pray and intercede for others. Unless and until you get a holy burden to pray, you will not be a real intercessor.

I am a passionate person by nature. Things I believe in, I believe in with all my heart. Things I don't believe in, I detest. And I especially feel that way when it comes to prayer.

I don't know how to pray for things I don't sincerely care about. In fact, I usually don't.

It doesn't make sense to me for people to pray for things they really do not want or need. You have to care about something or someone before you can really make intercession for them. But it is not difficult to care if you first learn to consider people's needs from a Godly perspective.

Why do I pray for somebody with cancer if I am not their close friend? Because cancer hits really close to home with me. I lost the most precious wife a man could have to a monstrous cancer. So when I hear that someone has cancer, I can really relate to what they are going through, and I feel more compassion to pray for them.

Why, you may ask, didn't I get a miracle for my wife when she had cancer?

Do you really want to know? Hold on, and I will tell you what I think.

Dixie and I had just celebrated our 25th wedding anniversary when the doctors found that she had Stage 3 colon cancer. It had already metastasized to her lymph nodes. For over a year, she had, on three different occasions, asked her doctor to examine her, but he repeatedly told her that she was young and she had no reason to believe that she had anything to worry about, so he ran no tests.

We finally went to a different doctor for another opinion, and he found the cancer with the first test. They removed a large segment of her colon the next day and told us they thought they got it all. Sure.

I immediately went on a 21-day fasting and prayer vigil for Dixie. The doctor started her chemotherapy and radiation treatments. That went on for a year. That was a very, very difficult year, but she got through it, and her first-year exam was a good report. That was followed by four pretty good years. At the five-year mark, they told us she was cancer-free.

But that same month, she became desperately ill. She was lethargic and weak. The doctor told her that he thought she had contracted West Nile Virus. He told her to go to bed until it ran its course. Five weeks later, it still had not run its course. She could hardly get out of bed.

They ran a fresh CAT scan, and said they wanted to do exploratory surgery. On my fifty-first birthday, the doctor met me in the hospital counseling room and told me that he found cancer throughout her body, and there was nothing else he could do for her. The tumors were everywhere. He performed a colostomy, and two nephrostomies - tubes running out her back from her kidneys, and put her on oxygen.

The next thirteen months were Hell on earth. In over thirty years of ministry, visiting sick folks and hospitals and intensive care units, I had never seen anyone suffer the way Dixie suffered in her final stages. The cancer got into the sciatic nerves in her hips, and the pain was unspeakable. In her last months, she required vast doses of morphine through an intravenous pump to mask the pain. No doctor or nurse I have spoken to since that time has ever heard of anyone taking the massive doses of pain drugs that she took.

During Dixie's last year, I spent more time in prayer than in any one year of my life. I fasted 21 days for her on one occasion, and 30 days on another occasion. Many nights, while I attended to her at her bedside, I spent the entire night on the floor in prayer, asking God to heal her.

Praying for Results

You don't have to believe me, but I will tell you anyway that we never expected her to die. From the first day I learned she had cancer, I made up my mind to trust God for her healing. She did too. All the saints in the Church we pastored were there for us, too. Ministers and friends all over the country called and sent letters of prayerful support. Everybody believed that God would heal Dixie. Some preachers came hundreds of miles to pray for her and express their faith that she would be healed.

We never discussed her dying. Never bought a cemetery plot. Never discussed a funeral. We believed she was going to get well.

Maybe you think I'm crazy. But I have seen far too many inexplicable miracles in my day to doubt that God can do a miracle like that. I am absolutely certain that He can.

So, just about two weeks before Dixie died, one night as she lay in bed, and I was tending to her, she said, "If I die, it's because God has something He wants to do with you, and He needs me out of the way." She wasn't just saying that for naught. She really, really believed it. I am not saying that I agreed with her, because I really did not want to believe that was true. But I can never forget that statement.

In her last year, she was in and out of the hospital many times and had several brushes with death. Despite all that, she continued to attend Church faithfully. She only missed Church a very few times during that entire year. Finally, the tumors did so much damage that she could not stand up. We got a wheelchair for her. She missed Church that Sunday. After I got home from Church, I tended to her; we talked, and fell asleep at about midnight. About an hour later, I was awakened as she went into a seizure. Twenty minutes later, as I sat beside her, holding her in my arms, she simply stopped breathing. It was the wee hours of Monday morning.

I called my children, and they came immediately. Then I called the mortician. And it was all over.

I went into shock. I didn't realize it at the time, and didn't really know it for months. But I knew it when I came out of shock about seven months later.

Praying on Purpose

On the Monday that she died, I sat down and wrote a vow to myself that I would not allow Dixie's death to destroy me, body, soul or spirit. I vowed to myself that I would never get bitter or accuse God rashly of anything. I vowed to myself that I would maintain a right relationship with God, and that I would continue in prayer and living for God. I made a firm declaration that I still believed that "ALL THINGS WORK TOGETHER FOR GOOD to those who love God, to them who are the called according to His purpose," (Romans 8:28). It was about a 300-word commitment to myself. And I have lived every word of it since then.

So why have I included this story in the chapter on "How to Intercede"?

Because I want you to know that if you are ever going to be an intercessor, you are going to have to learn to intercede for people no matter what kind of response you get from God.

If you think that by making a big commitment to intercession, God will just jump on His chariot and come running to you every time you pray, then you are going to crash and burn.

If my whole relationship with God had been predicated on whether or not God healed Dixie, that might have been the end of mine. And if my PRAYER LIFE had been predicated on whether or not Dixie was healed, then that might have been the end of my praying.

You must never fail to acknowledge that God is sovereign, regardless of how you live or how you pray. You must never get in a fight with God's sovereignty. He will hear and answer you according to His perfect will.

> "In Gethsemane the holiest of all petitioners prayed three times
> that a certain cup might pass from Him. It did not."
> *C.S. Lewis*
> *1898-1963*

I don't really think there is such a thing as a short-winded intercessor. If you don't have staying power in prayer, your days as an intercessor are numbered. If you are the kind to pray one prayer, then not pray anymore until you get what you asked for, you are never going to have the slightest idea what true intercession is all about. If you are only going to pray when there is a major crisis boiling in your life... Lord, have mercy on you.

Intercessors never quit. Intercessors don't know the meaning of quitting.

Intercessors are like Daniel. They pray under threat of death. They pray when the whole world says, "Stop praying!" They pray as a matter of principle. It is the right thing to do. Always. And if they go to prison, or a lion's den, or a dungeon, or a hangman's noose, oh, well. God is in control.

Intercessors are like Esther. She said, "If I perish, I perish." But I am going to pray and see what happens. Intercessors figure they have nothing to lose. And they don't.

Intercessors are like the Syrophenician woman. When she got a "NO" for an answer, she argued with God and won. She made her case and stayed on the job. Jesus changed His mind and performed her miracle, even after He had already refused to do so.

Intercessors are like the man who pounded on his neighbor's door at midnight, asking for food for his unexpected guests. You have to swallow your pride, throw convention out the window, and convince yourself that it doesn't matter what time it is or what anybody else thinks. Your need is bigger than any of the rest of the facts, and you are going to knock on Heaven's door until Somebody answers.

If I have learned anything about God over these years, it is that He really is in charge, and He does all things well. You can't second-guess God's strategy. He knows the end from the beginning, and He promised that He would never leave us or forsake us - that He would be with us as long as we would be with Him (2 Chronicles 15:2).

So what do you do if the thing or the person you are making intercession for does NOT get what you are praying for? You just keep praying. Either you are going to get a break-through, or you are going to get whatever alternative that God decides is better than what you are praying for. You must not doubt or criticize God's response. I know that whatever God does - after I pray - is what He really wants to do, so I accept the answer and give Him praise, in Jesus' name.

And as far as Dixie is concerned, as much as I miss her every day, and as much as my children and grandchildren miss her, nevertheless I know that she is, at this very moment, standing in the Presence of Jesus Christ, the holy angels, and all the saints who have already gone on (2 Corinthians 5:8, Revelation 6:11). It is really hard to believe that there is anything wrong with that. She is home free. How can I complain?

One morning, Ezekiel was prophesying before all Israel, warning of God's harsh judgments that were about to come upon Israel for their sins. In the afternoon, Ezekiel's wife died (Ezekiel 24:18). That night, Ezekiel was back out in the streets prophesying again. Sometimes, that is just the way God does things. You have to go with God's flow.

Keep on making intercession. The heartening thing about it all is that you ARE going to see many, many victories. You WILL get the answer you pray for again and again and again.

But sometimes God is going to say "NO," and there is not going to be a thing in this world that you can do to change His mind. More times than not, however, God will be pleased to give you the very desires of your heart. That is why you must make a career out of being an intercessor. By the grace of God, you are going to make a difference in your world.

Say it out loud: "I am an intercessor!"

"There is a place where thou canst touch the eyes
Of blinded men to instant, perfect sight;
There is a place where thou canst say, "Arise"
To dying captives, bound in chains of night;
There is a place where thou canst reach the store
Of hoarded gold and free it for the Lord;
There is a place–upon some distant shore–
Where thou canst send the worker and the Word.
Where is that secret place–dost thou ask, "Where?"
O soul, it is the secret place of prayer!
Alfred Lord Tennyson
1809-1892

Chapter 10

How to Pray

Prayer is art. It is both objective and subjective. You can be very, very specific, or you can pray in quite general terms. Prayer styles vary from person to person. Just like no two people will ever paint the same picture, no two people are ever going to pray the same prayer.

The amazing thing is that God responds to the infinite variety of prayers that are presented to Him around the clock.

I know that you and I cannot comprehend a God who can pay attention to a million prayers simultaneously, but take my word for it, He can. Just remember, He presides over a universe that is 28 BILLION light years across. Only ONE light-year is 5.8 TRILLION miles! He keeps your body functioning, although that requires micro-managing almost 100 TRILLION living cells simultaneously in your body. And there are seven BILLION of us on the earth right now. And then there are countless species of other miraculous creatures, too. If our God can keep all His Creation and all His Creatures running on schedule, don't you think for one moment that He can't pay attention to EVERY WORD you say and EVERY THOUGHT you think. When we say that God has infinite power, we are talking INFINITE. No limits whatsoever. He takes note of every sparrow that falls.

We have never preached God bigger than He really is. We have never overstated His abilities, and never asked for anything that He cannot do.

Consider this. The poor widow woman in 2 Kings 4 was down to nothing. All she had in her house was a pot of oil. The prophet told her to borrow all the pots in the neighborhood, which she obediently did. On orders from the prophet, she literally filled up every pot in town out of that one bottle. Then she sold all the oil and paid off all her bills.

Now, would you have ever thought to pray for something like that? God has tricks up His sleeve that you and I cannot even imagine. That's why we should be completely uninhibited when we pray. Jesus said that if you can believe it, you can receive it.

A preacher I know got a call from a businessman in his town.

"Preacher, I need prayer."

"What for?"

"My business is failing. I have a new car dealership that is on the verge of bankruptcy."

"What do you want me to pray?" the preacher enquired.

"I want you to pray that God will send a tornado and destroy this place."

The preacher was shocked, but just kept listening. The guy figured he could start over with the proceeds of the insurance claim he would file in the event of such a calamity.

The preacher prayed. That weekend, a Category 3 tornado swept through town and totally destroyed that car dealership. No one was hurt. But the businessman collected the insurance proceeds and was able to pay off his debts and open up a new dealership.

That is a true story.

You never know what God might do if you will pray.

It's time to throw out all your preconceived, self-limiting ideas about prayer and just get down in the trenches and conduct guerilla warfare in prayer.

I took my own advice. The Church building where I was pastoring in Birmingham needed a new roof which was going to cost an exorbitant price.

I prayed and asked God to give us a new roof. Would you believe that within a WEEK, a hailstorm came through town and damaged that old roof? The insurance adjuster came out and appraised the damage. The insurance company paid for a completely new roof, and we did not spend one dime out of pocket.

I know that sounds crazy. It almost sounds dishonest. But it was NOT. I never did anything dishonest in that situation. I only prayed for a new roof. If you need a miracle, God is not ashamed or embarrassed to do whatever He has to, to give you your miracle.

One of the biggest hurdles in learning how to pray is learning how to believe that God will respond to ANY prayer that is genuine and full of faith. You do NOT have to be eloquent, articulate or verbose. Your prayers do NOT have to be well-structured, grammatically correct or humanly impressive. But they do have to be real. There is NO REASON why you or anybody else cannot learn to pray powerful prayers that work. Just give it a try.

The thief on the cross beside Jesus only had minutes left to live. He was nearing his last breath. But he knew this man Jesus was the Son of God, and he could not restrain himself.

"He said unto Jesus,
Lord, remember me when thou comest into thy kingdom.
And Jesus said unto him, Verily I say unto thee,
To day shalt thou be with me in paradise."
Luke 23:43

With a NINE-WORD prayer, that fellow won the heart of the LORD of glory, and saved his eternal soul.

Nine words. God created the universe with only THREE words:

"Let there be..."

Stop worrying about your prayer skills. Just pray whatever you can find in your heart to pray. You may just find that you can get your miracle in only ONE word...

"Jesus!"

"Nothing shall be impossible to you."
Matthew 17:20

Chapter 11

You can Call on that Name

If you happen to be reading this book, and you are not a Christian, then it is very important that I make this next point.

I have absolutely NO use whatsoever for generic prayer; prayers not directed to anybody in particular, prayers to anyone other than Jesus Christ. There are non-religious people who practice prayer as a paranormal phenomenon, and sometimes achieve measurable results. I believe that such practices sometimes engage evil spirits (i.e., familiar spirits) that allure and deceive. Such praying leads to gross deceptions and are abominable in God's sight (Leviticus 19:31).

I am not a spiritualist. I do not practice spiritualism. I do not pray to anybody but Jesus Christ. All of my spiritual activity is proprietary between me and the God who created me. I intend to keep all my prayer, faith, and spiritual activity carefully within strict Biblical guidelines.

I don't pray to the Virgin Mary. Mary, the mother of the Christ child, is dead, and in Heaven, and is oblivious to everything going on down here on earth. The Preacher in Ecclesiastes 9 said, "**The dead know not anything**." I have found nothing in the Bible to convince me that the saints in Heaven have any knowledge of what is going on in the earth. The same chapter says that **the dead "hath not seen the evil work** that is done under the sun." Saints are very much alive in Heaven, but they are prevented from participating in earthly matters. You are wasting your precious time praying to saints, AND you are offending God. Not one single scripture in the Bible suggests in any way that we should pray to Mary or anybody else for that matter. Why go to Mary, anyway? Jesus is the answer! Only He has ALL power in Heaven and in earth (Matthew 28:18).

I don't pray to Buddha, or Krishna, or Santa Claus or the Easter Bunny. I don't burn incense to goddesses with elephant faces or which have a dozen arms. I don't pray to the sun, the moon or the stars.

There is NOBODY out there who cares about me but Jesus Christ. He is the great Creator, and He is the ONLY true and living God.

Now, we must acknowledge that there are many, many - countless - spirits out there that would LOVE for you to believe that THEY are the answer to all your problems.

If you want to buy Sylvia Brown's books, (or books by some other fortune-teller, soothsayer or witch) and let her teach you how to talk to your dead great-grandfather, you are really, really getting into deep waters - and into deep TROUBLE with God. **Stay away** from anybody or anything like that!

The Bible clearly teaches that there are spirit imposters, familiar spirits out there that would love to seduce and persuade you to believe in them.

That was the enormous trouble that King Saul got into when he went to the witch of Endor. That gal allegedly pulled up the spirit of the prophet Samuel for Saul. But make no mistake about it. **That was NOT Samuel**. No witch has the power or authority to call up the spirit of a dead Prophet, or any saint of God. That mistake cost Saul both his kingdom and his soul. (See my article: "The Witch of Endor" on my website at kenraggio.com.)

If you think Almighty God is going to subject the sanctified spirits of His best saints to the beck-and-call of demon-possessed witches, you really don't understand the way God operates. Those "ghosts" are called "familiar" spirits in the Bible. They are **devils** - **unclean spirits** - who pay close attention to things that men and women do, (so they become **familiar spirits**) and then act to deceive the people they are familiar with, to distract them away from God.

The great, great tragedy of seeking the help of familiar spirits is that those demon spirits can wow and bamboozle an uninitiated person into believing that they have just discovered **the power of God**. We have an entire generation that is fascinated with SPIRITS, but despises GOD, their Creator! That is the most dangerous thing you could ever do in this world – mistake a devil for God. And YES, demons CAN work miracles!

"For **they are the spirits of devils, working miracles**."
Revelation 16:14

Stay away from ANY spirit that is not of God. **Do not believe every spirit.** Try the spirits and know whether they are of God (1 John 4:1). If they don't meet crystal-clear Biblical guidelines, get out of there fast! Resist the Devil, and he will flee from you.

And last, but not least, I don't pray (or make confessions) to the local priest. For nearly two-thousand years, that harlot church has raped, killed and deceived multitudes of men and women who only wanted to find God, but instead got suckered into a Pandora's box of lies, perversions and unspeakable corruptions. **Don't go there!** If you need something from God, go straight to God.

If you want some godly saint to agree with you in prayer, or if you want your pastor to say a prayer for you, that is fine and good. Jesus said,

"If two of you shall agree on earth as touching anything that they shall ask, it shall be done for them of my Father which is in Heaven."
Matthew 18:19

It is good to have a GODLY prayer partner.

But do not ever think that **any** man is going to meet your need.

Jesus is the answer. Jesus is all you need. He has all power in Heaven and earth, and He can do what no other power in Heaven or earth can do. He is the great physician. He is the wonderful counselor. He is the mighty God.

What else could you possibly need? You can call on His name. **Jesus.** Demons tremble at the sound of that name.

Years ago, I knew of a Pentecostal woman who was standing in her garage in a Houston, Texas suburb when an intruder approached her with the intention of burglarizing her house. He was armed with a .38 caliber pistol.

I don't remember the details of what provoked the burglar, but apparently he was not expecting to find anybody at home. For whatever reason, he decided to shoot her. The moment she realized that this man was about to kill her, she screamed, "JESUS!!" **The bullet hit her in the chest** and literally bounced off her body and fell onto the pavement!

She was uninjured. The burglar was dumbfounded! He turned and fled. Her miracle was featured on the nightly news in Houston.

Prayer does not have to be elegant or articulate. But it does have to be with faith in the name of Jesus. Paul said that everything we do in word or deed should be done in the name of Jesus (Colossians 3:17).

Some dear friends of mine were pastoring a Church in the Dallas metro area. The pastor's wife had traveled to Lufkin to attend a Ladies Conference. After the conference, she was driving back to Dallas in a blinding rain. Up ahead of her, heading in her direction, a car had hydroplaned, and was rocketing into her lane. She was seconds from a high-speed head-on collision. Directly behind her was a large motor home. She could not slam on her brakes without being rammed from behind by the motor home. She screamed "JESUS!!" and closed her eyes.

Moments later, she found herself parked on the shoulder of the road. She turned around to see where the on-coming car had gone. It had collided head-on with the motor home.

The driver of the motor home was climbing out of his vehicle to examine the wreckage. He saw the preacher's wife sitting in her car, parked on the side of the road.

"WHERE DID YOU GO?? LADY!! WHERE DID YOU GO? That car was headed directly toward you, and you suddenly disappeared!! Where did you go??"

You don't have to believe that story, but she believes it. God moved her car out of the way of that potentially fatal accident.

You can call on that name. It only takes a second. Say it.

JESUS.

> "Hitherto have ye asked nothing in my name:
> ask, and ye shall receive, that your joy may be full."
> *John 16:24*

Chapter 12

Angels and Answers

I was preaching a series of meetings in Beaumont many years ago. I preached a sermon about "Angels" one night, enumerating the instances when angels ministered to believers, from Genesis to Revelation.

At the end of the service, a young man named Dennis came to talk with me. "I want to tell you a story, and you tell me if you think it was an angel," he said.

I listened to Dennis tell me about an accident he had been in two years previously. As he was driving down the service road along the freeway, doing about 50 MPH, an 18-wheeler pulled out from a side street and totally cut him off. Dennis had nowhere to go but directly into the 18-wheeler. He aimed the car between the wheels under the 50-foot trailer. As his car went underneath the trailer, it ripped the top of the car completely off. As it did, it hit him in the head, tearing a gash in his forehead.

As his car came to a stop, Dennis felt himself slipping into unconsciousness. Before he did, he noticed out of the corner of his eye a very large man, bright and shining, sitting in the front seat beside him. Dennis turned to look at him, and the man said, "Don't worry, Dennis. We will go for help."

The man then leaned toward him, lifted him up out of the car, and carried him across the freeway into the lobby of a large restaurant. He stood Dennis beside a telephone and helped him dial an emergency number. As the phone began to ring, Dennis turned to say, "Thank You" to the large man, and he had disappeared.

"Do you believe that was an angel?" Dennis asked me.

"Absolutely!" I said.

Praying on Purpose

"Are they not all ministering spirits,
sent forth to minister for them who shall be heirs of salvation?"
Hebrews 1:14

God has armies and agents of any and every kind to dispatch to your emergency, your problem, your need.

I could write another book on that subject alone. Maybe I will someday.

In 1997, right after Dixie's first cancer surgery, she was recuperating from so much treatment, and wanted to get out of the house for a few hours. We were both ragged from stress and exhaustion, and were under a great deal of financial stress at the time, having spent everything on medical treatments.

Nevertheless, we decided to spend a few hours having lunch at a nice cafe, and then browsing a few shops in a shopping village nearby.

We chose to browse around a quaint little Collectibles store. For years, I collected model lighthouses, and this store sold the kind that I liked. So we were just walking around doing some window shopping. I was totally broke and had no intention of buying anything.

I picked up an interesting looking porcelain figurine that was sitting on display. When I did, it slipped right out of my hand and crashed to the floor. I panicked. I couldn't believe I had done such a foolish thing.

I had no idea what the figurine was worth, but I picked it up and headed to the check-out counter. I showed the lady what I had done, and told her that I would gladly pay for it, whatever it cost. The price was not marked on the item, so she had to look in her price-catalog to find out.

It wasn't listed in her price-book. It was a limited edition porcelain that had been retired. If you know collectibles, then you know that "retired" means "valuable." I winced.

She had to call the owner of the store to find out what that figurine was worth. Dixie was standing beside me, and we were both waiting nervously, because we both knew this was going to cost an arm and a leg.

Praying for Results

"Six hundred dollars."

"What!? Are you sure??"

"Six hundred dollars."

I panicked. I didn't have six-hundred dollars to my name. I stood there, and under my breath, I whispered, "Dear Jesus, help me."

INSTANTLY, a woman **from the middle of the store** walked up behind us and pulled her wallet out of her purse. She looked at the clerk behind the counter and said, "I want to pay for that." She shoved a VISA card across the counter.

I looked at her incredulously. I looked at Dixie. She looked at me. I looked back at her and said, "Lady, I don't understand. What are you doing? Why are you paying for this? Do you know that they want six-hundred dollars for this thing?"

"Yes, I know. I just want to do it." I didn't know what to say. I stood there as she signed the charge ticket and handed the broken figurine to me. I looked at her and said, "No, you paid for it. It's yours." I handed it to her.

Then I told her how that Dixie had just been through cancer surgery and had been very, very sick and this was our first outing since her surgery. The lady just smiled and said, "Well, all I know is that I wanted to pay for this for you." We shook her hand, and walked out of the store. Never even got her name.

I don't know if that woman was actually an angel, or if angels carry VISA cards, but I do know that the Bible says,

> "Be not forgetful to entertain strangers:
> for thereby some have entertained angels unawares."
> *Hebrews 13:2*

If you walk with God, and trust your life to Him, and call on Him faithfully in prayer, you just can't do better than that. He is going to take care of you.

Praying on Purpose

"The angel of the LORD called unto him out of heaven, and said, Abraham, Abraham: and he said, here am I." *Genesis 22:11*

"The angel of God spake unto [Jacob] in a dream, saying, Jacob. And [he] said, here am I." *Genesis 31:11*

"The angel of the LORD appeared unto [Moses] …and said, Moses, Moses. And he said, Here am I." *Exodus 3:2-4*

"The angel of the LORD said unto [Balaam], … thy way is perverse before me." *Numbers 22:32*

"The angel of the LORD spake …unto all the children of Israel, …the people lifted up their voice, and wept." *Judges 2:4*

"The angel of the LORD …said unto [Gideon], The LORD is with thee, thou mighty man of valour." *Judges 6:12*

"The angel of the LORD …said unto [Manoah's wife], … thou shalt conceive, and bear a son." *Judges 13:3*

"An angel touched [Elijah], and said unto him, Arise and eat." *1 Kings 19:5*

"[God] hath sent his angel, and delivered his servants [Shadrach, Mesach, and Abednego]." *Daniel 3:28*

"The angel said unto him, Fear not, Zacharias: for thy prayer is heard." *Luke 1:13*

"The angel said unto her, Fear not, Mary: for thou hast found favour with God." *Luke 1:30*

"The angel said unto them, Fear not: for, behold, I bring you good tidings of great joy." *Luke 2:10*

"The angel said unto [Peter], Gird thyself, …and follow me." *Acts 12:8*

"The angel of the LORD encampeth round about them that fear him, and delivereth them." *Psalms 34:7*

Chapter 13

Praying in the Spirit

Some things are difficult to pray for. You don't know what to ask for. You don't know how to pray.

Your spirit feels the urgency of the need, but it is defiant. You want God to come on the scene and make a difference, but you don't know what to ask.

That is exactly the kind of situation that the Apostle Paul was referring to when he said,

"Likewise **the Spirit also helpeth** our infirmities:
for **we know not what we should pray for as we ought**:
but **the Spirit itself maketh intercession** for us
with groanings which cannot be uttered,
And he that searcheth the hearts knoweth what is the mind of the Spirit,
because **he maketh intercession for the saints**
according to the will of God."
Romans 8:26

The Spirit makes intercession.

That's what he said. Almighty God helps you make your case. He helps you express yourself. Not in the words of your native tongue, but in the language of the Spirit, you begin to pray.

That is all the same as if you stood before the Chief Justice of the Supreme Court trying to make your legal case, and you and your lawyers had completely run out of arguments. You knew that your appeal had already been articulated as best as it could be, and yet you could tell that the judges simply were not convinced.

Then suddenly, the Chief Justice himself began to articulate your argument more clearly, more explicitly, more convincingly than anything you and your lawyers had heretofore been able to express. He used exactly the right words; so much so that you stood in awe as the Chief Justice used legal vernacular that you had never even heard before.

Your lawyers fell backward as the case they had struggled exasperatingly with suddenly came into focus, and your case seemed suddenly completely logical and convincing!

With the perfect argument now made (by him), the Chief Justice leaned back, and the court ruled in your favor!

I realize that is a wildly hypothetical scenario that would never happen in the real world, but when it comes to praying in the Spirit, that is NOT wildly hypothetical. That is EXACTLY what happens every time a believer goes to God with an inexplicable problem, and the Holy Spirit begins to intervene in prayer.

When you are praying in the Spirit, Almighty God is arguing your case to Himself! It just cannot get any better than that.

That is certainly why Paul said,

> "I thank my God, I speak with tongues more than ye all."
> *I Corinthians 14:18*

Now, I know that a lot of people object to praying in unknown tongues. They argue that you should never speak in tongues if there is no one there to interpret. But that is a complete error.

> "But if there be no interpreter, let him keep silence in the Church;
> and let him speak to himself, and to God."
> *1 Corinthians 14:28*

That verse has nothing to do with praying privately in tongues. It only forbids someone from raising their voice in the midst of a congregation, and causing confusion. It clearly does not forbid me from speaking in tongues. Nothing in the scriptures forbids me to pray in tongues. It only teaches me not to disrupt a meeting by speaking in unknown tongues if no one is there to interpret.

Speaking in tongues is one of the most universal practices in the early Church. In Acts 2, the 120 disciples spoke in unknown tongues in the Upper Room on the Day of Pentecost. Nobody was standing around translating all of that praying. 3,000 people in the streets heard them, and after Peter preached to them, they, too, were filled with the Holy Ghost and spoke with other tongues. There were not 3000 extra translators standing around! EVERYBODY was talking directly to God as they prayed in the Spirit!

In every New Testament case where people received the Holy Spirit, they spoke in unknown tongues, (i.e., Cornelius and his household, the Ephesians, etc.)

Again, Paul said,

> "For he that speaketh in an unknown tongue **speaketh not unto men**,
> but unto God: for no man understandeth him;
> howbeit in the Spirit he speaketh mysteries."
> *I Corinthians 14:2*

Nobody has any business judging you as you speak in tongues. Speaking in tongues is a PRIVATE language between you and God. They may not like the fact that you speak in tongues, but there is nothing they can do about it. You are praying more effectively when you pray in the Spirit, than at any other time in your life.

By praying in the Spirit, you are able to pray things that you could not possibly pray otherwise. You are praying more wisely and more accurately than at any other time, because you are praying in the Spirit, a language that only God understands.

Lots of people who oppose speaking in other tongues love to insult people who speak in tongues, as if speaking in tongues is something that only wackos do. They believe that speaking in tongues is what people with mental disorders or severe emotional problems do.

I'm not going to deny that some Spirit-filled people have emotional problems, but that's all the more reason why they should be praying in the Spirit.

Paul said, "He that speaketh in an unknown tongue edifieth himself;" and "I would that ye all spake with tongues."

Any way you look at it, Paul heavily endorsed speaking in other tongues.

You EDIFY yourself - you build yourself up - when you speak in unknown tongues. How? God flows through you. God helps you pray. God is WORKING for your good when you pray in tongues.

I've been praying in tongues since I was eleven years old, and I am unabashedly unashamed of it. I believe that praying in tongues is as Biblical, as scriptural, as doctrinally correct as ANYTHING a Christian can do.

And to those who oppose it, I have a word from the LORD:

> "Wherefore, brethren, ...**forbid not to speak with tongues**."
> *I Corinthians 14:39*

But far more important than the issue of its legitimacy, speaking in tongues is EFFECTIVE.

> "For if I pray in an unknown tongue, my spirit prayeth,
> but my understanding is unfruitful. What is it then?
> I will pray with the spirit, and I will pray with the understanding also:
> I will sing with the spirit, and I will sing with the understanding also."
> *I Corinthians 14:17-18*

Praying in the Spirit is the only real way to pray in the midst of enemies. Speaking in tongues is cryptological. It is like spies sending secret codes in the presence of enemies. When you pray in the Spirit, Satan is powerless to intercept your prayers.

I am certain that Satan listens to us when we pray. And I am just as sure that he will do anything in his power to hinder us (Luke 11:52; Romans 15:22; I Thessalonians 2:18).

But when we pray in the Spirit, Satan is utterly clueless. It is impossible for Satan to "crack the code" of saints who pray in the Spirit. I feel certain that is one of the principle reasons why Jesus was so pressed to baptize everyone with the Holy Ghost.

> "But I have a baptism to be baptized with;
> and how am I straitened till it be accomplished!"
> *Luke 12:50*

John the Baptist knew, from the day he introduced Jesus to the multitudes, that the principal reason Jesus came to the earth was to baptize people with His Holy Spirit.

> "He that cometh after me is mightier than I, whose shoes I am not worthy to bear: **he shall baptize you with the Holy Ghost**, and with fire."
> *Matthew 3:11*

There is no more important reason why Jesus came into the world than to fill people with His Spirit. WHEN HE DOES, you will pray in the Spirit.

So, this all boils down to one overriding premise. Praying in the Spirit is one of the most rudimentary functions of being a child of God. If you do not pray in the Spirit, you are somehow missing out on the most basic, fundamental, essential activity for which you purported to become a Child of God.

Why do you NOT pray in the Spirit (if you don't)?

Begin right now. Isolate yourself in prayer. Shut out everything and everybody for a while. Get alone with God. Open up your heart. Let the Spirit come in. Then, let it flow.

You can do it. God will help you. He is the Chief Justice.

> "I never get out of bed in the morning without
> having communion with God in the Spirit."
> *Smith Wigglesworth*
> *1859-1947*

Praying on Purpose

"We can just pour out the fullness of our heart,
the burden of our spirit, the sorrow that crushes us,
and know that He hears, He loves, He understands, He receives; and
He separates from our prayer all that is imperfect, ignorant and wrong,
and presents the rest, with the incense of the Great High Priest,
before the Throne on high; and our prayer is heard,
accepted, and answered in His name."
A.B. Simpson
1843-1919

"Since the days of Pentecost,
has the whole Church ever put aside every other work
and waited upon Him for ten days,
that the Spirit's power might be manifested?

We give too much attention to **method** and **machinery** and **resources**,
and too little to the **source of power**."
Hudson Taylor
1832-1905

Chapter 14

Unimaginable Miracles

You do not have to know how God will answer your prayer. Sometimes, we just cannot imagine how a miracle could possibly happen. Big problems, bizarre problems, whatever problems you have - God can come up with answers that will blow your mind.

On a Friday night, I preached in a Church near Dallas. During the prayer time, a retired couple came to me asking for prayer. They told me that they had some terrible financial reversals that year, and their house was being foreclosed by the finance company.

They only owed $41,000 on a house and property that was very valuable. They were in danger of losing a lifetime investment. They were desperate for a miracle.

We joined hands and prayed the prayer of faith. I asked God to do whatever He had to do to save that couple's home from repossession. I frankly didn't have any idea how God could make that happen, but I knew when we prayed that they were going to get a miracle.

The next morning at 10 AM, we had another service in that Church. When I arrived at the building, I was intercepted by that same couple. They were both beside themselves with delight. They told me that when they got home from Church the night before, the telephone rang. It was a call from an estranged son from whom they had not heard in many years. They did not even know where he was. He told them that he had become very successful in business, and that he wanted to do something kind for them. He told them that he was sending them a check for $45,000. They only needed $41,000 to save their house.

God had done a miracle within an hour of the two-minute prayer we prayed. As a bonus, He brought their estranged son back into their lives. If you can believe, all things are possible.

Praying on Purpose

There is no need too strange or too out-of-the-ordinary for God to do a miracle. Never hesitate to ask God for anything you have need of.

Years ago, we purchased three acres of heavily-wooded property in the country, and planned to build a home there. I leased a large bulldozer for a week, and set out to clear the property in preparation for the house. On the last day of the week, I was bulldozing along a small creek that ran across the bottom corner of our property. I had been working all day long, and the sun was almost below the horizon. It was nearly dark.

All of sudden, I sensed that the dozer was sinking. The ground along the little creek was much more saturated than I realized, and before I could drive out of the bog, that 12-ton dozer sank down three feet into the mud.

I was not an experienced heavy-equipment operator, and I did not have any idea what I could do to get that dozer out of that mud. The dozer sank so deep, that the TOP of the tracks was under the mud. I climbed down, and walked around that situation, then climbed back on and started to pray. I was truly in a panic. I figured that it would cost me the price of another bulldozer rental to pull it out of the bog.

I literally prayed until I cried, "God, I have to have a miracle here! Please help me. I don't know what to do."

It was now completely dark, and I was sitting on a bulldozer sunk in a creek, several miles out in the county, hidden behind a line of trees, out of sight from the road.

But miracle of miracles! I saw a pickup truck drive by, and disappear over a hill. Momentarily, I saw that truck BACKING UP in the dark. He backed all the way down the hill and stopped at the place where the creek went under the road. He got out of his truck and began to walk over in my direction. I could not believe that he could even see me out in the woods.

"Looks like you've got yourself a bit of a problem," he said.

"Yeah. I didn't realize the ground was soft until it was too late. This thing started sinking and there was nothing I could do to get out."

Praying for Results

"Well, that's no problem. I have some equipment out at my place. I just live a few miles down the road from here. I will bring it down here first thing in the morning and help you out."

The next morning at sunrise, an 18-wheeler pulled up at my place with a bulldozer riding on its trailer. Two other trucks came in with a crew of men. They unloaded the dozer, drove it down to where mine was sitting, and went to work. In fifteen minutes, they had pushed my dozer out of the bog, and were loading up to leave.

I asked the guy how much I owed him for his help. He said, "What are neighbors for?" and waved me off. They got in their trucks and drove off, and God had given me the miracle I had prayed for.

Not long after that experience, I was emboldened to pray about bizarre needs. After clearing our property, I had dump trucks haul in a caliche base for the future driveway. Caliche is crushed sedimentary rock that is used to provide a hard base for driveways and roads. After a few rains, that material is almost as hard as cement, and provides a good underlayment for asphalt or cement.

I later needed to run about 150 feet of water line along that driveway. Unfortunately, when I started to dig a trench with a small trenching machine, it proved to be almost impossible to break into. I needed a large, diesel-engine trenching rig to do the job. But that meant another large expense for renting another machine and having it delivered and returned.

I stood on my driveway and prayed. I said, "God, I need some help with this trench. I cannot dig this trench with the equipment I have, and I can't afford the equipment I need right now."

You don't have to believe this story if you don't want to, but WITHIN AN HOUR, a telephone company crew stopped on the road in front of my property. On the back of a flatbed trailer was a large, diesel trenching machine. I stood there in awe. Then I backed my shoulders and walked down the hill to the road. I walked up to the guy who was driving the truck.

Praying on Purpose

I said, "Hey, is there any chance I could get you to do a little trenching job for me while you are here?" He said, "Where do you need it?" I showed him that I needed a trench from the road, up the hill along the driveway for about 150 feet. He said, "That shouldn't be a problem."

He got on the trenching machine, started the engine, backed it off the trailer, and headed up that hill, trenching as he went. In less than thirty minutes, I had my trench.

"How much do I owe you?"

"Not a thing," he said. I handed him a $20 dollar bill for his trouble. I went back to my work, and he went back to his.

And God had answered another bizarre prayer for me, within an hour of my praying it.

About three years later, after we built a house and a large barn on that property, I needed another miracle. I was working out in the yard one evening. Our part of the country had been under a severe drought for three years. At last, several of our largest trees had succumbed to the drought. I looked at several 40-60-foot-tall pine trees that were dead from the drought. About four of those trees were standing near the house and the barn, and would eventually threaten those structures if they fell.

I knew that it would take several thousand dollars to hire a crew to take those trees down, since they were so near the buildings. At about 7:00 PM, as the sun was going down, I stood out in the middle of the driveway (just like I had the time before) and said, "God, I really need a miracle to get those trees down and off this property. I wish that you would send me a solution to this problem."

The next morning, at about 8 AM, a black pickup truck drove onto our property. A man got out and came to knock on the door. "I'm running a logging company that is working down the road. I just wonder if you have any trees on your property that you would like to sell."

"I don't have any trees to sell," I told him, "but I have several dead pine trees that I sure do need removed."

He wanted me to show the trees to him. I walked the property and pointed out the dead trees.

"I'll send some equipment by here this afternoon, and we will get those trees out for you."

A few hours later, one of the biggest rigs I have ever seen drove up on my property. The tires on that rig were nearly six feet tall, and it had a giant circular saw on the front end, and claws that easily reached around the largest tree and literally held it vertical while the saw cut it away from the ground.

I watched as that giant rig drove up to one tree after another, put its enormous steel arms around it and held it as the rig drove forward with the massive circular saw, and within seconds, cut the tree off close to the ground. The driver then backed up with the tree still standing in its arms, and gently laid the tree down on the ground. In less than two hours, he had cut and removed every dead tree on my property, and was GONE!

I simply shook my head in amazement. Within less than 24 hours after I stood in the driveway and asked God to help me get rid of those trees, those trees were gone. And it cost me absolutely nothing.

I call that a miracle. And I call it an answer to prayer.

So the next time you find yourself looking into the face of an exasperating problem, wondering how in the world you will ever find a solution, why don't you go stand out in the driveway and ask God to do a miracle? In Jesus' name.

"Call unto me, and I will answer thee,
and shew thee great and mighty things,
which thou knowest not."
Jeremiah 33:3

"Therefore I say unto you, What things soever ye desire, when ye pray, believe that ye receive them, and ye shall have them."
Jesus
Mark 11:24

"Let us therefore come boldly unto the throne of grace, that we may obtain mercy, and find grace to help in time of need."
Hebrews 4:16

Chapter 15

"Life or Death" Prayers

On October 14, 1987, an 18-month-old toddler named Jessica McClure of Midland, Texas fell into an abandoned well. Her frantic young mother called for help, and within minutes, rescue workers began arriving on the scene. For the next 58 hours, a tense drama ensued.

Little Jessica had been playing in the yard with other small children. Her mother left them briefly to go into the house and answer the phone, when somehow the well's covering, apparently an old flower pot, was removed, and the child fell into the well.

When they finally found her, she had fallen down an 8-inch-wide casing to around 22 feet deep. One leg had been pinned upward against her chest, restricting its circulation. They lowered a microphone down the shaft and Andy Glasscock, a local policeman, spent most of those three days lying on his stomach trying to maintain communications with the child.

Rescuers were forced to drill another shaft parallel to the one she was in. They had to dig below the point where she was, to prevent the shaft from collapsing on top of her. The drilling was long and tedious, due to a layer of extremely hard rock that quickly wore down the bits that were being used. One worker after another was dropped into the shaft with jackhammers and drills, and pulled back to the surface completely exhausted.

Television crews quickly moved in, and CNN provided round-the-clock world-wide coverage of the episode. The crowd of rescue personnel, media reporters, and local residents was so large that few people would leave the scene for fear of not being able to return. Many from the media who had come from great distances were never able to get close to the scene.

Around the world, "Baby Jessica" provoked an outpouring of prayers and sympathy. Rescuers could not give her food or water, not knowing the extent of her injuries. They believed she could survive three or four days without water. They lowered a hose for fresh air, and another with warm air to prevent hypothermia. From Wednesday morning to late Friday evening, the intense drama dragged on.

Finally, at noon on the third day, drillers completed the rescue shaft and a larger horizontal tunnel at the bottom for easier access. Reporters stood on ladders around the perimeter trying to catch a glimpse of what was going on.

Robert O'Donnell was chosen to make the rescue, because he was thin, at six feet tall and 145 pounds. He did not tell anyone that he was claustrophobic. According to Lisa Belkin of the New York Times, O'Donnell "lay down on his back and wriggled head first through the cross-tunnel, with his arms out in front of him. The air was wet and sticky, and within moments he was bathed in sweat. It was like trying to slither through a tightly wrapped sleeping bag, he would tell reporters later."

He wormed his way through the tunnel until he reached the shaft that held Jessica. She was wedged against raw rock above him. He could see one leg dangling, but she was in a split. He spoke to her using the nickname her parents told him to use. "Juicy, I'm here to help you."

He tugged on her foot. She was stuck too tightly, and he had no space to maneuver. He cursed. Then he prayed. Finally, he realized that he could not move her. He had to go back up the shaft so the diggers could widen the tunnel. He promised her he would be back, and they lifted him out.

They almost refused to let him make the second try, because doctors felt that he was too distraught. But he prevailed. For the second time, he disappeared down the hole. When he reached the end of the tunnel, he coated the walls with K-Y lubricating jelly. He pulled on her, moving her just a fraction of an inch with each tug. Finally, she worked loose, and dropped into the tunnel with him - nose to nose.

"You're out, Juicy," he told her. He wiggled back through the tunnel, where another paramedic, Steve Forbes, waited behind him with a backboard used for accident victims. Workers lifted Steve and Jessica up the shaft, 29 feet, where the entire world was awaiting.

Praying for Results

One photographer, who would later win a Pulitzer Prize for his photograph, stood in the basket of a local telephone company cherry picker overlooking the well, and snapped the photo as Jessica, wrapped in gauze, first appeared in daylight.

ABC, NBC and CBS networks all interrupted their programming to make the announcement. "Live, and direct from Midland, Texas," Dan Rather said, "Jessica McClure is up. She's alive. What a fighter."

O'Donnell paused for a few moments, still in the tunnel, getting his thoughts together. "I was totally exhausted. Totally elated, too. I've saved other people's lives before, but there'll never be anything like this again."

When Jessica emerged, Church bells rang all around Midland. Her rescue was credited mostly to paramedic Robert O'Donnell and police officer William Andrew Glasscock, Jr.

"Baby Jessica" is now a grown woman, married and mother of a child.

For years, Robert O'Donnell was bombarded with media attention for his heroic act. The daring rescue itself, coupled with the unbelievable bombardment of media inquiries, produced what doctors called Post-Traumatic Stress Disorder in Robert. He struggled with emotional issues for years. Then, in 1995, O'Donnell put a .410 shotgun in his mouth and committed suicide. Saving the baby's life ultimately cost Robert his life.

The same man who had so heroically wormed his way down into a would-be tomb to free an 18-month-old baby girl, at long-last, succumbed to the trauma of the entire experience.

Not just anyone could do what Robert O'Donnell did that day. I, for one, could never descend into such a shaft because I would be entirely too claustrophobic. My body could not withstand the anxiety of such close quarters.

But miraculous rescues take place in the world somewhere every single day. How many times has some ordinary person experienced a sudden rush of adrenaline and "super-humanly" lifted a vehicle off of a victim lying under it? How many times a day do firefighters plunge into a burning inferno to save the life of some stranded person? How many times do Coast Guard personnel rescue a drowning one at sea, or a helicopter pilot rescue a mountain climber or a skier from an avalanche?

If you live long enough, you will eventually awaken one day to discover that someone you love dearly has fallen down a well of sin. You will literally be shocked with the horror that is unfolding. At first, you may try to deny it. Your belief system may be temporarily suspended. Then the reality that your loved one is in a life-or-death crisis will occur to you.

You will not have to debate within yourself what to do. You will look at that hole in the ground, and nothing on earth can keep you from going down into it. No matter that you are claustrophobic. No matter that it will put your own life at risk. There is only one reality. Your loved one has to be saved.

Upside down into the darkness you go. It is a race against the clock. It is now or never.

If you don't pray, somebody is going to die and go to Hell. If you don't pray, Satan is going to abduct the very one whose soul means more than all the world to you. If you don't pray, you will never be able to forgive yourself for not trying.

That is the kind of praying that Jesus Christ did when He showed up at midnight in the Garden of Gethsemane. He told His disciples to sit and wait while He went to pray. He took only Peter, James and John. Then He began to be sorrowful and very heavy. He said, "**My soul is exceeding sorrowful, even unto death**: tarry ye here, and watch with me. And he went a little further, and fell on his face, and prayed, saying, O my Father, if it be possible, let this cup pass from me: nevertheless not as I will, but as thou wilt." His sweat was like drops of blood.

Jesus went down the shaft. He put our needs ahead of His own. He knew that He was going to die, but there were souls to save, and He was the only one who could save them. Nobody could comprehend the trauma He was going to endure. The cursings. The beatings. The stripes and the wounds and the pain and the blood. The nails. The thorns. The cross. The darkness. The earthquake. The horror of it all.

Praying for Results

But three days later, He returned from the hole in the earth. He had conquered death, Hell and the grave. No one had ever done it before.

Your passionate, gut-wrenching prayers are going to be effectual. Your tears are going to touch the heart of God. Your agony in the face of devastating defeat is going to produce a triumph greater than anything you ever imagined.

When it is over, you will face the conflicting emotions of great joy over your victory, and great exhaustion from the effort.

In the end, you may feel as though you can never endure another ordeal such as that. But pray on. As long as you live, you are an intercessor.

Pray for your family. Pray for your friends. Pray for your neighbors. Pray for your nation and for all those who have rule over you. Pray even when it feels like you are sweating blood.

When you see those precious souls returning from what seemed to be certain destruction, the exhilaration of it all will be a great reward.

But that is not all. When you stand in the presence of Almighty God someday, and look around and see all the souls who were saved from death, your reward will be eternal in the heavens.

Therefore...

Pray. Pray as if it is a matter of life or death. Because it is.

"For these things I weep; my eyes run down with water;
because far from me is a comforter, One who restores my soul.
My children are desolate because the enemy has prevailed."
Jeremiah
Lamentations 1:16

Praying on Purpose

"There is no power like that of prevailing prayer,
of Abraham pleading for Sodom,
Jacob wrestling in the stillness of the night,
Moses standing in the breach,
Hannah intoxicated with sorrow,
David heartbroken with remorse and grief,
Jesus in sweat of blood.
…always there is the cost of passion unto blood.
Such prayer prevails.
It turns ordinary mortals into men of power.
It brings power.
It brings fire.
It brings rain.
It brings life.
It brings God."
Samuel Chadwick
1860-1932

"The Church that is not jealously protected
by mighty intercession and sacrificial labors
will before long become the abode of every evil bird
and the hiding place for unsuspected corruption.
The creeping wilderness will soon take over that Church
that trusts in its own strength and forgets to watch and pray."
A.W. Tozer
1897-1963

Chapter 16

Fasting and Praying

A distraught father came to Jesus because his young son had frequent, life-threatening seizures causing him at times to fall into water and even into a fire. The man had already taken the boy to Jesus' disciples, but they could not cure him.

Jesus was sorely displeased with their failure and openly expressed His displeasure. Then He rebuked the devil in the boy, and the devil immediately departed from him. The child was instantly cured.

The disciples came to Jesus privately and asked, "**Why could not we cast him out?**"

His answer was straightforward. "**Because of your unbelief.**"

He lectured them briefly, telling them that faith – if only as small as a grain of mustard seed - could move a mountain.

But unbelief prevents miracles. Unbelief is the product of the carnal mind.

The carnal mind is enmity (hostility) against the mind of God (Romans 8:7). The Spirit of God says, "All things are possible," but the carnal mind says, "It cannot be done." The mind of God says one thing, but the carnal mind contradicts it.

When Jesus told the Pharisees, "Ye are of your father the devil"(John 8:44), He was speaking of their carnal minds.

Satan is the father of carnal thinking. Satan perverted the pure minds of Adam and Eve in the Garden by planting thoughts into their heads that were lies - contrary to the mind of God. Before Satan did that, Adam had never had a thought contrary to the mind of God.

In that instant, Satan became the father of the carnal mind. Since that time, men have continued to think contrary to the mind of God.

All carnality is hostile to faith.

"It is the **Spirit** that quickeneth [**gives life**]; the **flesh profiteth nothing**."
John 6:63

Therefore, if you want to see the will of God accomplished, you must absolutely SUBDUE your carnal mind. Your carnal thoughts MUST be totally overruled if you want to see the glory of God.

You cannot think according to the carnal mind and see the glory of God. It is impossible. The flesh profiteth NOTHING.

Your flesh can ONLY doubt God.

"They that are in the flesh CANNOT please God."
Romans 8:8

"Therefore, brethren, we are debtors,
not to the flesh, to live after the flesh.
For if ye live after the flesh, ye shall die:
but if ye **through the Spirit**
do mortify the deeds of the body, ye shall live.
For as many as are led by the Spirit of God,
they are the sons of God."
Romans 8:12-14

We must MORTIFY the deeds of the body in order to see the life of God working freely in our lives. **MORTIFY means to put to death, kill.**

That is what FASTING is all about. Fasting is about crucifying the flesh. Fasting is ONE of the many ways that we go about crucifying the flesh. Fasting is one of the CURES for unbelief.

Consider this. The ORIGINAL SIN committed by Adam and Eve was an out-of-control appetite. God had clearly commanded Adam not to eat the forbidden fruit. Naturally, THAT was the one single thing that Satan desperately wanted them to do.

Satan appealed to the appetites of their flesh, and won. As a result, sin came into the world. That is the most ominous five words that can be uttered – **"Sin came into the world."** Think about it.

Sin came into the world because Adam and Eve did not control their appetites.

Like it or not, **your fleshly appetites are the most hostile enemies against God**. If we did not so freely yield to the desires of our flesh, we could do the will of God. But therein lies the problem.

SIN occurs when our carnal appetites overrule the will of God.

We do not restrain the flesh as we should, so it characteristically betrays God. Satan has made it his permanent business to tempt and tease all your carnal appetites until the day you die.

Now, let's get back to the story of the demon-possessed boy.

After telling them that their UNBELIEF had prevented the boy from having a miracle, Jesus told the disciples:

> "Howbeit **this kind goeth not out but by prayer and fasting.**"
> *Matthew 17:21*

You cannot cast out devils with the carnal mind. The carnal mind is allied with the Devil. It descends from its father the Devil. Your carnal mind is itself the child of the Devil.

You must always distinguish between the carnal mind and the mind of the Spirit. Every thought and every act you ever commit will fall into one of those two categories. It will either be carnal or spiritual.

The difference between that which is carnal and that which is spiritual is determined by its obedience or conformity to the Word and will of God.

If your lifestyle conforms to the image of the Son, by being mindful and obedient to the will of God, then you are walking in the Spirit. Paul said,

> **"Walk in the Spirit, and ye shall not fulfil the lusts of the flesh**."
> *Galatians 5:16*

As long as your thinking and living does not contradict the mind of God, you are on safe ground. Anytime your behavior contradicts the Word, you are on carnal, sinful ground.

> "The flesh lusteth against the Spirit, and the Spirit against the flesh:
> these are contrary to one another."
> *Galatians 5:17*

Therefore, if we are to do the will of God, we must conquer our flesh. We must attain to the mastery of our flesh. That does not suggest that the flesh can be permanently subdued. Paul said, "**I die daily**,"1 Corinthians 15:31.

It is a perpetual, ongoing effort. Every morning that you wake up, you must face another day of warfare with your carnal mind. Every day, you must master that devilish contrary will.

That is where FASTING comes in. Fasting is at the top of the list of weapons we can and must use to subdue the lusts of the flesh.

Fasting addresses the problem of proud flesh. When we deprive our bodies of food for a time, it naturally weakens the flesh. When we accompany our fast with PRAYER, our spiritual man is strengthened.

Fasting puts down the flesh. Prayer lifts up the Spirit.

But there is more to fasting than meets the eye. Any Christian who has any real experience with fasting and prayer can tell you that **there is something very supernatural about fasting and prayer. Fasting indeed has a supernatural effect on your life. Fasting breaks yokes.**

I began the practice of fasting and prayer when I was a teenager. In the past forty-five years or so, I have spent countless days in fasting and prayer. And I have seen miraculous results again and again and again.

Praying for Results

From my school days, I learned that any time I faced a major decision or a crisis of some kind, it was time to fast and pray. It was following fasting and prayer that some of the first ministry opportunities opened up to me. It was following fasting and prayer that I received direction to attend Bible college. While at Bible college, I committed to a three-day fasting and prayer vigil during which I received an answer from God about my specific calling. I could write another book simply about my own experiences in fasting and prayer.

After Bible college, I took a permanent position on the staff of a large Church. Every Tuesday and Thursday was a designated fast day for the entire Church. Everyone was called to fast until 3 PM every Tuesday and Thursday. Then, every year, the entire Church was called to a 30-day fast during the month of October. The Pastor, myself, and many of the other members of the congregation joined in that 30-day fast. During that time, we ate no solid foods. We only drank liquids like water, tea, coffee, orange juice, or other low-calorie drinks.

The results were measurable. We saw countless miracles, signs and wonders, as well as large numbers of people receiving the baptism of the Holy Ghost.

One notable miracle which I will never forget occurred in 1972, in a special Sunday service following a time of Church-wide fasting and prayer.

An elderly lady came for prayer. Her vision was failing. She had lost an eyeball many years earlier to a disease. The doctors had removed the eyeball from its socket. She only had one eye to see with, and vision in that eye was beginning to fail. She came for prayer and a miracle.

I was sitting at the grand piano when she came across the platform to be prayed for. I was no more than fifteen feet away from her as she stood for prayer. Suddenly, she began to worship loudly. **She declared that she could see.**

At first, nobody realized what was happening. Then she explained, "I can see out of my right eye!!" That was preposterous. She had no eyeball in her right socket. But she reached down and took a Bible off the pulpit. She opened it up and began reading it aloud. It didn't make any sense.

The Pastor asked her, "Are you seeing out of your socket?" She said, "Yes!" He placed his hand completely across her left eye, and about 600 people witnessed this lady reading about a dozen verses from the Bible with an empty eye socket!

I know it sounds incredulous, but I saw it with my own eyes.

If I tell you that I believe in miracles - believe me.

Fasting breaks yokes. Jesus said, "This kind goeth not out but by fasting and prayer."

Fasting has a supernatural effect in the spirit world. Demons are dealt a crippling blow when we fast.

I have two theories which I cannot prove, but I believe they are true.

1. **Fasting precipitates divine retribution.**

   I believe that because Adam and Eve sinned by yielding to their physical appetite (eating the forbidden fruit), **as an act of retribution, God honors** the man or the woman who FASTS. God responds to fasting and prayer by manifesting His supernatural power.

   In other words, since the ORIGINAL SIN was OUT-OF-CONTROL EATING, God appears to show respect to the person who DENIES HIS APPETITE to do the will of God, by granting supernatural power against his adversaries. Fasting inspires God to miraculously intervene in behalf of the one who fasts and prays.

2. **Fasting reduces Satan's access to our carnal desires.**

   Satan leads us into sin by appealing to our physical appetites (lusts). But when we fast (deny or mortify our flesh) those temptations fail. Unclean spirits cannot accomplish their evil schemes. God miraculously intervenes when a believer sacrifices his appetite to the will and purpose of God. Unclean spirits are frustrated and defeated.

That makes sense to me. And I think it is true.

Praying for Results

For that reason, I continue to practice fasting and prayer. I have seen supernatural things happen at the end of the first day of a fast. At other times, I have fasted three days, ten days, 21 days, 30-days, and once, I even fasted 40 days. You can say whatever you want, but I have seen God intervene in the most amazing ways as a result of fasting and prayer.

Consider these Biblical examples of fasting:

When Moses fasted forty days, **he came down from the mountain with the Ten Commandments**. When rebel enemies rose up against him, **God opened the earth** and swallowed them alive.

Again, Moses fasted forty days, and prevailed with God **not to destroy Israel** for worshiping the golden calf.

Elijah fasted for forty days after his grueling ordeal with Ahab, Jezebel, and hundreds of false prophets. Afterward, the still, small voice of God spoke to him and told him to go to Damascus and anoint Hazael as the next King of Syria, anoint Jehu as the next King of Israel, and Elisha as the prophet in his room - quite an outcome for a forty-day fast. **Two kings and a prophet came from that fast.**

Daniel fasted and prayed twenty-one days, after which **the angel Gabriel visited him** and showed him **epic prophecies pertaining to the Last Days**.

Jesus fasted forty days in the wilderness. **He overcame Satan** himself in a great victory, and that **launched the greatest ministry ever known.**

Cornelius was the first Gentile upon which the Holy Ghost fell. An **angel of the Lord appeared to him WHILE HE WAS FASTING** AND PRAYING, and instructed him to call for Simon Peter, who came and showed him the way of salvation. **Cornelius' fast opened the door to the Gentile Church.**

After the Church at Antioch engaged in a period of fasting and prayer, God ordered them to lay hands and Barnabas and Saul and send them into the missionary work. **Paul's great ministry began at the conclusion of a corporate fast.**

You cannot imagine how God will respond when you commit yourself to a season of fasting and prayer.

There is nothing complicated about a fast. Just do it, and see what God will do. One day. Three days. Ten days. Whatever. Just obey your heart, and God will honor it.

"**Prayer is reaching out after the unseen;
fasting is letting go of all that is seen and temporal.**
Fasting helps express, deepen, confirm the resolution that
we are ready to **sacrifice anything, even ourselves**
to attain what we seek for the kingdom of God."
Andrew Murray
1828-1917

"When the saint ceases to seek after holiness, purity,
righteousness, truth; when he ceases to pray,
stops reading the Word and **gives way to carnal appetites**,
then it is that Satan comes."
Smith Wigglesworth
1859-1947

Chapter 17

Confrontational Prayer

I preached in a Church in Mississippi many years ago. A man in that Church told me a story about his wife's ordeal with cancer. She was a young woman who had never had any children when the doctors told her that she had a fast-growing cancer of the womb. They urged her to immediately have it removed surgically lest it quickly spread throughout her body. But she did not want to lose her womb, because she wanted to have children.

So she refused to have the surgery and set out to pray and believe God for a miracle. For nine months, the cancer continued to grow. Every time she saw the doctor, it was worse. But one night, while standing in front of her fireplace praying and seeking God, a miracle happened. She literally passed the cancer right out of her body. She went to the doctor the next day and he examined her, then ran tests. He said, "It's a miracle. I can't find any cancer in your body." As time passed, the miracle was confirmed. It really was a miracle. That lady eventually had children of her own, from the very womb that had at one time been consumed by cancer.

That miracle would never have occurred without nine months of persistent, even obstinate, confrontational prayer and faith. It takes real faith and a lot of grit to carry a massive cancer for nine months without yielding to the temptation of surgery.

Smith Wigglesworth was often called to the bedside of the sick and dying. His manner of prayer would be considered terribly peculiar today, if not downright offensive, because Wigglesworth was unusually obstinate and confrontational in prayer. In many cases, he required everyone else to leave the room, then proceeded to either kneel or prostate himself on the floor and pray (often quite loudly) for the sick until they were fully recovered. It was not unusual for him to stay for hours, even all day long or all night long in passionate prayer for the one in need. His results were astonishing. He was renowned around the world for the amazing number of remarkable miracles and healings that occurred in his ministry. Some reports say that he raised as many as twenty-three people from the dead in his lifetime.

I call his kind of praying **confrontational prayer** because it is hard-headed, obstinate and unrelenting. In these days, it is a **highly uncommon type of prayer**. It is praying that says, "I am going to pray and believe until God answers my prayer, or until He undeniably says 'No.'"

I once heard someone say,

"If you ever truly make up your mind, you will never change it."

If you ever make up your mind that you will pray until you get the victory, then nothing can stop you. You will pray until you receive what you ask from Him, or until God firmly says 'No.'

We have no reason to believe that wishy-washy prayer ever works. Real prayer is the matchless weapon of men and women who are genuinely consecrated to getting the job done, come Hell or high water.

In his book entitled "Barriers to Christian Belief," Leonard Griffith, former pastor of the famous City Temple in London, said that one of the major obstacles and stumbling blocks that hinders people from being a Christian is "unanswered prayer."You probably know that feeling. Few things are more discouraging than unanswered prayer.

But it is inevitable that every one of us will face that obstacle of unanswered prayer sooner or later. We cannot abandon our duty to make intercessory prayer merely because the last time we prayed, God denied our request.

I don't think that you or I have ever been quite as insulted as the Syrophenician woman was insulted when Jesus refused to heal her daughter because (He said) it was not appropriate to cast the Jews' bread to the dogs.

Most of us would have turned and walked away, feeling deeply insulted, angered or even embittered by such a derogatory statement. But not her.

She was undaunted by what only seemed to be legitimate obstacles. She said, "Yes, LORD: yet the dogs under the table eat of the children's crumbs."

Hers was **confrontational prayer;** uncommon prayer; **"won't take 'NO' for an answer"** prayer.

And it worked! Jesus gave the woman her miracle! We must not stop praying when prayers go unanswered. Dr. Jack Hyles called it, "How to argue with God and win."

The Apostle Paul was a man who prayed INCESSANTLY.

> "For God is my witness, ...that **without ceasing**
> I make mention of you always in my prayers."
> *Romans 1:9*

> "I beseech you, brethren, ...that ye **strive together with me**
> in your prayers to God for me."
> *Romans 15:30*

> "**[I] cease not** to give thanks for you,
> making mention of you in my prayers."
> *Ephesians 1:16*

> "We give thanks to God **always for you all**,
> making mention of you in our prayers."
> *1 Thessalonians 1:2*

> "I exhort therefore, that, ...**supplications, prayers, intercessions**, and giving of thanks, be made for all men."
> *1 Timothy 2:1*

> "...**without ceasing** I have remembrance of thee
> in my prayers night and day."
> *2 Timothy 1:3*

> "I thank my God, **making mention of thee always** in my prayers."
> *Philemon 1:4*

Prayer needs a sharp cutting edge. Don't let your prayers get dull. Too many modern Christians have no spiritual cutting edge. A real, evidential consecration sharpens prayer. Relentless perseverance sharpens prayer. Earnest commitment sharpens prayer.

> "If my people, which are called by my name,
> shall **humble themselves, and pray**,
> and **seek my face**, and **turn from their wicked ways**;
> then will I hear from heaven, and will forgive their sin,
> and will heal their land."
> *2 Chronicles 7:14*

From the earliest days, effectual prayer has been inextricably linked to the consecration of the people who pray. Without a genuine consecration and dedication to God, accompanied by a diligent, faithful habit of prayer, there can be no denying that your prayers lose their cutting edge.

Men and women who daily walk with God in consecrated, holy living have an advantage that cannot be denied. In fact, it is MORE than a mere **advantage**.

Consecration validates prayer. Prayer WITHOUT a real consecration may be completely ignored!

> "If I regard iniquity in my heart, the Lord will not hear me."
> *Psalms 66:18*

Few people nowadays have that kind of consecration, either to holy living or to unwavering prayer.

I am referring to a kind of consecration that says, "I won't eat for three days, or ten days, or twenty-one days."

Or it says, "I will hide myself in a prayer closet somewhere, and I won't come out until I have made my petitions known to God."

Or it says, "No man or devil will hinder me or prevent me from making intercession in behalf of these things. I will cancel my activities and give myself completely to touching God for these needs. Nobody will stop me."

Praying for Results

I once knew an elderly, saintly lady who told about an episode that took place when she was a young mother. In the days before advanced medicine and high-tech hospitals, her baby became deathly ill. She prayed and prayed, but the child only got worse. At last, she called a doctor, who made a house call. He found the child critically ill, severely dehydrated, and semi-conscious. He told her that the child was too far gone. There was nothing he could do to save it. He told her that she should prepare for the baby to die.

Weeping, she ran out her back door in to the back yard and literally screamed at God to help her and save her baby. By the time she went back into the house, the child had begun stirring, and before the day was done, it was again full of life.

There is no way that a double-minded man will ever get the kind of response from God that die-hard prayer warriors get. To be a man or woman of unrelenting faith like her or Wigglesworth, it takes a single mind. It takes made-up mind.

It takes consecrated, confrontational prayer.

That kind of praying is totally alien to most professing Christians today. We have a whole generation of silly, light-weight, carnally-minded Christianettes who would curl up and die under a hot sun. In a real crisis, they lose the faith. They have never prayed a passionate prayer in their life. They have never been on their face with tears and weeping. They have never walked the floors for hours, or pushed away from the dinner table in order to get a miracle - a real miracle - from God.

They live in a phony, euphoric spell of "HAPPINESS" that they have created for themselves. They are delusional. They can't even discuss demons. They haven't a clue what demon possession or demon oppression is, and if they do, they haven't a clue what to do about it.

They won't admit when Satan is afflicting them with sin, sickness and other problems. But make no mistake about it. Our problems are not mere flesh and blood problems.

"For we wrestle not against flesh and blood,
but against **principalities**, against **powers**,
against the **rulers of the darkness of this world**,
against **spiritual wickedness in high places**."
Ephesians 6:12

Our enemies are not obnoxious bosses, or uncooperative school teachers, or cranky check-out clerks. Our enemies are far more diabolical. They are from Hell itself, and they intend to do far more than spoil your happy mood. Jesus said,

"The thief cometh not, but for **to steal, and to kill, and to destroy**."
John 10:10

Hell wants you DEAD! If God won't allow Hell to KILL you, then Hell will afflict you with every imaginable malady and woe.

Jesus therefore commissioned his ministers to **countermand those evil works** when He commanded them to

"...**heal the sick, cleanse the lepers, raise the dead, cast out devils**."
Matthew 10:8

That task cannot be accomplished without direct confrontation.

We MUST **confront sickness**. We MUST **confront disease**. We MUST **confront death**. We MUST **confront devils**. If we don't, they will simply continue to rule the day. In the end, you will be defeated.

You cannot continue to treat your problems as if they are psychosomatic - "all in the head." A P.M.A. (Positive Mental Attitude), mind-over-matter approach will never get you the victory over Hell's insurgencies.

Practicing phony JOY and phony HAPPINESS won't work either. Living in a state of DENIAL will have little or no effect on the final outcome. People tell us just to get our minds off the problem, refuse to think about them. "Think positive." I'm not slamming positive thinking, but that is **not** the cure in real spiritual warfare.

If the best weapon I have against the great problems of my life is DENIAL or POSITIVE THINKING, then shoot me now, and put me out of my misery, because I don't believe either of those tactics has any real power to save, heal or deliver.

IGNORING SATAN DOES NOT DEFEAT HIM.

Pretending that things are well when they are not well is nothing but wilful ignorance, and it has no beneficial effect on reality.

Don't lie to yourself. Refusing to acknowledge Satan's presence or Satan's work does NOTHING to defeat him. Ignoring Satan does NOT make him go away. On the contrary, **ignoring Satan only gives him a license to kill, steal and destroy in broad daylight.**

Some "hyper-positive" Christians would condemn me as a pessimist right about now, but I deny the charge. I do not see the Apostles and early saints practicing mind-over-matter hyper-positivity. They hated devils and did not mind getting in their faces.

People who are fighting Hell day and night do NOT need to see a secular counsellor, a psychologist, a psychiatrist, or some other hotshot who can never actually fix their problems. Spiritual warfare cannot be won with Zoloft, Wellbutrin, Prozac or Valium. If Satan wants to destroy your relationship with God by messing with your mind, your finances or your health, then nothing in the world can stop him. **Only real spiritual warfare that includes prayer, fasting, and faith in God can do what you need done.**

It may be depressing to see what Satan is doing to knock me out, but antidepressants are not going to fix that. I am going to have to get my victory in Jesus.

We MUST be confrontational with the enemies of our souls.

But instead of declaring spiritual warfare, we regularly take our physical infirmities to the doctors, clinics and hospitals. We take our legal dilemmas to lawyers and politicians, our financial problems to bankers and accountants. For every problem, we turn to the "arms of the flesh."

We don't think we need miracles any more. It is too easy just to pick up our prescription at the pharmacy and get this over with so we can pick up the grandkids at Little League and carry on with life. We don't have time for the things of God. We can get along without Him.

We do not realize how we offend God by our constantly trusting in the flesh. We have almost completely eliminated our dependence on God.

> "**Thus saith the LORD; Cursed be the man that trusteth in man,**
> and maketh flesh his arm, **and whose heart departeth from the LORD.**"
> *Jeremiah 17:5*

It is very simple to calculate why we do not get as many miracles as saints in previous times did. **We don't think we need God.**

> "...The Church has more **faith in the world and the flesh**
> **than in the Holy Ghost**, and things will get no better
> till we get back to His realized presence and power."
> *Samuel Chadwick*
> *1860-1932*

We have health insurance, life insurance, home insurance, car insurance, disability insurance, and all other kinds of insurance. We have Medicare, Medicaid, and food stamps. We have X-rays, MRIs, CT scans, antibiotics, surgeons, dentists and psychiatrists. We have 401K plans, I.R.A.s, stock portfolios, and investment managers. Why do we need God? State Farm, Merrill Lynch, Blue Cross, Chase Bank and F.E.M.A. have us covered.

I will tell you why we need God. **We need God because He is our Creator, and He CREATED US to need Him.** He is our Father. He is our Savior. He is our mighty Counsellor. He is our great Physician: Jehovah Rapha, "The LORD that Healeth Thee." He was wounded for our transgressions, bruised for our iniquities, and **with His stripes WE ARE HEALED.**

We are so addicted to happiness that comes from having money, houses, possessions, friends, and THINGS, that **when we have a nice home**, a nice car, a good job and good health, **we think we have no need of God.**

Solomon knew there are **grave perils** in that kind of thinking. He prayed,

"Remove far from me vanity and lies: **give me neither poverty nor riches**;
feed me with food convenient for me: **Lest I be full, and deny thee**,
and say, **Who is the LORD?** or **lest I be poor, and steal**,
and take the name of my God in vain."
Proverbs 30:8-9

"Who is the LORD?" Solomon's inference here is EXACTLY what I have
been talking about. That is what WE do. We are subconsciously thinking,
"Who is the LORD?" I have Dr. So and So. I can go to the Emergency
Room. I can borrow the money at the bank. Who is the LORD?

We now have multitudes of young professing Christians who know
absolutely nothing about calling for the elders of the Church, anointing the
sick with oil, laying hands on the sick, or casting out devils.

"Is any sick among you?
let him call for the elders of the church;
and let them pray over him,
anointing him with oil in the name of the Lord:
And the prayer of faith shall save the sick,
and the Lord shall raise him up;
and if he have committed sins, they shall be forgiven him."
James 5:14-15

I remember a childhood incident that illustrates what I am talking about.

City road crews had been replacing sewer lines under the street in front of
our house. When they were finished, they put a temporary coat of oyster
shell on the street until the asphalt pavement could be repaired. My little
brother was out riding his bicycle, and when he rode across that large
patch of loose shell, he lost his balance and tumbled face-forward into the
sharp-edged shell, ripping huge, long, horrible gashes all across his face.

Now, in this 21st Century, we would quickly dial 911, and within minutes
an ambulance, a fire truck, police and paramedics would be on the scene.
But in 1960, that is not what happened.

My mother gathered him up and quickly washed and cleaned his face as best she could, then we jumped into the car and sped away to find a PREACHER! Our Church happened to be in the midst of a week of revival services, and there was an evangelist in town. We took my brother to see the **preacher!** He laid hands on him and prayed for him. That was a long time ago, and I honestly do not remember all the details of what happened after that. But I do know that he had a quick healing on his face, and afterward he had no scars remaining from the injuries.

There was a day when Christians believed that the prayers of a real man of God were more beneficial than emergency treatments in a hospital. People genuinely believed that God would heal and deliver, AND HE DID.

What happened between THEN and NOW?? Satan has deluded us and inebriated us with material amenities. Our Churches are flooded with powder-puff preaching that is non-confrontational with sin or Satan. More preachers are preaching "dream big dreams," worldly success and prosperity, and all kinds of positive thinking. Meanwhile, Satan is having a field day. Carnality and worldliness are flooding the Church, and Christians are turning into carnal, worldly, sports and entertainment zombies.

It is time for somebody to stand up and declare war on sin and Satan. It is time for confrontational praying. It is time to cast out devils, heal the sick and bring back the mighty miracles of Pentecost.

"**Prayer is a weapon**, a mighty weapon in a terrible conflict.
Our prayers are to be a continual, conscious, earnest **effort of battle,
the battle against whatever is not God's** will."
P. T. Forsyth
1848-1921

"Pray often; for prayer is a **shield** to the soul,
a **sacrifice** to God, and a **scourge** for Satan."
John Bunyan
1628-1688

Chapter 18

Binding and Loosing

Most Churches nowadays rarely speak of the Devil, and if they do, it is more often in a mocking, comedic way. According to George Barna's surveys, only about **36% of professing Christians** actually believe that Satan is a real being. That obviously means that those same people are in complete denial that there is such a thing as spiritual warfare. No confrontational prayer or fasting.

In most Churches, **fasting,** if practiced at all, is more like joining Weight Watchers or going on the South Beach diet. No TRUE fasts. No real hunger. No hardcore self-denial. No face-to-the-floor prayer meetings. No agonizing, travailing prayer. No earnest contending for the faith.

Just JOY and HAPPINESS.

There is a lot of superficial happiness around; happiness that comes from worldly pleasures and social engagements. It is temporal happiness; a paper-thin veil that dishonestly and deceptively masks the pernicious spiritual needs in our lives.

It is phony happiness that works like Tylenol - it deadens the pain, but does **nothing** to cure the illness.

It is a happiness that deceptively hides the sinful, worldly, carnal, evil essence below the surface that will eventually smother all life out of you.

Lest we forget, **one of the primary purposes of prayer is to destroy the works of the devil - to terminate evil works**, whether they are works of the flesh or the works of Satan. Jesus said,

"I will give unto thee the keys of the kingdom of heaven: and whatsoever thou shalt **bind on earth** shall be **bound in heaven:**

and whatsoever thou shalt **loose on earth** shall be **loosed in heaven**."
Matthew 16:18-19

BINDING. Binding what?? Binding devils. Binding unclean spirits. Binding rebellion, pride, lust, and every unclean spirit that you can imagine. Now that is WARFARE.

LOOSING. Loosing what?? Loosing men, women and children who are either possessed or oppressed by Satan and his minions.

> "Is not this the fast that I have chosen?
> to **loose the bands of wickedness**,
> to **undo the heavy burdens**,
> and to **let the oppressed go free**,
> and that ye **break every yoke**?"
> *Isaiah 58:6*

By the will of God, God's people are ordained to loose sicknesses, diseases, mental disorders, life crises of every kind, which are works of unclean spirits. **Bind the evil. Loose the good.**

So you don't believe all those things are caused by spirits anymore? You think you are now enlightened? You think everything can be treated with Ritalin, Valium, Prozac, Zoloft, Haldol or some other mind-numbing or mind-altering drug. Hell celebrates such inexcusable ignorance.

You can accuse me of having an archaic point of view if you want. Call me a dim-witted simpleton if you want. But I will tell you what I know is true.

A lady came to a Church we were pastoring. Her upbringing had been in the Church of Christ, but she had married a Pentecostal backslider, and learned of the Jesus' name, Holy Ghost way from her in-laws. God filled her with the Holy Ghost, and she was madly in love with God and Church and Pentecost. But her husband was furious. He did not want her to go near a Church. He wanted her to be at home, away from God and religion.

He had been a hot-headed, pistol-packing, drug addict for many years, and everybody knew it. The more his wife tried to assimilate into all the activities of the Church, the angrier he became. At first, he manifested his displeasure by ranting and raving against her and their children. As weeks went by, he grew more belligerent, and the cursings became more and more frequent and more violent. He began throwing things and breaking things. Then he began threatening their lives. The drugs only made it more nightmarish. She had very little opportunity to speak of her dilemma to anyone, but the bruises told the story.

He didn't like me because I encouraged his wife and children to come to Church. One day, I saw him in a place of business, and he quickly pelted me with some pretty barbed comments. Still, I defended their desire to live for God and be faithful to the House of God. That only exasperated him, and made him more hostile. He dropped a few subtle threats at that time.

At home, his wife and children were utterly terrified by his threats and his abuse. I came to believe that he was genuinely demon-possessed.

Finally one evening he came knocking on the front door of our home. He was obsessed, belligerent, and ready to fight. He was already in a boiling rage when I opened the door.

He stepped into the door, forcing me to step backward as he came. For the first few minutes, he maintained relative calm as he stated his complaints. Again, I assured him that I would do nothing to prevent his family from coming to Church. He laid into me, leaning into my face and pounding his finger on my chest.

Then, he began to curse, and swear, and yell at me. I pointed my finger in his face and said, "I rebuke you in the name of Jesus. I bind every foul spirit in you, and I command them to come out, in Jesus' name."

He froze. He looked at me totally stunned. He stood there for a moment staring me directly in the eyes. Then he fell down on his knees and started crying. He grabbed my ankles and said, "Brother Raggio, PRAY FOR ME! I NEED HELP! PRAY FOR ME!"

I laid my hand on his shoulder and began to pray for him. He took my hand and said, "I want to go out there to the Church house, and I want you to cast all these devils out of me, and I want to get right with God."

"Let's go!" I said. He and I walked out the front door, and over to the Church next door. We went inside, and he fell down at the altar and began to pour his heart out to God in profuse repentance.

I stayed with him for two hours. I cast out devils, and he repented, and before we finished, God had filled him with the Holy Ghost. It was an exhilarating deliverance.

That Sunday, he was sitting in Church with his wife and children. When we sang, he sang. When we worshiped, he worshiped. During the preaching, he sat on the edge of the pew and soaked in every word.

I have never seen a man make a more radical change so quickly in all my life. He and his wife have been faithful to Church ever since that day many years ago.

So you can call it negative if you want, but rebuking foul spirits and casting out devils is **not** negative. It is the most **positive** work of God. Casting out devils displaces evil principalities with the rightful Kingdom of God.

Jesus said,

> "But **if I with the finger of God cast out devils**,
> no doubt **the kingdom of God is come** upon you."
> *Luke 11:20*

Casting out devils ushers in the Kingdom of God. When saints of God become obstinate about putting sin, Satan and sickness out of business, THAT is the work of God.

We need preachers and saints who strike terror in demons and evil men.

The Prophet Samuel had been God's prophet in Israel, but the people wanted a king like the other nations. God had always been their King, and Samuel felt very strongly that they were making a grave mistake by demanding an earthly king. He rebuked the people, and **prayed that God would send a terrible rain on their fall harvest fields, "that ye may perceive and see that your wickedness is great,"**1 Samuel 12:17.

Praying for Results

"So Samuel called unto the LORD;
and **the LORD sent thunder and rain** that day:
and **all the people greatly feared the LORD and Samuel**."
1 Samuel 12:18

The man of God prayed that God would manifest His displeasure and strike fear in the hearts of the people. **God answered Samuel by raining on their harvest**. Samuel's prayer effectively decreed that God should destroy their crops!

Modern Christianity has either forgotten or is ignoring the potential of obstinate, confrontational prayer. Almost all the prayer we hear of is prayer for material blessings. We rarely hear of a prayer of rebuke, or a prayer of judgment.

Make no mistake about it. God often uses frightening tactics to demonstrate His displeasure with evil men.

When evil men crucified Jesus Christ, the **sun went dark**, the **earth quaked**, the **veil of the Temple was rent**, and many **dead came out of their graves**. When the spectators saw "those things that were done, **they feared God greatly**," Matthew 27:54.

Jesus TAUGHT us to FEAR GOD.

"I will forewarn you whom ye shall fear:
Fear him, which after he hath killed hath power to cast into hell;
yea, I say unto you, Fear him."
Luke 12:5

The world needs to know that God and His saints and ministers still have power and authority over sin and evil.

The world needs to know that God is still in control of Heaven and earth. They will never know that unless and until RIGHTEOUSNESS confronts, refutes and challenges UNRIGHTEOUSNESS.

Truth must confront error. Holiness must confront the profane. Purity must confront the defiled.

Martin Luther, an Augustinian monk in the Roman Catholic Church, read the Bible for himself, and discovered that Catholicism was in grave transgression of the Holy Word of God on many points. In 1517, he wrote his "Ninety Five Theses," a carefully prepared list of Biblical objections to the selling of indulgences, the Papacy and other Catholic heresies, and posted it on the door of the All Saints' Church in Wittenberg, Germany. That was the opening salvo of the Protestant Reformation, and the first major assault in centuries of doctrinal blows against Roman Catholicism.

Luther's daring confrontation with Catholicism resulted in his excommunication by the Pope, and his condemnation to death by Holy Roman Emperor Charles V in 1521. But Luther was rescued from execution by Frederick III of Saxony, who hid him in the Wartburg Castle, during which exile, Luther translated the entire New Testament into the German language.

Luther's challenge emboldened many others who would follow him to resist the deceptive evils of the Catholic Church and pursue Biblical Truth instead. Step-by-step, and point-by-point, courageous students of the Bible eventually dismantled the entire Roman Catholic catechism and reconstructed a more Biblical interpretation of Christianity. John Calvin, a young Catholic Priest who renounced the Catholic Church, was largely responsible for carrying Luther's torch and engaging Europe proper in the Reformation.

In the British Isles, King Henry VIII helped facilitate the breakaway of the Church of England from the Roman Catholic Church. But Anglicanism (Church of England) retained too many sympathies for Catholicism, and many more reformers arose to precipitate a much more non-conformist revolution.

There were principally TWO MAJOR COMPONENTS that drove the Reformation. 1) Men's profound love for the pure Word of God, and 2) **Intense consecrations that included PIETY (holiness) and great PRAYER, often with FASTING.**

The Reformers earnestly besought God for His assistance in being delivered from the errors of Catholicism and other enemies of Truth.

Praying for Results

In Scotland, a man name John Knox worked against all odds - often as a fugitive - to take Christianity another major step further away from Catholicism. Influenced early on by John Calvin, and licensed by the Church of England, Knox withstood persecution, imprisonment and even enslavement of Kings, Queens and high Church officials to bring about the Scottish Reformation which eventually took the form of the Scottish Presbyterian Church. So formidable were the prayers of John Knox that the Queen herself stood in terror of them.

> **"I fear the prayers of John Knox**
> **more than all the assembled armies of Europe."**
> *Mary, Queen of Scots*
> *1542-1587*

Four centuries later, Protestantism finally stripped away enough of a thousand years worth of Catholic heresies to expose the TRUE New Testament Apostolic Pentecostal Holiness Church.

To be sure, **we are not engaged in flesh and blood warfare**. God has not called us to kill anybody. This war is about pulling down strongholds of Satan. Even Jesus' disciples did not really understand that at first.

> "They went, and entered into a village of the Samaritans,
> to make ready for Him. **And they did not receive Him,**
> because His face was as though He would go to Jerusalem.
> And when His disciples James and John saw this, they said, Lord,
> **wilt thou that we command fire to come down from heaven,**
> **and consume them, even as Elias did?**
> But He turned, and rebuked them, and said,
> **Ye know not what manner of spirit ye are of.**
> **For the Son of man is not come to destroy men's lives, but to save them."**
> *Luke 9:51-56*

James and John were so disturbed that the Samaritans were rejecting Jesus, they wondered if they should call down fiery judgments on them. **They DID have a Biblical precedent:** Elijah had called down fire from Heaven, and then slain the abominable prophets of Baal, in 1 Kings 18.

Nevertheless, Jesus reminded them that the RULE is that **He came to SAVE MEN, and DESTROY EVIL WORKS**.

John later wrote,

> "He that committeth sin is of the devil; for the devil sinneth from the beginning. **For this purpose the Son of God was manifested, that he might destroy the works of the devil.**"
>
> *1 John 3:8*

God is longsuffering. He is in no hurry to destroy the wicked. But make no mistake about it. God WILL destroy the wicked eventually.

So today, our mission on earth is not to see how many sinners we can destroy, but how many sinners we can save.

But IN THE COURSE OF SAVING SINNERS, it is virtually inevitable that the man or woman of God will sooner or later have a serious confrontation with the powers of Hell that oppose saving grace.

In Acts 13, Paul was on the Isle of Paphos, where "a prudent man," a deputy named **Sergius Paulus, "desired to hear the Word of God."**

Unfortunately, an unbelieving Jewish **sorcerer named Barjesus** [translated Elymas] "**withstood them, seeking to turn the deputy away from the faith**." Paul refused to allow this evil man to interfere with his soul-winning effort. **Paul miraculously pronounced blindness on the evil man.**

> "Then Saul, (who also is called Paul,) filled with the Holy Ghost, set his eyes on him, And said, O full of all subtilty and all mischief, **thou child of the devil, thou enemy of all righteousness,** wilt thou not cease to pervert the right ways of the Lord? And now, behold, the hand of the Lord is upon thee, and **thou shalt be blind, not seeing the sun for a season**. And immediately there fell on him a mist and a darkness; and he went about seeking some to lead him by the hand. **Then the deputy, when he saw what was done, believed,** being astonished at the doctrine of the Lord."
>
> *Acts 13:9-12*

Paul decreed, by the Word of the Lord, that Elymas the sorcerer should be smitten BLIND! And God performed Paul's decree that day. Elymas immediately went blind.

Such an act in these days would probably end up with the police being called to the scene, and charges filed against the preacher! But God did not have a problem with it! In fact, THAT ACT led to the deputy believing the Gospel!

You can decree blindness. You can decree silence. You can decree that an evil work will cease and come to naught.

We have either forgotten or abandoned the notion that a man or woman of prayer has such unimaginable options in prayer. Our politically-correct generation intimidates Christians, and as a result, we hesitate to pray for things that are not popular.

King Ahab and Queen Jezebel were the most vile, despicable, and despotic rulers. The Prophet Elijah was upset because Ahab and Jezebel were leading Israel into grievous sin and idolatry.

So Elijah prayed that God would halt the rain in Israel, as a sign to rebuke the wicked King Ahab, and to punish sinful Israel. Elijah prophesied to King Ahab that there would be no dew or rain in Israel except by his word only.

"Elias was a man subject to like passions as we are,
and **he prayed earnestly that it might not rain**:
and it rained not on the earth by the space of three years and six months.
And **he prayed again, and the heaven gave rain**,
and the earth brought forth her fruit."
James 5:17-18

God answered, and it did not rain for over **three and a half YEARS**!!

Do you think you could pray a prayer that powerful? Why not? Is there some kind of fundamental difference between you and I and Elijah? The Bible says there isn't! James said that Elijah was a man **subject to like passions as we are.**

Praying on Purpose

We may perceive Elijah to somehow be super-human, or superior to us in some way, but he clearly was NOT. Read his story, and you will see a man of hot temper, frustrations, suicidal tendencies, and plain old misbehaving. But Elijah knew how to pray the prayer of faith, and Almighty God knew how to dry up the Heavens for him.

Elijah's prayers moved God. When we articulate our confidence in God, He rewards our faith with astonishing miracles. Not only did God send the drought to punish Ahab and Jezebel, but He also protected Elijah from the same drought and famine that plagued them.

> "So he went and did according unto the word of the LORD:
> for he went and dwelt by the brook Cherith, that is before Jordan.
> And the **ravens brought him bread and flesh in the morning,
> and bread and flesh in the evening**."
> *1 Kings 17:5*

God rules the elements, and He is perfectly capable of rebuking the elements in behalf of a man or woman of faith.

Many years ago, while I was pastoring in Southeast Texas, my wife and I were driving into a shopping center parking lot when a huge, terrible-looking tornado began to dip down right in front of us from some low-hanging, very dark clouds. This tornado was going to be massive and it was already close to the ground. I stopped the car and jumped out and stood with my hand pointing at the tornado and said, "I rebuke you in the name of Jesus! Go back into those clouds! I command you tornado to disappear!" I don't mind telling you that my heart was racing as I looked that monster cyclone moving in my direction.

Dixie and I were absolutely amazed at what happened. That tornado immediately began to withdraw back into the clouds above, and in less than a couple of minutes, it had completely vanished.

"Coincidence!" you say? Don't say it! "With God, all things are possible."

> "What manner of man is this, that even the winds and the sea obey him!"
> *Matthew 8:27*

Chapter 19

Speak to the Problem

God told Moses to **speak to the ROCK**, "and it shall give forth its water."

Jesus **spoke to the STORM** and said, "**Peace! Be still!**" The storm ceased.

Many, many miracles in the Bible were performed **simply by decree**.

Tell the problem what to do, in Jesus' name.

Blessings and curses come by decree.

A decree is an authoritative order having the force of law.

God **decrees** blessings. God **decrees** curses. In Genesis 1, God **decreed** Creation:

- "Let there be light."
- "Let there be a firmament."
- "Let the waters ...gather together."
- "Let the dry land appear."
- "Let the earth bring forth [grass, herbs, fruit trees]."
- "Let there be lights [in the Heavens]."
- "Let the waters bring forth [living creatures]."
- "Let fowl multiply in the earth."
- "Let the earth bring forth [creatures, cattle, beasts, etc.]."
- "God blessed them, saying, Be fruitful."

This is God's modus operandi. It is His intentional way.

> "**I have declared** the former things from the beginning;
> and they went forth out of my mouth, ...and **they came to pass**."
> *Isaiah 48:3*

Jesus instructed His disciples to "**say unto this mountain**, be thou removed, and be thou cast into the sea," Matthew 21:21.

He said, "**Say unto this sycamine tree**, Be thou plucked up by the root, and be thou planted in the sea…" Luke 17:6.

The Centurion in Matthew 8 understood the **power of an authoritative order** when he asked Jesus to heal his servant. "**Just speak the word, and my servant will be healed!**" He knew that Jesus did not have to touch the man, nor even be near him.

A single decree from the mouth of Christ was all the Centurion sought. And that is all he needed. Across the miles, the Word of Christ healed the servant at the very moment it went forth.

The Word of God can bless or curse.

When four men let down the palsied man on a bed through the roof for Jesus to heal him, Jesus said,

> "**Arise, and take up thy bed, and go thy way** into thine house."
> *Mark 2:11*

The crippled man immediately arose, obeyed and walked.

But when Jesus saw a fruitless fig tree, **He cursed it**, saying,

> "**Let no fruit grow** on thee henceforward for ever.
> And presently **the fig tree withered away**."
> *Matthew 21:19*

The spoken Word of God is more powerful than a nuclear bomb. It can kill, or it can give life and healing. The Word of God spoken by faith can save, heal and deliver. The Word of God can raise the dead.

Peter was called to Joppa where a saintly disciple named Tabitha had died. They led him into the room where she lay. He put them out of the room, knelt down, said a brief prayer, then said to her, **"Tabitha, arise."**

She opened her eyes, saw Peter, and sat up.

She rose from the dead by a decree - an authoritative order.

When we operate by faith in the name of Jesus, we have His authority and His power.

Technically, we do not have to ASK. We can authoritatively command a miracle if we genuinely believe that what we desire is acceptable to God, and that He will perform it. The element of faith must be there.

If the life of God dwells in you, then the miracles of God will flow through you. The same life that is in the ROOT is in the BRANCH. If it is in God, it is in Christ. If it is in Christ, it is in me and you, if we have the Spirit of Christ dwelling in us.

Jesus saw a man who had a withered hand. He said to him, "**Stretch forth thy hand.**" He **decreed (authoritatively ordered)** him to so something that he otherwise could not do. As the man attempted to obey, his hand was healed. "It was restored whole, like as the other," Matthew 12:13.

Jesus stood at the tomb of Lazarus, who had been dead for four days. The corpse already stank from corruption. Jesus instructed them to take away the stone, then gave thanks, and said, "**Lazarus, come forth.**" Lazarus stood up and walked out. **By decree.** Yes, Jesus raised Lazarus by decree - an authoritative order having the force of law.

Paul told the Romans that we do not need to go to Hell or the grave to bring Christ up, neither do we have to go to Heaven to bring Him down.

> "**The word is nigh thee, even in thy mouth, and in thy heart:**
> that is, **the word of faith**, which we preach."
> *Romans 10:8*

You do not need a vision of Christ, nor a visitation from an angel to have the power of God working presently in your life. The Word of God by faith is able to do any and every miracle that you need.

If you cannot believe that your prayer or your decree is going to produce a miracle, you may as well skip it. A doubtful prayer or a doubtful decree will not produce a miracle. Never.

And that's not my opinion either. It is the word of God:

> "Let him **ask in faith, nothing wavering**.
> For he that wavereth is like a wave of the sea
> driven with the wind and tossed,
> For **let not that man think that he shall receive any thing** of the Lord."
> *James 1:6,7*

Wavering means "to exhibit irresolution or indecision." So, what do waverers get? Nothing.

An angel visited Paul while he was passenger on a ship battered for many days by a violent storm. "Fear not, …God hath given thee all them that sail with thee," Acts 27:24. Paul declared the word of the angel to the men, saying, "**I believe God, that it shall be even as it was told unto me**."

When you know that God is for a thing, you have no reason to doubt or fear. Likewise, **if you have the Word of God in your heart** (I am talking about the whole Word of God, from Genesis to Revelation), then you already know what God is **capable** of doing, what He is **willing** to do, and the **terms** upon which He will do them.

Based on your knowledge of God's Word, and in conjunction with the faith of God that dwells in your heart, **you should then be able to boldly decree a miracle** in any given situation.

When you do, you will be operating by faith in the power and authority of God's Word, so you have every reason to believe that the miracle will come to pass.

In a Church service one day, I asked a group of people to make known their need for a miracle. A sixteen-year-old boy quickly raised his hand and said, "I need a job!" I immediately said, "In the name of Jesus, we are getting you a job right now!"

Less than thirty minutes later, just as that service ended, a lady who did not even attend our Church walked into the building. Someone said, "There is a job for Terrance!" She was the manager of a large store nearby.

I looked at her and said, "Do you need some help at your store?" She said, "I do. One of my boys just quit Friday night!" I looked at Terrance and said, "There is your job!" She looked at him and said, "Just come in and fill out the application, and I will approve it." He got a job before he ever left the building.

Coincidence? I think not. **That miracle came by decree.**

When I was a boy, our family owned a little camp in the woods on Village Creek in East Texas where we vacationed two or three times a year. Daddy and Mother had spent a few days there when, at just about dawn, a knock on the door brought a warning that heavy rains upstream were sending flash floods that would soon submerge everything in the area.

They were warned to get out of the area as fast as possible, so they hurriedly put their most important things in the car and started to leave. Rising waters had already reached the rear wheels of the car, and they had to get help pulling it out.

My dad drove quickly down the narrow dirt roads as they rose and fell. Flood waters were surging through the low spots. In the first low area, waters came up to the hood of the car, but he pressed forward. But in the second low spot, the wheels came up off the ground and the car began to float. The engine died. Water flowed above the hood and lapped against the windows.

Momentarily, my dad panicked, then reached for the ignition key. **"IN JESUS NAME, START!"** He began praying in the Holy Ghost, speaking in tongues. Miraculously, the engine, which was totally under water, started, and he held the wheel firmly forward. In a few moments, the car regained traction and he drove to higher ground. God saved them and the car.

Speak to your car. Speak to your disease. Speak to your rock. Speak to your problem. Speak to your need. Tell it what to do. In Jesus' name.

Examples of Speaking to the Problem

"Jesus answered and said unto him, **Get thee behind me, Satan.**"
Luke 4:8

"There met him ten men that were lepers,
…He said unto them, **Go shew yourselves unto the priests**.
…as they went, they were cleansed."
Luke 17:12-14

"Jesus said unto him,
Receive thy sight: thy faith hath saved thee.
And immediately he received his sight."
Luke 18:42-43

"A certain man was there, which had an infirmity thirty and eight years.
…Jesus saith unto him, **Rise, take up thy bed, and walk**.
And immediately the man was made whole,
and took up his bed, and walked."
John 5:5,8-9

"He found a certain man named Aeneas, …sick of the palsy.
And Peter said unto him, Aeneas,
Jesus Christ maketh thee whole: **arise, and make thy bed**.
And he arose immediately."
Acts 9:33-34

"There sat a certain man at Lystra, impotent in his feet,
being a cripple from his mother's womb, who never had walked:
The same heard Paul speak: who stedfastly beholding him,
..Said with a loud voice, **Stand upright on thy feet.**
And he leaped and walked."
Acts 14:8-10

Chapter 20

Blessings and Curses

God Himself decreed countless **blessings** and **curses** from ancient time, which can NEVER be reversed. For example, God told Abram,

"I will make of thee a great nation,
and **I will bless thee**,
and make thy name great;
and thou shalt be a blessing:
And **I will bless them that bless thee**,
and curse him that curseth thee:
and in thee shall all families of the earth be blessed."
Genesis 12:2-3

Concerning Sarai, his barren wife, God told Abram,

"**I will bless her**, and give thee a son also of her:
yea, **I will bless her**, and she shall be a mother of nations;
kings of people shall be of her."
Genesis 17:16

The power of the **blessing** and the **curse** does not belong to God alone. Every man or woman of God is empowered to pronounce the blessings and curses of God.

Consider Noah.

Noah blessed two of his sons, Shem ("Canaan shall be his servant") and Japheth ("God shall enlarge him"), but because one of his sons had committed some kind of breach of trust with him, he decreed that Ham's descendants, Canaan, would be "a servant of servants," Genesis 9:25.

And there are many examples:

- Melchizedek, King of Salem, **blessed Abraham** (Genesis 14:9).
- Abram **blessed Ishmael** (Genesis 17:18,20).
- The LORD Himself **blessed Isaac** (Genesis 25:11; 26:12).
- Abraham **blessed Eliezer's search** for Isaac's bride (Genesis 24:7).
- Isaac **blessed Jacob** (Genesis 27:23,27; 28:1).
- Jacob **blessed Joseph's sons**, Ephraim and Manasseh (Genesis 48:22).
- Moses blessed the artisans who created items for the Tabernacle (Exodus 39:43).
- Moses and Aaron blessed the children of Israel at the dedication of the Tabernacle (Leviticus 9:23).

There are countless other examples throughout the Bible.

Almighty God honors the decrees of His saints, whether they are blessings or curses. He empowers His saints to make decrees in His name, invoking His power and His authority.

These are not to be reckless decrees. They are not to be foolish decrees. Every decree must be WORD-perfect decrees; decrees that agree 100% with the Word of God.

Balaam is the first glaring example of a man who broke God's rules of blessings and curses. **Balaam was offered a bribe** to curse Israel and bless the Moabites. King Balak of the Moabites sent representatives to Balaam saying,

> "Come now therefore, I pray thee, curse me this people;
> for they are too mighty for me: peradventure I shall prevail,
> that we may smite them, and that I may drive them out of the land:
> for I [know] that **he whom thou blessest is blessed**,
> and **he whom thou cursest is cursed**."
> *Numbers 22:6*

At first, Balaam refused to do so. He prayed that night, and **God specifically told him not to bless them**. So Balaam sent the men away. But Balak sent more representatives, and this time he offered him a great reward if he would curse Israel and bless Moab.

Again Balaam refused, BUT he told them to wait while he went and asked God about it one more time. Naturally, God again told him not to bless them or curse Israel.

"God came unto Balaam at night, and said unto him,
If the men come to call thee, rise up, and go with them;
but yet the word which I shall say unto thee, that shalt thou do.
And **Balaam rose up in the morning,
and saddled his ass, and went with the princes of Moab**."
Numbers 22:20-21

RIGHT HERE is the most important element of the entire story of Balaam.

God told Balaam, "**If the men come to call thee,** …go with them."

BUT the men DID NOT COME TO CALL on Balaam. Instead of **waiting** to see if the Moabites would return to him, **HE got up in the morning and WENT TO THEM!!**

(Who knows whether they would have come on their own? Perhaps God would have stopped them.) **THAT was Balaam's grave sin.**

We can only deduct from the later scriptures that **Balaam was motivated by the reward that King Balak had offered him**. Otherwise, he would have had no reason to go to them.

If Balaam had NOT gone to meet the Moabites, that might have been the end of the story. The remainder of the story might never have happened if Balaam had stayed in his tent that morning.

YOU AND I MUST BE EXTREMELY CAREFUL NOT TO BE ENTICED BY THE REWARDS OFFERED BY GOD'S ENEMIES!!

That means that we must soberly reject all enticements to bless any enemies of God or to curse any of the TRUE people of God. There is a frightening episode in Balaam's story to prove my point. You surely remember the story of Balaam's donkey. **The angel of the LORD stood in the way** to stop Balaam from going to negotiate with the Moabites.

At first, the donkey saw the angel with its sword drawn, and ran off the path into a field. Balaam smote him for his behavior.

Again, the donkey tried to avoid the angel, and ran into a stone wall along a vineyard, crushing Balaam's foot. Again, Balaam smote the donkey.

The third time, the angel blocked the path, so the donkey fell down under Balaam. Balaam smote him the third time.

God opened the mouth of the donkey to speak. Balaam threatened to kill the donkey, but God opened Balaam's eyes to see the angel. Balaam fell with his face to the ground.

The angel rebuked him for smiting the donkey, and warned him that **if the donkey had not stopped, the angel would have KILLED Balaam, because what he was doing was PERVERSE**.

> "I went out to withstand thee,
> because **thy way is perverse before me**:
> And the ass saw me, and turned from me these three times:
> unless she had turned from me,
> surely now also **I had slain thee**, and saved her alive."
> *Numbers 22:32-33*

At that point, God told Balaam to go with the Moabites, but to ONLY SAY WHAT HE GAVE HIM TO SAY.

But his re-entry into the negotiations emboldened the Moabites to press for more concessions from Balaam.

The next thing that happened was that King Balak took Balaam to the top of a mountain and showed him the vast multitude of Israel in the valley below.

Balaam made Balak build seven altars and offer seven oxen and seven rams on them.

But God still refused to cooperate. Balaam told the men,

> "Behold, I have received commandment to bless
> and he hath blessed; and I cannot reverse it."
> *Numbers 23:20*

The enemies of Israel continued to press Balaam to curse Israel and bless the Moabites. Again, Balaam refused, saying,

> "How shall I curse, whom God hath not cursed?
> or how shall I defy, whom the LORD hath not defied?"
> *Numbers 23:8*

Again, Balak, King of the Moabites attempted to coerce Balaam to curse Israel, to which Balaam replied,

> "Behold, I have received commandment to bless:
> and he hath blessed; and I cannot reverse it."
> *Numbers 23:10*

In desperation, the evil king said,

> "Neither curse them at all, nor bless them at all."
> *Numbers 23:25*

But Balaam persisted in taking God's position, saying of Israel,

> "Blessed is he that blesseth thee, and cursed is he that curseth thee."
> *Numbers 24:9.*

Balak was enraged.

> "I called thee to curse mine enemies, and, behold,
> thou hast altogether blessed them these three times."
> *Numbers 24:10*

Now, if all you knew about Balaam is what I have just told you, you would be surprised to learn that **God hated Balaam in the end**.

In almost every stage of the story, Balaam took a strong stand to bless Israel, and refused to bless the Moabites, their enemies.

But God did not see it that way, because of the fact that IN THE VERY BEGINNING, Balaam was even WILLING to consider blessing Moab.

My friend, I beg you to consider this enormous principle.

Based on this story of Balaam, we should learn that **it is not good enough to bless only the righteous and curse only the wicked**. Balaam was true to that principle.

The grave ERROR OF BALAAM was that he ever considered compromise in the first place.

Balaam's sin was no small sin.

Balaam had two empirical facts to base his decisions on.

1. Israel was God's blessed people.
2. The Moabites were the enemies of God's people.

Nothing else mattered. The only other consideration in this equation was the reward that Balak offered Balaam if he would curse Israel.

(King Balak erroneously believed that Balaam could actually curse God's people.)

The fact that Balaam WENT TO NEGOTIATE reveals the fact that he had a mercenary motive. He was looking for a way to collect the reward that Balak offered.

Several later scriptures revealed that Balaam did in fact receive hire from Balak, and that he somehow played a role in enabling Balak to seduce the Israelites to sin in whoredoms and idolatry, which God punished by sending a plague upon them. The New Testament confirms this assessment.

> "...the children of Israel, **through the counsel of Balaam, ...commit{ed} trespass against the LORD** in the matter of Peor, and there was a plague among the congregation of the LORD."
> *Numbers 31:16*

> "...they hired against thee Balaam the son of Beor
> ...to curse thee."
> *Deuteronomy 23:4 (see also Nehemiah 13:2)*

> "Balaam also the son of Beor, the soothsayer,
> did the children of Israel slay with the sword..."
> *Joshua 13:22*

Now in modern times, we have a warning from the Apostle Peter not to be guilty of the sins of Balaam, "...who **loved the wages of unrighteousness**," 2 Peter 2:15.

Jude pronounced woes on those in Christianity who sell out to the world, the flesh or the Devil. "**Woe unto them**! for they **...ran greedily after the error of Balaam for reward**," Jude 1:11.

John, in the Book of Revelation, prophesied by the Spirit of Christ against those in the Church who "hold **the doctrine of Balaam**, who taught Balac to **cast a stumblingblock** before the children of Israel, to eat things sacrificed unto idols, and to commit fornication," Revelation 2:14.

Those words are the most explicit descriptions of Balaam's error.

- **Loved the wages of unrighteousness.**
- **Ran greedily after reward.**
- **Taught enemies to cast a stumblingblock before God's people.**
- **Caused God's people to become idolatrous.**
- **Caused God's people to be sexually immoral.**

So Balaam ultimately DID NOT BLESS ISRAEL. He cursed them by his acts of greed. **You curse God's people when you bless his enemies**.

That temptation and snare is just as poisonous today.

Jude 1:11 listed three primary sins in the last days:

1. **The Sin of Cain** - worshipping God while doctrinally incorrect.
2. **The Sin of Balaam** - receiving reward for standing with enemies.
3. **The Sin of Korah** - leading rebellion against God's men of Truth.

Blessing and curses.

You can bless only those things that God is willing to bless.

You can curse only those things that God is willing to curse.

You are not free to bless anything that countermands Truth, righteousness or holiness. You are not free to curse anything that is True, right or holy.

So obviously, a saint must respect the SOVEREIGNTY of God. We are not free to bless or curse anything contrary to the will and purpose of God.

Our blessings are restricted to things that are not offensive to God. We cannot bless something that God is unwilling to bless. **Our curses** are restricted to things that are not acceptable to God. We cannot curse something that God is unwilling to curse.

In a nutshell,

- **It is the business of Godly people to bless and encourage righteous causes.**
- **It is the business of Godly people to curse and silence evil works.**

Jesus said,

> "I give unto you power to tread on serpents and scorpions,
> and over all the power of the enemy:
> and nothing shall by any means hurt you."
> *Luke 10:19*

That power to oppose the enemies of God RESIDES in the Spirit-filled believer. You don't have to wait on it. You don't have to call it down from Heaven. Take it and use it ON THE SPOT, any time the need arises!

Bless the righteous. Curse the works and powers of evil.

Now this kind of power and authority is nothing to be handled playfully. There are **users**, and there are **abusers** of decrees.

Praying for Results

We live in a convoluted Christian environment where charlatans and hucksters in abundance love to throw around decrees like Mardi Gras candy. "I decree a new house for you!" "I decree a new job for you!" "I decree a pay raise and a bonus!" "I decree a new car!"

They are **abusers**, and that is **abuse**.

Neither Jesus Christ nor the Apostles were frivolous with their decrees. The miracle working power of God is not a toy to be played with, nor is it circus magic. Those who abuse the authority that is in Christ may soon find it not only revoked, but also blowing up in their faces.

When Simon the sorcerer saw that through the laying on of the Apostles' hands, people received the baptism of the Holy Ghost, he offered them money to give him that gift to do the same.

> "But Peter said unto him, **Thy money perish with thee**,
> because thou hast thought that the gift of God
> may be purchased with money.
> Thou hast neither part nor lot in this matter:
> for **thy heart is not right in the sight of God**."
> *Acts 8:18-21*

People who abuse, or would abuse, the gifts and powers of God are interlopers. Their hearts are not right. In every generation, there have been men who misused and abused the gifts of God. It is up to you and me to ascertain that the power of God is held in sacred trust. Our prayers, our lives and our ministries must be SOBER, RIGHTEOUS, and TRUE.

When we invoke the name of Jesus for ANY cause, it must not be used frivolously.

> "Thou shalt not take the name of the LORD thy God in vain;
> for the LORD will not hold him guiltless
> that taketh his name in vain."
> Exodus 20:7

The scriptures often warn us to beware of imposters, false apostles, false workers and other deceivers.

"For there are many unruly and vain talkers and deceivers,
…Whose mouths must be stopped."
Titus 1:10

Nevertheless, the power of a child of God to bless or curse is profound.

Look at Peter and John walking up the steps of the Beautiful Gate of the Temple. There, lying on the ground, is the cripple man who has NEVER WALKED in his entire life, begging for alms just like he always has.

But today, something different is going to happen, because Peter is not going to act like everybody else this time. Peter fastened his eyes on the beggar and said, "Look on us."The man thought Peter was going to give him alms. But Peter surprised him.

"Silver and gold have I none; but such as I have give I thee:
In the name of Jesus Christ of Nazareth rise up and walk.
And he took him by the right hand, and lifted him up:
and immediately his feet and ankle bones received strength.
And he leaping up stood, and walked,
and entered with them into the temple,
walking, and leaping, and praising God."
Acts 3:6-9

Four simple words! "**Rise up and walk!**"

That man DANCED!! He jumped up and down!

There was not a speck of hesitation in Peter's voice that day. He was so charged with divine energy that the poor cripple was just a lightning rod.

Peter was so electrified with the power of God. He had seen **Christ, risen** from the dead. He had watched Him **ascend into heaven**, and heard the **angels speak**. He had seen **tongues of fire** fall in the Upper Room. He and 120 had spoken in **unknown tongues** as the Spirit gave them utterance. He had preached a **powerfully anointed message** to a massive crowd and **3,000 more were baptized in the Holy Ghost**, speaking in tongues.

Peter knew as well as any man who had ever lived that our God is an awesome God. Spontaneously - with no premeditation or foreknowledge - he blurted out to the lame man, **"Rise up and walk!"**

If it had not been the crippled man, no doubt it would have been someone else that day - struck by Peter's "lightning" of faith.

How can you or I replicate such an event? How much more difficult is it for ME to say, "Rise up and walk!"?

It's all about what is in your heart. Peter's heart was full of God - His Word, His Christ, His Spirit, and a great, great testimony of what God had already done. Peter could hardly contain himself.

- IF WE are mindful of the enormous TRUTH of the Word of God that we hear preached in our Churches every Sunday, AND...

- If WE truly celebrate every time we see sinners converted, baptized in Jesus' name and filled with the Holy Ghost, AND...

- IF WE walk daily with the testimonies of what God has already done for us, we will very likely feel the kind of inspiration and boldness that Peter felt that day.

In Acts 5, Ananias and Sapphira sold a possession and donated the proceeds to the Apostles. But they represented their donation to be the total amount of the sale. They lied.

Peter asked Ananias, "why hath Satan filled thine heart to lie to the Holy Ghost? ...thou hast not lied unto men, but unto God," Acts 5:3-4.

Ananias fell dead. Young men carried his corpse away. Three hours later, Sapphira came in, not knowing what had happened.

Peter asked her, "How is it that ye have agreed together to tempt the Spirit of the Lord? behold, the feet of them which have buried thy husband are at the door, and shall carry thee out."

Peter pronounced a death sentence on Sapphira.

She too fell dead, and they buried her beside her husband.

> "And **great fear came upon all the church,**
> **and upon as many as heard these things**."
> *Acts 5:11*

Many years ago, I heard a story about Rev. N.A. Urshan, who had been preaching a large Ministers' Conference in California. In the middle of his sermon, a wild man came into the conference cursing and blaspheming God, and making sordid threats against Bro. Urshan. According to the version of the story that I heard, he paused his sermon and looked down the aisle at the man, who had seriously interrupted the conference.

"Sir, God either save you or kill you."

The man dropped dead in the aisle. When the details came out about who the strange man was, he was deeply involved in witchcraft and the occult, and had come to curse the Pentecostal Church that day. **But the man of God had the last say.**

I charge you, in the name of Jesus, to **bless the right** and **curse the wrong**. I am not talking about calling fire down on anybody. But I am talking about using the power of God that dwells inside of you to further the cause of God.

Bless good and Godly men, women and children. Bless good and Godly works.

Curse evil beliefs, false doctrines, evil attitudes, evil works, and carnal or worldly ways.

Pray or pronounce the blessings of God on men of good will, and pray that God will stop the mouth of lions.

> "The immediate purpose of prayer is
> the accomplishing of **God's will on earth**;
> the ultimate purpose of prayer is the **eternal glory of God**."
> *Warren Wiersbe*
> *1929-*

Chapter 21

Prevailing Prayer

Men and women have been getting miracles from God for eons when they believed. Jesus said,

> "What things soever ye desire, when ye pray,
> believe that ye receive them, and ye shall have them."
> *Mark 11:24*

I know the objections. I have had them myself. I have allowed my doubting mind to argue with God all day long. You know what came of it? Nothing! Absolutely nothing, unless you want to count disappointment as something.

Can you demonstrate the kind of faith that prevails with God? Why not? What keeps you from declaring unabashedly, "I believe Jesus can perform MY miracle, no matter what!"

Mileage? No problem! Complexity? No problem! Circumstances? No problem. "What things soever you shall ask in my name!"

WHATSOEVER you ask.

I can't see where that excludes any legitimate request of any kind.

If you are a died-in-the-wool skeptic, you are probably asking, "Do YOU always get your miracle like that?"

I'm glad you asked.

No.

I don't always get what I ask, because just like most people, I don't always ask in faith. I have issues with doubt. I have issues with fear. I have issues with unbelief. So do I get miracles on those terms? Not on your life.

Praying on Purpose

There was an old man of God who lived to be more than 90 years old. He never spent one night in a hospital in his lifetime. He was known far and wide as a man of great faith. Hundreds, if not thousands of people claim to have been healed and received amazing miracles when he prayed for them. He even raised several people from the dead in his lifetime.

But the real story behind the story is that that old gentleman's great faith came through devastating experiences. As a young man, he spent days in prayer and fasting for a sister who was critically ill. After coming in from an intense prayer meeting in the woods, his sister still died in his arms. And that happened not just one time. A second sister also died in his arms, even after he had exhausted himself in fervent prayer.

So, did his losses dissuade him from being a miracle worker? Did the death of his dear ones cause him to dismiss God as a healer or a miracle worker? As I see it, the exact opposite is true! The record of his lifetime revealed that those losses did nothing but make him more determined to find the real source of the miracle-working power of God.

And he DID find it, and over his many years he performed countless amazing miracles by that same faith in God.

There is little in the world to challenge your faith more than failure.

My wife died in my arms at 2:48 in the morning. I was holding her when she drew her last breath. She was only 50 years old. There was no one else left in the house but God and me. During the six years she had been sick, I had prayed as hard and long as any man ever prayed for his wife.

I could have stopped believing in miracles right then and there.

But something happened in me that night that made me forever determined not to allow her death to make me turn my back on the eternal Truth that **God is and always will be a miracle worker**.

We must not allow ourselves to be a victim of our losses, defeats, or failures. We must not lose our determination to stand upon the Word of God, or to claim the miracles, signs and wonders He PROMISED that we could have! Satan would be delighted if we quit, but this is not about him.

Praying for Results

Hannah was barren for many years, but she prayed, and miraculously bore Samuel. Samuel became one of the greatest prophets of all time **because of a mother's prevailing prayer.**

One of the best teachers of any great truth is failure. Sometimes, the most powerful lessons are learned through trial and error. Unfortunately, in some cases, we only learn through a process of elimination. After we have tried everything the WRONG way, we decide to try something that turns out RIGHT. **We must learn to prevail in prayer**, against every hindrance.

Our **perseverance** will impact not only our own lives, but also the lives of our descendants and all who know us. Entire generations of civilization have been lost to sin because their fathers gave up on God. Entire nations have been alienated from God because their fathers lost their faith in God. Tragically, the circumstances of each new generation are handed to them from their forefathers. If forefathers fail, whole generations are lost.

But by the same logic, entire families and communities have come to the knowledge of God because of a few godly ancestors. One man's faith or failure can have a long-standing "ripple-effect."

Jacob had failed many, many times in his life. But he never stopped pursuing the blessing of God. At last, he prevailed.

"Jacob was left alone;
and there **wrestled** a man with him until the breaking of the day.
And when he saw that he prevailed not against him,
he touched the hollow of his thigh;
and the hollow of Jacob's thigh was out of joint,
as he wrestled with him.

And he said, Let me go, for the day breaketh.
And he said, **I will not let thee go, except thou bless me**.

And he said unto him, What is thy name?And he said, Jacob.
And he said, **Thy name shall be called no more Jacob, but Israel:
for as a prince hast thou power with God and with men,
and HAST PREVAILED. ...And he blessed him there**."
Genesis 32:24-29

You can talk about **Jacob's prevailing prayer**, and how it blessed him. But I want you to consider that **Jacob's ordeal with the angel that night was not merely about Jacob.**

Jacob was fighting for you and me that night. If Jacob had not prevailed with God, we would never have heard the name "ISRAEL."

Israel is here today because of prevailing prayer, and Israel is our link to God. In Israel, all the nations of the earth are blessed.

PREVAILING PRAYER is the lifeline to more of God than any of us can imagine.

One of the worst indictments on modern Christianity is its inability to engage in prevailing prayer. Most modern Churches don't have the withal to call a prayer line where the sick and infirm stand before a powerful man of God and receive a miracle ON THE SPOT!

We have entire "Christian" denominations whose doctrinal platforms officially deny that God even does miracles today! That kind of spiritual environment has a malignant, deadly effect on the entire "Christian" community.

Compare that to the ancient Christian practices.

Jesus told the early believers that they were going to receive **POWER** after they received the Holy Ghost. That word in Greek ("dunamis") could be translated **DYNAMITE** in English. **Explosive power. More power than a human can contain.**

Ask yourself, "Have I ever felt that kind of power in me? Is there any of that dynamite in me?" Have you ever felt so "high" on the faith of God that you were ready to boldly command a miracle without even a speck of reluctance or hesitation, and **with an unstoppable determination to prevail with God in prayer**?

That is how you command a miracle. Speak the positive word of faith in God, and you will have what you ask.

So what is the best way to embark on a life of prevailing prayer? How does someone who has rarely, if ever, practiced commanding miracles?

If the only way you can believe in miracles is to vaguely and impotently throw a prayer into the wind and "hope for the best," you will probably never see many miracles as a result of your praying.

Jesus trained His disciples by making them follow Him around the countryside while He performed all kinds of miracles. He put His power to the test as they looked on.

Jesus turned the water into wine "on demand." They needed it right then, and He did it right then. The wedding celebration was almost over, and soon folks would be going home. It was now or never. Get the water pots. Fill them up. Pour them out. The wine was flowing.

On demand. A miracle on demand.

Why is it important for me to talk to you this way? Because most of us are content to pray a generic prayer, and walk away and leave it all to the wind. If a miracle comes, fine, but if it doesn't, we just won't speak of it again. **That is not the way we should deal with it.**

God has given us His great power. It is an insult to God not to use it.

If you do not have the faith to command a miracle, or declare a miracle or at the very least EXPECT a miracle, then I would like to know, "WHY NOT?"

Is it because you think that somehow OTHER people can do it, but you can't? Do you think other people have great faith, but you can't?

God called you out of darkness into His marvelous light so you would show forth His praises. You were not born to run around helpless and ashamed of your Christianity. God did not create you to spend your time on earth as a powerless, defenseless victim of circumstances.

"I GIVE YOU POWER!" Jesus said.

What are you going to do with that power? Die in your misery? Take a whipping from every problem that ever comes down the pike?

What a tragic fate! **You can do better than that.**

"God is going to do a great thing for you!" How difficult is that to say? Is there any reason why those words will not come out of your mouth? It is the stuff of miracles.

Words produce miracles.

God Almighty created the whole universe with nothing but words. Jesus performed countless miracles with nothing but words. Elijah called down fire from heaven with nothing but words.

Stop and think about it. Everything in the universe is the product of thought. When John wrote in John 1:1, "In the beginning was the Word. And the Word was God…," the Greek root for 'word' is 'LOGOS', which means, "thought or arrangement."

So God was THOUGHT. Arrangement.

And God SAID… "Let there be…" and there WAS.

We are made in the image of God. We see because God sees. We hear because God hears. We feel because God feels. And we THINK because God thinks.

But do we SPEAK as God speaks?

"But," you may say, "ME speaking is not the same as God speaking!"

It is certainly true that a lot of what we say is not the way God speaks.

But what if you DO speak as God speaks? What if you DO speak creatively in His name?

Put these three things together. **Faith. Words. Expectation.**

There is no "magic formula." There is no special phrase, nor mantra, nor chant to perform. But there is infinite power simply in the name of Jesus.

It is not good enough just to hear somebody else's story.

YOU can prevail with God. God will do miracles for YOU, if you will have them.

What does it take to have a miracle?

Throughout the entire length of this book, I have shown you countless examples of prayers that prevailed.

It is now time to digest everything that has been said, and put it into action. It is now time to get your miracles.

It is time now for PREVAILING PRAYER.

Just do it.

Don't make it complicated or difficult.

One preacher I know who has performed as many miracles as any preacher I ever knew, told me that the first thing you have to do is just "turn your brain off."

I knew what he meant. You have to cut off the source of unbelief. You have to silence your carnal mind. You have to shut out all the arguments. You have to deprive doubt of its voice.

Get after it.

Prevail!

"Prevailing, or effectual prayer, is that prayer
which attains the blessing that it seeks."
Charles G. Finney
1792-1875

"It is the habit of faith, when she is praying, to use pleas.
Mere prayer sayers, who do not pray at all,
forget to argue with God; but **those who prevail
bring forth their reasons and their strong arguments**."
Charles H. Spurgeon
1834-1892

"All great soul-winners have been men of much and mighty prayer,
and **all great revivals have been preceded and carried out
by persevering, prevailing knee-work in the closet**."
Samuel Logan Brengle
1860-1936

"When thou prayest, enter into thy closet,
and when thou hast shut thy door,
pray to thy Father which is in secret;
and thy Father which seeth in secret shall reward thee openly."
Matthew 6:6-7

Chapter 22

A Quiet, Solitary Place to Pray

So, now it is time to pray.

Talking about prayer is not praying. Telling stories about prayer is not praying. Reading books about prayer is not praying. Listening to sermons about prayer is not praying.

Sooner or later, prayer is going to have to find a TIME and a PLACE.

Maybe we should speak of the PLACE first. Do you have a PLACE to pray? Where will it be?

There are many places that will suffice to pray when you are not bent down in major intercession. I spend a very large part of all my driving time praying. If I am in the car, I am usually praying. I have a pocket-size voice recorder that has my entire prayer list on it. I call hundreds of names out to Jesus as often as I can. But that is not my most serious prayer time.

You can pray throughout the course of your day in every imaginable situation. If you are eating lunch alone, you can pray for a while. Anytime you are waiting, for whatever reasons (an appointment, an arrival, you name it), you can pray.

But if you want to be a true intercessor, you need an appointed time and place to pray.

Do you have a solitary place in your home? Consecrate it to daily prayer.

Move the furniture around to facilitate your praying. I have known people who had a cabinetmaker build a custom-made altar where they could kneel and pray in their home, and others who dedicated a closet or a spare room to prayer. Both of those practices have great value.

But the most important thing is that you find a place where you can forget about everything else and be uninterrupted for whatever period of time that you need to pray.

I owe a debt of gratitude to two praying grandmothers who influenced me profoundly as a child. One of them, my "Granny" used to go to the ladies' prayer meeting each week down at the old Church house. Several of the older ladies met in the Church auditorium one morning each week, for no other reason than to pray.

Although I was only about eight or nine years old, I was already playing the organ for Sunday services in our Church. The ladies who attended the weekly prayer meeting asked me to softly play hymns while they prayed. I played songs like, "Sweet Hour of Prayer," and "What a Friend We Have In Jesus," "Take the Name Of Jesus With You," and so many other songs while they prayed, usually for about an hour.

Those were defining moments in my childhood. The images of those old ladies kneeling around the altars and among the pews are forever etched into my mind. There is no more beautiful sight on earth than the sight of godly men or women on their knees in earnest prayer, lifting their voices, often with tears, calling on the God of Heaven in behalf of themselves and all those they love.

That experience helped me learn the importance of prayer. By the time I was a teenager, I had already learned the significance of fasting and prayer, and had established those routines in my own life. I believed that every time a major decision needed to be made, I should fast and pray for direction. I can think of dozens of times when my choices or decisions were completely determined by an answer I received during a time of fasting and prayer.

When I finally went off to Bible College at the age of 17, I felt the first order of business was to enter into prayer for my own future and ministry.

I lived on the fourth floor of the Bible college dorms. On the third floor there was a large, open prayer room where all the male students living there could find a place to pray. Altar benches were built all around the walls of that room, and a row of altars went down the center of the room, from one end to the other.

Right away, I decided that I needed to enter into a three-day prayer and fasting vigil. I wanted God to show me clearly what I was supposed to do with my life. First thing in the mornings, I went to the prayer room and prayed until I had to leave to go to classes. As soon as classes were over, I returned to the prayer room and stayed for the remainder of the day.

At the end of the third day, God gave me several verses of scripture that I believed were His explicit answers to me. I memorized those verses, and quoted them often to myself for many years to come. The answer that I received during that time of fasting and prayer literally guided my decisions for several years.

A few years after I married Dixie, and our sons were still small, I reached another crossroads in my life. We were on staff at a Church in Texas when I began to feel a great need to get alone with God for prayerful intercession about the future of our ministry.

This time, I chose a spare bedroom in our home. I took a three-day Sabbatical, and told Dixie that I planned to spend the next three days alone in that room, fasting and praying for an answer from God about our destiny.

I literally closed the outside world out for three days. I prayed and studied the Word, wrote notes, and meditated on spiritual things. On the third day, I wrote down a list of five things that I felt particularly distressed about, and asked God to give me clear answers for all five of those particular things.

> "An honest man with an open Bible and a pad and pencil
> is sure to find out what is wrong with him very quickly."
> *A.W. Tozer*
> *1897-1963*

That evening, as the sun went down, I came out of that spare room, and asked for something to eat. Just as I sat down at the dining room table, the telephone rang. When I hung up from that phone-call, ALL FIVE of the things on my prayer list had been answered - in less than THIRTY MINUTES after completing my prayer and fasting vigil.

Later that night, another call came from someone out-of-state that literally changed the direction of our lives. I will always believe that God initiated those phone calls in direct response to that prayer and fasting vigil.

I am telling you these things because I want you to see that PRAYER CHANGES THINGS.

"The effectual fervent prayer of a righteous man availeth much."
James 5:15

God honors an honest pursuit of His will, and He will intervene.

"It is God's will... that **the prayers of His saints**
should be one of the great principal means
of carrying on the designs of Christ's kingdom in the world.
When God has something very great to accomplish for His Church,
it is His will that there should precede it
the **extraordinary prayers of His people**;
...when God is about to accomplish great things for His Church,
He will begin by remarkably **pouring out**
the spirit of grace and **supplication**."
Jonathan Edwards
1703-1758

So, find a place to pray. If you cannot find any privacy in your home, your Church is the next best choice. Day or night, God's house is supposed to be a house of prayer. I would not expect the average layperson to be so powerfully attracted to having a solitary prayer meeting alone in a darkened Church building, but in over forty years of preaching in hundreds of Churches across the United States, those experiences have been absolutely critical to my salvation.

I am reminded right now of so many times when I stayed, locked up in an empty Church sanctuary, alone with God and the angels, seeking the blessings and the will of God for my life. They are without doubt some of the most valuable experiences of my life.

Praying for Results

But you do not have to be in a Church house to pray. It could be anywhere you find a place that can be sanctified unto prayer.

In the early 1980s, my wife and I went through a great trial. We sought God for several months about a complex situation. One night, I was the guest preacher in a Church in Bryan/College Station, Texas. After the service was over, my wife and children went on to bed, but I stayed at the Church. I intended to stay at the Church and pray through the night until I got an answer from God about our situation.

I walked those aisles and prayed until five o'clock in the morning. I told God everything I could think of to persuade Him to work out a particular situation for us. Finally, I could stay awake no longer, and went home and went to bed.

Only three hours later, at 8:00 AM, I received a very important and entirely unexpected phone call out of the blue. That phone call was probably the most important phone call I had ever received until that time. After about six hours of intense prayer, our lives were again changed dramatically by intense intercessory prayer.

> "Oh, what peace we often forfeit!
> Oh, what needless pain we bear!
> All because we do not carry
> everything to God in prayer!"

If praying in your local Church is not an option, find a place. Any place.

One of my old pastors suffered a massive heart attack in the early years of his ministry while he was still young. Those were the days before open-heart surgery was an option. He faced the prospect of either dying, or at least having to give up the ministry.

He said good-byes to his wife and children, and checked into a small hotel nearby to get alone with God. If my memory serves me correctly, he spent five days alone in that hotel, fasting, praying, and asking God for a miracle. When he left that hotel days later, he went back to his Church and ministry, and never again IN HIS LIFE did he have another episode with his heart. He lived to be 86.

Praying on Purpose

Find a place to pray. Sit in a chair, lie on the floor, kneel by a bed, walk the floor, or whatever suits you. Just find your place to pray, and get started. Now is better than later.

Even as I write this, I am saying a prayer that the very next time you set out to seek the Lord in this fashion, you will find Him to be more real, more powerful and more wonderful than at any time before in your life.

> "Whole days and weeks have I spent
> prostrate on the ground in silent or vocal prayer."
> *George Whitefield – 1714-1770*
> *(Evangelist during "The Great Awakening" of Britain and America)*

Spurgeon's Boiler Room

Five young college students were spending a Sunday in London,
so they went to hear the famed Charles Haddon Spurgeon
preach at the Metropolitan Tabernacle.

While waiting for the doors to open, the students were greeted
by a man who asked, "Gentlemen, let me show you around.
Would you like to see the heating plant of this Church?"

They were not particularly interested, for it was a hot day in July.
But they didn't want to offend the stranger, so they consented.
The young men were taken down a stairway, a door was quietly opened,
and their guide whispered, "This is our heating plant."

Surprised, the students saw 700 people bowed in prayer, seeking a
blessing on the service that was soon to begin in the auditorium above.
Softly closing the door, the gentleman then introduced himself.
It was none other than Charles Spurgeon.

Chapter 23

God's House of Prayer

Typically once or twice each week, I go to Church, either into the main Sanctuary or into the Prayer Room, to spend time alone with God. Sometimes, I stay there for an hour. At other times, I may stay for three or four hours. It may be during the day time, or it may be at night, even in the wee hours. When I go to the Prayer Room, it is because I want to conduct serious business with God. I consider that to be some of my most valuable and intense prayer times.

In my sixty-one years, I have spent literally thousands of sacred hours alone in Church houses - praying, reading my Bible, and seeking the will of God. And I will confide to you that the Prayer Room is the most luxurious amenity in my life. There is no place on earth more comforting or more sacred than the place where I get alone with God in prayer. I would rather have a Prayer Room than a luxury car, an RV, a yacht, or anything else I can think of.

Jesus quoted the prophet Isaiah when He said,

> "Mine house shall be a house of prayer for all people."

A Church is not supposed to be merely an assembly hall where lectures are given. One large Church where I served on staff as a young man had a sign over the Sanctuary entrance: "Where People Meet God."

If people do not meet God at Church, then what is Church for?

Simeon and Anna were in the Temple the day that Joseph and Mary brought baby Jesus to be dedicated. But their presence was no coincidence. Simeon and Anna were regulars in the Temple. Anna "was a widow of about fourscore and four years [84], **which departed not from the temple, but served God with fastings and prayers night and day**," Luke 2:37.

If you make a habit of seeking God regularly, it is certain that the Lord, whom you seek, will suddenly come to His Temple.

King David also had a deep love for the House of God. He said,

> "A day in thy courts is better than a thousand [elsewhere]."
> *Psalms 84:10*

In the great crises of his life, David ran to the House of God for refuge.

In the beginning, Churches were not Rock-and-Roll Concert venues. They were not Drama Theaters. They were not basketball courts. They were not community centers, soup kitchens, or recreation centers.

The House of God was, and should be, a holy, sacred, sanctified, and consecrated house where people can always go to pray.

Today's Churches are often multi-purpose, multi-cultural activity centers. In many cases, they are used more as gymnasiums for youth to hang out, or cafeterias for seniors to have pot-luck dinners, or sound stages for musicians to jam in, than for sacred purposes.

The sad reality is that many Churches are so much like Grand Central Station with activities that it would be almost impossible to find a quiet, undisturbed place to pray.

Why do we feel that it is so important to conduct our social activities in the House of God, yet we seldom think to use it for the far-more-important, divinely-ordained purpose of prayer?

From the beginning, the Church was NOT such a recreational center. People came to the House of God to spend holy, consecrated time in the presence of God. Today, if you go to a typical Church house to pray, you may find that there is no privacy or no sanctity whatsoever. The Church house has been hijacked for secular purposes. We have forgotten that the most important furnishings in a Church are the ALTAR and the PULPIT.

That kind of invasion of the holy place was the cause of Jesus' outrage in John 2:14-16:

Praying for Results

"And when he had made a scourge of small cords,
he drove them all out of the temple, and the sheep, and the oxen;
and poured out the changers' money, and overthrew the tables;
And said unto them that sold doves, **Take these things hence**;
make not my Father's house an house of merchandise."

More details of that scenario are recorded in Matthew 21:12-14:

"And Jesus went into the temple of God,
and cast out all them that sold and bought in the temple,
and overthrew the tables of the moneychangers,
and the seats of them that sold doves,
And said unto them, It is written,
My house shall be called the house of prayer;
but ye have made it a den of thieves.
And the blind and the lame came to him in the temple;
and he healed them."

The Church must be first and foremostly a house of prayer. If we will cleanse the House of God, and re-consecrate it as a House of Prayer, the blind and the lame will be healed, and many other miracles will follow.

Prayer has always been the precedent and prelude to every spiritual revival throughout the ages.

When the Holy Ghost first began to fall in America in 1901, it began at a small Bible School in Topeka, Kansas, organized by Charles Parham.

For three weeks, forty students met together in the Chapel for fasting and intercessory prayer. On New Year's Eve, 1901, the Spirit came upon the first of them, and she began to speak in other tongues as the Spirit gave the utterance. That week, twelve seekers received the Baptism of the Holy Ghost - the first notable outpouring of the Holy Ghost in modern times!

When the epic revival began in Los Angeles at the Azusa Street Mission, pastored by William Seymour - that sweeping revival was preceded by weeks and months of intense, almost non-stop prayer meetings by the hundreds of people from that community. That revival in 1906 was so powerful, that by 1909, over 50,000 people around the country had received the Holy Ghost as a result of the ministry of the Azusa Street Mission. Ultimately, virtually all of the modern "Latter Rain" (Holy Ghost outpouring) that spread around the world (now numbering in the hundreds of millions of believers) was traced back to the prayer meetings organized by William Seymour.

Revival does not come by basketball tournaments, outdoor concerts, free hot dogs, or charity runs.

Revival comes by prayer.

And that is true of both personal revival and Church-wide revival.

When we restore the priority of prayer in our lives, miracles will begin happening. Your life has never been so rich as when you regularly and habitually enter into the House of God to pray.

> "**They that wait upon the LORD** shall renew their strength;
> they shall mount up with wings as eagles;
> they shall run, and not be weary;
> and they shall walk, and not faint."
> Isaiah 40:31

The next time you sense your need to get alone with God, go to the House of God, and pray.

You will eventually realize that it is the one place you should have discovered from the very beginning.

> "Shut the world out,
> withdraw from all worldly thoughts and occupations,
> and shut yourself in alone with God,
> to pray to Him in secret.
> Let this be your chief object in prayer,
> to realize the presence of your heavenly Father."
> *Andrew Murray*
> *1828-1917*

Chapter 24

Into The Most Holy Place

I did not originally plan this chapter, but as I came to the conclusion of this book, I realized that OUR APPROACH unto God is an enormous element of the process of prayer. It is essential that we enter into God's presence in the right manner. Therefore, I want to show you **the PRELUDE to prayer**.

My primary point of reference is the original **Tabernacle plan**. As you remember, the **Ark of the Covenant** represented the **Presence of God** in the midst of the Children of Israel.

God actually spoke audibly to Moses from between the wings of the **Cherubim** on the **Mercy Seat**, which sat atop the Ark. So Moses' approach to the Ark of the Covenant is the ultimate example of our approach to God.

Here is one of the greatest truths we will ever know about approaching God.

The Ark of the Covenant did not sit out in the sunshine. It was not exposed to the elements. It was not accessible to anyone but Moses (Exodus 25:22) and the High Priest.

The Ark of the Covenant sat within the **Most Holy Place**, beyond the **Holy Place**, inside the Tabernacle, inside the Courts of the Tabernacle.

NOBODY could even SEE the Ark of the Covenant without going through carefully prescribed procedures to get there. (When the Tabernacle was in transit, the Priests COVERED it during its transport, and the people could not see it.)

1. First, Aaron, and all subsequent High Priests were required to wear meticulously designed **Holy Garments** when they went into the **Most Holy Place**.

2.   He had to make a sacrifice at the **Altar of Sacrifice**.

3.   He had to wash at the **Brazen Laver**.

4.   Then he had to enter the **Inner Court**

5.   He had to eat at the **Table of Shewbread**.

6.   He had to offer incense at the **Altar of Incense**.

7.   He was illuminated by the **Golden Candlestick**.

8.   Then, if he was a HIGH Priest, he could enter beyond the **Veil**, only ONCE A YEAR into the **Most Holy Place**.

Now, since Jesus Christ died at Calvary, the VEIL of the Temple is rent, and ANY true Christian (who is by divine decree, one of His kings and priests) may enter into the Most Holy Place.

HOWEVER, it is important to note that even though a New Testament believer may now enter into the Most Holy Place, HE STILL HAS TO GO THROUGH THE SANCTICATION PROCESS!

Symbolically and typologically, every New Testament Christians must:

1.   **Put on Holy Garments.** (Holiness) This tells us that we must not approach God in a common or profane way. We must put away the sins of the flesh and spirit before we make our approach to Him. This speaks of holiness and purity. "**Holiness ...without which, no man shall see God**," Hebrews 12:14.

2.   **Offer a sacrifice of blood at the Altar.** (Repentance) Everything that happened in the Tabernacle began at the Brazen Altar. Animals were killed, blood was shed, and the carcases were burned. Since the Garden of Eden, God has required death for sin.

   At the Altar, the debt began to be paid, the blood was shed, and remission of sins became possible. Without shedding blood, there can be no remission for sins (Hebrews 9:22).

Animal blood appeased God until the perfect Lamb was slain - Jesus Christ. ALL remission of sins ultimately comes by HIS blood.

We do not need to sacrifice animals for their blood. Jesus shed His blood to pay for our sins if we will repent and turn from them.

3. **Wash at the Brazen Laver.** (Water Baptism) That is fulfilled when we are baptized by immersion in the name of Jesus Christ for the remission of our sins. Exodus 30:21-22 tells us that "they shall **wash with water that they die not**." You must be washed in water before you approach the Holy Place.

    In order for OUR sins to be remitted, we must **REPENT at the altar** and be **baptized in Jesus' name for the remission of our sins** (Acts 2:38). **That obedience** appropriates the Blood of Jesus, which then washes away our sins.

4. **Enlightened by the Golden Candlestick and the Oil.** (Baptism of the Holy Ghost). This tells us to be filled with the Spirit of God - the Holy Anointing Oil. It is the light of the Spirit that enables us to see our way to the glory of God.

5. **Eat bread at the Table of Shewbread.** (Jesus Christ, Word of God, Bread of Life) That is fulfilled when we study the Word of God with faith in the Lord Jesus Christ.

6. **Offer incense at the Altar of Incense.** (The Prayers of the Saints) This is the last piece of furniture before reaching the Ark of the Covenant. It is fulfilled when we come boldly before Him in prayer.

7. **Stand before the Ark of the Covenant**, from which we can then hear the voice of God.

Now you may think that you can run recklessly into the Presence of God, but in God's order of things, technically, that simply is not true. BEFORE WE EVEN BEGIN TO PRAY, there are certain conditions which we must meet, and certain things that we should do.

Two verses quickly come to my mind that indicate two conditions that we must meet before we pray:

1. **"If I regard iniquity in my heart, the Lord will not hear me,"** Psalms 66:18.

    You cannot run haphazardly from the Outer Court into the Most Holy Place. You must put away your sins and sanctify yourself by God's due process.

    Now I can hear somebody objecting, saying, "BUT WHEN JESUS DIED ON THE CROSS, THE VEIL OF THE TEMPLE WAS RENT, SO I CAN GO INTO THE MOST HOLY PLACE!"

    Stop! Just because the VEIL was opened, we may not presume that the ALTAR, GOLDEN LAVER, ALTAR OF INCENSE, TABLE OF SHEWBREAD, and CANDLESTICK have no more significance! They still have profound significance.

    Although we may indeed go into the Most Holy Place, we must STILL proceed through the proper processes up to the Ark of the Covenant. Before we hear from God at the Ark of the Covenant, **we must PUT AWAY all iniquity from our hearts**.

    - **Put on Holy Garments** (a holy life) in the tradition of the **Priest**
    - **Repent** at the **Altar of Sacrifice**
    - **Wash** (by baptism) at the **Brazen Laver**
    - **Eat Bread** at **Table of Shewbread** (faith in Christ, Bread of Life)
    - **Light the Oil** (Holy Ghost baptism) in the **Golden Candlestick**
    - **Pray** at the **Altar of Incense**

2. **"He that cometh to God must believe that he is, and that he is a rewarder of them that diligently seek him,"** Hebrews 11:6.

    That text reminds me that I MUST HAVE FAITH in God if I hope to receive anything from Him.

    "The just shall live by faith."
    Habakkuk 2:4; Romans 1:17; Galatians 3:11

It is our FAITH that enables us to partake of the Tabernacle plan vicariously. Of course, there is no PHYSICAL Tabernacle or Temple in existence today. So the entire process is a process that occurs SPIRITUALLY by faith.

Lest there be any doubt in your mind that these things are legitimate claims, I will remind you that God warned a man **would be struck dead if he was not properly sanctified to approach the Ark.**

Since the days of Moses, men enquired of the LORD before the Ark of the Covenant. But in the days of Eli, when the Ark had been in the Tabernacle at Shiloh, the Philistines captured it and carried it away. But **God punished them for profaning it.** Consequently, the Philistines returned it, and it was stored away for nearly eighty years.

David started to move it to Jerusalem, but he did not take care to sanctify the priests in advance, and Uzzah died when he touched it. People often handle holy things recklessly, but God is holy and must be approached on His sacred terms.

> "Because ye did it not [sanctify yourselves] at the first,
> the **LORD our God made a breach upon us**,
> for that **we sought him not after the due order**."
> *1 Chronicles 15:13*

"We sought him not after the due order."

This is the entire purpose of this chapter - to impress upon you the sober reality that **we should take care to approach God "after the due order."** Before you pray, SANCTIFY YOURSELF. Prepare yourself according to God's sanctifying process - which I have just outlined for you.

> "The faith which has not a **sanctifying** influence on the character
> is no better than the faith of devils."
> *J.C. Ryles*
> *1816-1900*

"**The sanctified body** is one whose hands are clean.
The stain of dishonesty is not on them,
the withering blight of ill-gotten gain has not blistered them,
the mark of violence is not found upon them.
They have been **separated from every occupation**
that could displease God or injure a fellow-man."
A.B. Simpson
1843-1919

"Our sanctification is a process wherein we are coworkers with God.
We have the promise of God's assistance in our labor,
but His divine help does not annul our responsibility to work."
"**Work out your salvation** with fear and trembling," Philippians 2:12.
R.C. Sproul
1939-

"Sanctification is not a mystical, magical process.
It is the result of having our steps
ordered by the Word of God.
It is our coming into conformity to the image of Christ.
It is in the daily keeping of the commandments of God
that the man or woman of God is sanctified.
Jesus prayed that we would be
'sanctified through the Truth,' (John 17:19).
Truth floating in the air does not sanctify us.
Truth guiding our steps sanctifies us."
K. R.

"Order my steps in thy word:
and let not any iniquity have dominion over me."
Psalms 119:133

Chapter 25

Let Us Pray

Using Prayer Starters

The remainder of this book, "Praying on Purpose, Praying for Results," will have a completely different style than what I have used so far.

In these remaining pages, I am asking you to pray with me for a while. I want you to say some prayers with me.

I know that everyone has their own style of praying, and I do not want to infringe on your sacred territory, nor do I want to take away anything whatsoever from your private prayer time.

I am not asking you to abandon your own manner of praying. But I am asking you to join with me in some sample prayers, in the hopes that I will be able to take you into some fresh new thoughts and desires, which will bring about a new and higher level of praying.

Because I have ministered to and prayed with countless multitudes of people in more than forty-five years of ministry as a Pastor and as an Evangelist, I have learned that many people just cannot find the words to pray effectually.

For that reason, I am submitting to you, in these next pages, a wide variety of prayers – **Prayer Starters** - in many categories. I want to help you learn how to pray more effectively.

The following prayers are not intended to be memorized or recited.

I do not encourage vain repetitions. But I do encourage you to pray along with me in the prayers that I am providing here. They are not perfect prayers. My great desire is that as you pray with me, you will suddenly be inspired to pray for things above and beyond anything I have written here. I would be delighted for that to happen, and would be thankful that we were actually making progress together in this effort.

Praying on Purpose

Every day for more than five years, I have written four 100-word Bible lessons that have circulated by Internet into every nation (236 in all, including islands) on earth. At this writing, my subscribers in 215 nations are learning daily lessons from the Word of God. These mini-lessons, also published in my new book, "MY DAILY BIBLE COMPANION," have produced thousands of remarkable responses from my readers.

As a result, I am now encouraged to use the same teaching method with these lessons on Prayer.

I will present to you **a series of 100-word Prayer Starters** on a wide variety of topics. I believe that among these prayers, you will discover something that will help you become more effective in your praying.

I believe these short prayers will stimulate your mind, and help you realize more precisely what prayer is all about. These prayers will help you see the reasons why you pray, and help you to be more specific in your appeals to God.

It is my hope and desire that as you pray these prayers with me, you will begin to realize that your prayers have far more potential than you ever dreamed or imagined.

Here is what to do.

1. As you read the prayers that follow, **pray them out loud**. Practice praying more specific prayers. Search your heart for more things, and add your own personal requests to the ones you find here. After you have prayed a certain prayer with me, add your own requests to them.

2. I have taken **more than 150 pages of my own personal prayers** that I have prayed over various things for more than a decade, and **broken them down into small segments,** then **rewritten** them as **Prayer Starters**, and placed them more-or-less categorically by title.

You will certainly not feel all the same priorities that I feel. **I am not trying to force a prayer style onto you**. Your prayers may have a completely different range of urgencies than mine. Your priorities will be different than my priorities. If you do not like a particular line in these prayers, then mark it out, and write a different line in the margins. As much as you can, make these prayers your prayers, in your own words.

3. **Choose the prayers that seem most important to you today.** These prayers have evolved from the prayer notes I have used for many years. I have revised and simplified them pretty radically for this book, because I want you to be able to use them for any purpose. I have rewritten them to make them usable by anyone, instead of for my own specific requests. As you read them, and pray them out loud, make any changes you want.

4. **Decide which prayers you should pray most frequently**, and which ones you will pray weekly, monthly, etc. Naturally, there are some things and some people for whom you will want to pray every single day. Other things are not so urgent, but you do not want to neglect.

> Pray as much as you can,
> for as many things as you can,
> as often as you can,
> in Jesus' name.

In the following chapters, you will find a volume of prayers on many, many topics. Use those that you think are appropriate to your needs, and skip over the rest.

> "God shapes the world by prayer.
> The more praying there is in the world
> the better the world will be,
> the mightier the forces against evil..."
> E.M.Bounds
> 1835-1913

Praying on Purpose

Sweet Hour of Prayer! Sweet Hour of Prayer!
That calls me from a world of care,
And bids me at my Father's Throne
Make all my wants and wishes known.

In seasons of distress and grief,
My soul has often found relief,
And oft escaped the tempter's snare,
By thy return, Sweet Hour of Prayer!

Sweet Hour of Prayer! Sweet Hour of Prayer!
The joys I feel, the bliss I share,
Of those whose anxious spirits burn
With strong desires for thy return!

With such, I hasten to the place
Where God my Savior shows His face,
And gladly take my station there,
And wait for thee, Sweet Hour of Prayer!

Sweet Hour of Prayer! Sweet Hour of Prayer!
Thy wings shall my petition bear
To Him whose Truth and faithfulness
Engage the waiting soul to bless.

And since He bids me seek His face,
Believe His Word and trust His grace,
I'll cast on Him my every care,
And wait for thee, Sweet Hour of Prayer!

Sweet Hour of Prayer! Sweet Hour of Prayer!
May I thy consolation share,
Till, from Mount Pisgah's lofty height,
I view my home and take my flight.

This robe of flesh I'll drop, and rise
To seize the everlasting prize,
And shout, while passing through the air,
"Farewell, farewell, Sweet Hour of Prayer!"

William W. Walford
1845

Chapter 26

Pray With Me

The following prayers are not intended to be model prayers or prayers to recite again and again. I am not trying to put words in your mouth. These are merely **Prayer Starters**.

I can think of so many people right now that I have prayed with, only to discover that they were nigh unto speechless. We now have a generation of young people who have NEVER seen their elders pray. Most of them have NEVER been in a truly intense prayer meeting, NEVER been in an altar, and NEVER been on their knees to pray. That is one of the saddest tragedies of our time.

Nevertheless, that is one of the reasons why I have included this section to this book. I know that **many people need someone to teach them to pray**.

These Prayer Starters are only sample prayers to help you think about what you should be praying for. I am simply trying to give you a push in the right direction, **like putting a charger on a low battery**.

The following prayers will take a very simple format.

I will provide a 100-Word Prayer Starter for each of many significant ELEMENTS of prayer. This is simply to help you focus and be reminded of the kinds of things to pray on each topic.

For example, I will provide a Prayer Starter for each of several elements of **Repentance** (i.e., Contrition, Confession, Repentance), **Thanksgiving** (i.e., Thanks, Praise, Worship, etc.).

You need not pray every one of these topics every time you go to pray. That is strictly up to your personal desire and discretion. I am only trying to help you pray more effectively. I pray that each topic will help you.

Prayer Was Made Unto God Without Ceasing

"How significant the picture of the Apostolic Church:
Peter in prison.
The Jews triumphant.
Herod supreme.
The arena of martyrdom
awaiting the dawning of the morning
to drink up the Apostle's blood.
And everything else against it.

'But prayer was made unto God without ceasing,' **Acts 12:5.**

And what was the sequel?
The prison open.
The Apostle free.
The Jews baffled.
The wicked king eaten of worms.
A spectacle of hidden retribution.
And the Word of God rolling on in greater victory."

Andrew Murray
1828-1917

Chapter 27

Approaching The Mercy Seat

Prayers of Preparation

Entering Into His Presence

Heavenly Father, I come to You today in much the same manner that Aaron the High Priest entered into the Tabernacle, and ultimately into the Most Holy Place. I want to enter into Your Presence. I reverently enter into your courts, sanctifying myself body, soul and spirit for this sacred time. As Aaron put on his holy, priestly garments, I put on clean spiritual garments, "hating even the garment spotted by the flesh," Jude 1:23. I put away carnality, worldliness and every sin as I approach your Throne today, in Jesus' name.

Entering Into His Gates With Thanksgiving

Lord, as the Priest entered the Tabernacle, he came first to the Altar of Sacrifice where he would slay the sacrificial animal, shedding blood that would atone for his sins and the sins of the people. I thank you today for the Blood of the Lamb of God, Jesus Christ, who was slain for me at Calvary. Because of your precious sacrifice, I do not have to bring a lamb, bullock or goat. I lay myself on your Altar as a living sacrifice, which is my reasonable service, giving you thanks with a life of submission because of your grace and mercy toward me.

A Sacrifice of Praise

"Jesus ...that he might sanctify the people with his own blood, suffered without the gate. ...Let us offer the sacrifice of praise to God continually, that is, the fruit of our lips giving thanks to his name," Hebrews 13:12-15. Lord, I thank you and praise you for your precious blood that cleanses me today. I thank you that I need not bring a living animal to the Altar because you gave your body and your blood for the remission of my sins, and I praise you for that. I bless you today for what you did on the Cross for me.

The Washing Of Regeneration

Lord, as the Priests washed themselves at the Brazen Laver, I am thankful that I am washed, "not by works of righteousness which [I] have done, but according to [your] mercy [you] saved [me], by the washing of regeneration, and renewing of the Holy Ghost," Titus 3:5. Thank you, Jesus, for the opportunity and privilege to be baptized in your name, for the remission of my sins (Acts 2:38). "Even baptism doth also now save [me] (not the putting away of the filth of the flesh, but the answer of a good conscience toward God,)" 1 Peter 3:21.

The Bread Of Life

Thank you, Lord, for the Bread of Life, Jesus Christ. The Old Testament Priests ate bread from the Table of Shewbread, which foreshadowed your Body and your Word. I am blessed to eat of "the true bread from heaven. For the bread of God is he which cometh down from heaven, and giveth life unto the world," John 6:32-33. I am so thankful that I know who Jesus is. I bless your Holy Name, Jesus. Please feed me all the days of my life. Fill my soul with your Word and your Spirit, and teach me Thy ways.

The Golden Candlestick

Jesus, I am so thankful to be filled with your Spirit, baptized in the Holy Ghost, and speaking in tongues as your Spirit gives me the utterance. I know that the oil of the Holy Spirit is the power of God in my life (Acts 1:8). The oil and fire of the Holy Ghost is your Spirit enlightening me on the path of life. As the Golden Candlestick illuminated the Holy Place, I want your Spirit to illuminate every nook and cranny of my life, my family, and my world, in Jesus' name. Keep me full of your Spirit always.

The Altar Of Incense

Lord, I come before you, as before the Altar of Incense in the Holy Place. I am overwhelmed by the privilege you give me to "come boldly unto the Throne of Grace, [to] obtain mercy, and find grace to help in time of need," Hebrews 4:16. I am thankful that I "know that [you] hear us, whatsoever we ask, and we know that we have the petitions that we desired of [you],"

1 John 5:15. No one ever cared for me like you, Jesus. May every prayer I pray be to accomplish your perfect will, and to glorify your great name.

The Most Holy Place

I am thankful that the Veil of the Temple was rent when you died on the Cross. You have given me the incomprehensible privilege of entering into the Most Holy Place where I can make my most intimate and needful petitions known to God my Creator. Thank you for letting me stand before the Mercy Seat where I may hear your voice, know your will, and receive all that I need from you. Thank you for the Blood, the Water, and the Spirit that have sanctified me and made me worthy to enter into your Holy Presence. I bless your Holy Name forever.

The Ark Of The Covenant

Lord Jesus, I am overwhelmed by the promise of everlasting life that you have given me in the NEW Covenant of your blood. I am thankful that I will not be judged and condemned by the Old Covenant or the Law that sat within the Ark, but that I will be granted entrance through the gates of your eternal city of New Jerusalem because of your amazing grace that proceeds from the Mercy Seat. I pray that I will never frustrate the grace of God (Galatians 2:21) but that I will always "walk worthy of God, who hath called [me] unto His kingdom and glory," 1 Thessalonians 2:12.

The High Priest put on Holy Garments
BEFORE...
- he entered the Tabernacle
- he ministered at the Altar of Sacrifice
- he washed at the Golden Laver
- he lit the lamps on the Candlestick
- he ate of the Shewbread
- he offered incense at the Altar
- he entered God's Presence at the Ark

**He put off profane things
and put on holy things.**

**We should likewise
put off profane things
and put on holy things
BEFORE we seek GOD.**

The Tabernacle Plan

Ark of the Covenant
• The Presence and Voice of God

Altar of Incense
• Prayers (of the Saints)

Table of Shewbread
• Bread (Jesus, Word of God)

Candlestick
• Spirit (Baptism of Holy Ghost)

Laver
• Water (Baptism in Jesus' Name)

Altar of Sacrifice
• Blood (Christ)

The **Entrance** of the **Tabernacle** led into the **Outer Court** where the **Priest** first encountered the **Altar of Sacrifice**, then the **Brazen Laver**.

The **Inner Court** was the **Holy Place**. It contained the **Golden Candlestick**, the **Table of Shewbread**, and the **Golden Altar of Incense**.

Through the **Veil**, the **Priest** entered the **Most Holy Place** containing the **Ark of the Covenant**.

Chapter 28

Prayer Starters

Personal Prayers

Faith, Belief, Trust

Lord, I know that, "without faith it is impossible to please [you]: for he that cometh to God must believe that He is, and that He is a rewarder of them that diligently seek him," Hebrews 11:6. I totally believe that you are the only true and living God, and Creator of all things. There is no God beside you. You are the sovereign King and Master of the universe, embodied in Jesus Christ. All things were made by you for your glory and pleasure. I trust your providence over my life. My faith is in you alone, Master.

Contrition, Brokenness, Humility

Lord, your Word says that you resist the proud, but give grace unto the humble, James 4:6, and that you "dwell in the high and holy place, with him also that is of a contrite and humble spirit," Isaiah 57:15. I humble myself, ashamed of all my faults and failures, my sins, carnality, worldliness, vanity and pride. I want to dwell in your holy, righteous Presence. You said, "whosoever shall exalt himself shall be abased; and he that shall humble himself shall be exalted," Matthew 23:12. Nothing in my hands I bring, simply to the Cross I cling ("Rock of Ages, Cleft for Me")

Confessing Sins, Admitting Guilt

Moses taught the people, "When he shall be guilty... he shall confess that he hath sinned," Leviticus 5:5. Lord, I admit and confess that I have sinned against you. No sin is without consequence. Isaiah said, "Your iniquities have separated between you and your God," Isaiah 59:2. David said, "My iniquity have I not hid," Psalms 32:5. I am sorry that I have grieved your Holy Spirit. Your Word says, "If we confess our sins, [you are] faithful and just to forgive us our sins, and to cleanse us from all unrighteousness," 1 John 1:9-10. These are the sins I have committed:

[Take time to enumerate the sins that have not been repented of.]

Repentance

Lord, you and John the Baptist both began with, "Repent, for the Kingdom of Heaven is at hand." Peter preached repentance on the Day of Pentecost. Repentance means to turn around and go back (to righteousness). I want to return to innocence, pure and holy living, and obedience to your will. I renounce and put away all my sins now. I mortify the lusts of the flesh, lusts of the eye, and the pride of life. I crucify the works of my flesh. I do not want sin to be my eternal ruin. I resolve to do only what is right in your eyes.

To Be Forgiven, Pardoned, Spared

Nehemiah said, "Thou art a God ready to pardon, gracious and merciful, slow to anger, and of great kindness," Nehemiah 9:17. "It is of the LORD'S mercies that we are not consumed, because his compassions fail not," Lamentations 3:22. Thank you, Lord, for sparing me from deserved judgment, condemnation and destruction. I beg Your forgiveness for ALL my heinous, reprehensible failures. Please forgive me for every inappropriate thing I have ever said or done. Please wash away all my sins in Your precious blood, Jesus. I ask You to forgive me for all my folly, all my sins, disobedience and failures.

Thy Will Be Done

Jesus submitted His flesh to the will of God at Gethsemane, sweating as it were great drops of blood. Sometimes, my will is equally stubborn, struggling to have my own way. "Nevertheless not my will, but Thine, be done." I only want Your perfect will. NOTHING that I want is as good as what YOU want. Please ignore any request I make that contradicts your will or purpose for my life. I want to be flawlessly obedient. Show me when I displease you, and how to do perfectly. "Thy Kingdom come, thy will be done, on earth as it is in Heaven."

Relationship, Fellowship With God

Enoch walked with you. Abraham was your friend. Moses said, "...that I may know thee, ...shew me thy glory," Exodus 33:13,18. David said, "When thou saidst, Seek ye my face; my heart said unto thee, Thy face, LORD, will

I seek," Psalms 27:8. Paul said, "That I may know him, and the power of his resurrection, and the fellowship of his sufferings," Philippians 3:10. Lord, I want to walk with you, too. Show me your glory, the power of your resurrection, and the fellowship of your sufferings. Let me hear your voice and feel your touch. Reveal yourself to me.

No Relationship, No Fellowship With Evil

"If we say that we have fellowship with him, and walk in darkness, we lie, and do not the truth: But if we walk in the light, as he is in the light, we have fellowship one with another," 1 John 1:6-7. Lord, stop me - prevent me - from walking in darkness and losing fellowship with you. "I would not that ye should have fellowship with devils," 1 Corinthians 10:20. "And have no fellowship with the unfruitful works of darkness, but rather reprove them," Ephesians 5:11. God, embolden me to break every unequal yoke with unbelievers 2 Corinthians 6:14, in Jesus' name.

Teach Me, Lead Me, Guide Me

Evil men "spend their days in wealth, and in a moment go down to the grave. ...they say unto God, Depart from us; for we desire not the knowledge of thy ways," Job 21:13-14. Not so with me, Lord! "Search me, O God, and know my heart: try me, and know my thoughts: ...see if there be any wicked way in me, and lead me in the way everlasting," Psalms 139:23-24. "Shew me thy ways, O LORD; teach me thy paths. Lead me in thy Truth, and teach me," Psalms 25:4-5. "For thy name's sake lead me, and guide me," Psalms 31:3.

Wisdom, Knowledge, Understanding

The wise man said, "Wisdom is the principal thing; therefore get wisdom: and with all thy getting get understanding," Proverbs 4:7. "O the depth of the riches both of the wisdom and knowledge of God! how unsearchable are his judgments, and his ways past finding out!" Romans 11:33. I love your laws, your commandments, your precepts, your doctrines, your Truth! "For the LORD giveth wisdom: out of his mouth cometh knowledge and understanding. He layeth up sound wisdom for the righteous," Proverbs 2:6-7. Fill my heart and mind with all wisdom, knowledge and understanding to do your perfect will.

Commitment, Perseverance, Faithfulness

"Praying always ...and watching thereunto with all perseverance [persistency]," Ephesians 6:18. "It is required in stewards, that a man be found faithful," 1 Corinthians 4:2. Even ministers' wives must be "faithful in all things," 1 Timothy 3:11. Lord, you said, "Fear none of those things which thou shalt suffer: ...be thou faithful unto death, and I will give thee a crown of life," Revelation 2:10. I am persuaded that you will keep everything I commit unto you," 2 Timothy 1:12. Therefore, I commit everything - my life, my health, my family, my finances, my soul, my all - to you. Help me to be faithful and to persevere.

Consecrate, Dedicate, Sanctify, Fulfill Divine Purpose

Lord, in every generation, you have called your people to consecrate themselves to holiness. "Consecrate yourselves today to the LORD, ...that he may bestow upon you a blessing this day," Exodus 32:29. "Sanctify yourselves therefore, and be ye holy: for I am the LORD your God," Leviticus 20:7. "As he which hath called you is holy, so be ye holy in all manner of conversation; Because it is written, Be ye holy; for I am holy," 1 Peter 1:15-16. I consecrate myself to live a holy life to your glory. Keep me "unspotted from the world," James 1:27.

Submission, Servanthood, Sacrifice

Lord, your Word instructs us to, "Obey them that have the rule over you, and submit yourselves," Hebrews 13:17, and to, "Submit yourselves therefore to God," James 4:7. While most men seek to rise above other men, your Word tells us to be their minister-servant and a living sacrifice (holy and acceptable to God). "Whosoever will be great among you, let him be your minister; And whosoever will be chief among you, let him be your servant," Matthew 20:26-28. Teach me to take the lower seat, serve YOU, and serve others for your sake. I surrender all!

Truth, Righteousness, Holiness

David prayed, "Lead me in thy Truth," Psalms 25:5, and "Lead me, O LORD, in thy righteousness," Psalms 5:8. Zacharias prayed that we may serve God, "in holiness and righteousness, all the days of our lives," Luke 1:75. Lord, I "yield [my] members servants to righteousness and holiness," Romans 6:19. I gird my loins with Truth, with a breastplate of righteousness, Ephesians 6:14. In righteousness, I will be established, Isaiah 54:14. I will follow peace and holiness, Hebrews 12:14. I bought scriptural, doctrinal Truth, and will never sell it, Proverbs 23:23 The anointing of God "is truth, and is no lie," 1 John 2:27.

First Thing, Highest Priority

Lord, constrain me to keep first things first. Moses defined the top priority for all men. "Hear, O Israel: The LORD our God is one LORD: And thou shalt love the LORD thy God with all thine heart, ...all thy soul, ...all thy might," Deuteronomy 6:4-5. Jesus said, "The first of all the commandments is, Hear, O Israel; The Lord our God is one Lord: And thou shalt love the Lord thy God with all thy heart, ...this is the first commandment," Mark 12:29-30. Help me understand the nature of your Oneness, and love your true identity above all other doctrines and beliefs.

Responsibility, Accountability, Excellence

"Every one of us shall give account of himself to God," Romans 14:12. Jesus said, "Every idle word that men shall speak, they shall give account thereof in the day of judgment," Matthew 12:36. "Unto whomsoever much is given, of him shall be much required," Luke 12:48. Lord, help me to practice the highest level of sobriety, integrity and excellence in my speech and my actions. Constantly remind me that I must put your Kingdom ahead of all things worldly. "Seek ye first the kingdom of God, and his righteousness; and all these things shall be added unto you," Mathew 6:33.

Witness, Testimony, Reputation

Jesus told His disciples that they would be His "witnesses" after they were baptized in the Holy Ghost Acts 1:8. After Pentecost, they said, "We are His witnesses ...so is also the Holy Ghost," Acts 5:32. Jesus' entire plan for perpetuating the Church was by the power and witness of the Holy Ghost in His disciples. Nothing born of my flesh or my carnal mind is a true witness of Christ. Lord, please cause my entire reputation to be defined by the supernatural works of the Holy Ghost in my life, not by any foolishness or folly that springs from my old sinful nature.

A Stepping Stone, Not A Stumblingblock

Paul said, "Be ye followers of me, even as I also am of Christ," 1 Corinthians 11:1. Jesus, help me be your faithful follower, so that others will follow you by my example. You suffered for us, "leaving us an example, that [we] should follow [your] steps," 1 Peter 2:21. Teach me to patiently endure sufferings, trials or tribulations for your name's sake, so that others will be inspired, but never misled by my example. Prevent me from ever causing any reproach or offense. Lord, help me to be obedient, clean, holy, pure, Godly, and virtuous, for all to see, in Jesus' name.

Fruitfulness

Jesus, you said, "Ye have not chosen me, but I have chosen you, and ordained you, that ye should go and bring forth fruit, and that your fruit should remain," John 15:16. I want to be a profoundly effective and fruitful soul-winner, teacher, mentor, intercessor, worshiper, and believer. I covet your blessing and anointing on every facet of my life, my family, and my ministry for your name's sake. Help me multiply every talent I possess, so that I will give you many more in return, and hear you say, "Well done, thou good and faithful servant," Matthew 25:21.

Thankfulness, Gratitude, Acknowledging Your Goodness

"Enter into his gates with thanksgiving, and into his courts with praise," Psalms 100:4-5. "When ye will offer a sacrifice of thanksgiving unto the LORD, offer it at your own will," Leviticus 22:29. "Tell all thy wondrous works," Psalms 26:7. Lord, I give you a free-will offering of thanks for every blessing, every favor, provision, answers to prayer, open doors, miracles and more. Thank you for saving my eternal soul from Hell, for the New Birth by the Blood of Jesus, the waters of baptism in Jesus' Name, the infilling of the Holy Ghost, and for Truth, righteousness, and holiness.

For These Things I Give You Thanks

Here is only a partial list of the countless blessings I thank you for. For spiritual blessings, physical blessings, financial blessings, things pertaining to family and friends, the Church, the Kingdom of God, and my eternal salvation. For all blessings - past, present and future - Thank you, Jesus!

Prayer List #1 - Things I Thank and Praise God For

Praise, Glory, Honor and Laud

"Let us offer the sacrifice of praise to God continually, that is, the fruit of our lips giving thanks to his name," Hebrews 13:15. Almighty God, with all that is within me, I praise you. For your wonderful works and your mighty acts, I praise you. For the infinite miracles of Creation alone, you deserve praise and glory. Lord Jesus, for all that you are and all that you do, I magnify, glorify and worship you from the depths of my soul. With raised hands, singing, shouting, dancing, leaping, playing instruments and in every way that I can find, I will praise you forever.

Worship, Adore, Revere

In Greek, "worship" means "to kiss, or lick like a dog, bow, prostrate oneself." Moses taught, "Thou shalt worship no other god: for the LORD, whose name is Jealous, is a jealous God," Exodus 34:14. "Give unto the LORD the glory due unto his name: ...worship the LORD in the beauty of holiness," 1 Chronicles 16:29. Lord, I am so small and you are so great. I humbly worship, reverence and adore you in Spirit and in Truth. Kneeling. Bowing. Prostrate. I love you, exalt you, extol you. You are glorious, worthy, majestic and divine. The Mighty God in Jesus Christ.

Revelation of God

"Eye hath not seen, nor ear heard, neither have entered into the heart of man, the things which God hath prepared for them that love him," 1 Corinthians 2:9. "It is the glory of God to conceal a thing: but the honor of kings is to search out a matter," Proverbs 25:2. Lord God, please reveal ALL your essential truths to me and my loved ones, including the infinite wonders about your Godhead, your name, your baptism, your Spirit, your holiness, your great commandments, your great commission, and your abundant life. Give us the Spirit of wisdom and revelation, Ephesians 1:17.

True Doctrine, Instruction, Teaching, Precepts, Principles

"The way of man is not in himself: it is not in man that walketh to direct his steps," Jeremiah 10:23. I MUST HAVE your doctrines, your precepts. "For precept must be upon precept, precept upon precept; line upon line, line upon line; here a little, and there a little," Isaiah 28:10. Lord, "Order my steps in thy word," Psalms 119:133. "Through thy precepts I get understanding: therefore I hate every false way," Psalms 119:104. I crave to understand every absolute, infallible, and fundamental Truth of your Word so I will never err in anything that pertains to eternal life. Teach me, Lord!

One Lord, One Faith, One Baptism

Lord, in the midst of pervasive doctrinal irregularities and contradictions throughout so-called Christendom, I only want to know the infallible Truth. Please deliver me from all false teachings and false doctrines. "There is one body, and one Spirit, even as ye are called in one hope of your calling; One Lord, one faith, one baptism, One God and Father of all, who is above all, and through all, and in you all," Ephesians 4:4-6. I want to be in your One Body. I want to be filled with your One Spirit. I want to be baptized in your One Baptism.

Eyes to See, Ears to Hear, Heart to Know

Lord, I do not want to walk as Godless men, "in the vanity of their mind, having the understanding darkened, being alienated from the life of God..., because of the blindness of their heart," Ephesians 4:17-18. "If the blind lead the blind, both shall fall into the ditch," Matthew 15:14. You said, "Blessed are your eyes, for they see: and your ears, for they hear. ...many prophets and righteous men have desired to see those things which ye see, and have not seen them," Matthew 13:15-17. Lord, bless my eyes and ears to see and hear every truth about you.

Overcoming The Sins Of The Flesh

"Adultery, fornication, uncleanness, lasciviousness, Idolatry, witchcraft, hatred, variance, emulations, wrath, strife, seditions, heresies, Envyings, murders, drunkenness, revellings, and such like: ...they which do such things shall not inherit the kingdom of God," Galatians 5:19-21. "...filled with all unrighteousness, fornication, wickedness, covetousness, maliciousness; full of envy, murder, debate, deceit, malignity; whisperers, Backbiters, haters of God, despiteful, proud, boasters, inventors of evil things, disobedient to parents, Without understanding, covenantbreakers, without natural affection, implacable, unmerciful," Romans 1:28-31. Lord, lead me NOT into temptation, but deliver me from ALL evil. Help me overcome all EVIL with all GOOD, Romans 12:21, in Jesus' name!

Correction, Reproof, Chastisement

"All scripture is given by inspiration of God, and is profitable for doctrine, for reproof, for correction, for instruction in righteousness: That the man of God may be perfect, throughly furnished unto all good works," 2 Timothy 3:16-17. "My son, despise not the chastening of the LORD; neither be weary of his correction: For whom the LORD loveth he correcteth; even as a father the son in whom he delighteth," Proverbs 3:11-12. Lord, I love your rebukes above the praises of men. Show me my errors, and correct me, even BEFORE I sin, that I may only do righteousness all my days.

Deception, Delusions, Lies, Apostasy

"Many deceivers are entered into the world," 2 John 1:7. "Take heed that ye be not deceived," Luke 21:8. Paul warned that Satan would come with "all power and signs and lying wonders," 2 Thessalonians 2:9, and there will come "a falling away," 2 Thessalonians 2:3. "Take heed unto thyself, and unto the doctrine; continue in them: for in doing this thou shalt both save thyself, and them that hear thee," 1 Timothy 4:16. "If there come any unto you, and bring not this doctrine, receive him not into your house, neither bid him God speed," 2 John 1:10. Jesus, deliver us from all seducing spirits and doctrines of devils.

Redeem The Time

"Walk circumspectly [diligently, perfectly], not as fools, but as wise, redeeming the time, because the days are evil," Ephesians 5:15-16. "Walk in wisdom ...redeeming the time," Colossians 4:5. "Ye know not what shall be on the morrow. For what is your life? It is even a vapour, that appeareth for a little time, and then vanisheth away," James 4:14. "This night thy soul shall be required of thee: then whose shall those things be, which thou hast provided?" Luke 12:20. Lord, stop me from wasting precious time. Cause me to spend every minute soberly and righteously for your glory.

Fruit Of The Spirit

"The fruit of the Spirit is love, joy, peace, longsuffering, gentleness, goodness, faith, meekness, temperance: against such there is no law. ...Let us not be desirous of vain glory, provoking one another, envying one another," Galatians 5:22-23. "Whatsoever things are true, ...honest, ...just, ...pure, ...lovely, ...of good report; if there be any virtue, and if there be any praise, think on these things," Philippians 4:8. O Lord, please help me to crucify my flesh with all its lusts, and manifest only the beautiful fruit and virtues of the Holy Spirit, now and ever, in Jesus' name.

Intentions, Declarations

As a man "thinketh in his heart, so is he," Proverbs 23:7. From "the abundance of his heart, his mouth speaketh," Luke 6:45. Everything in my heart affects my intentions, and those intentions define my declarations and all my future deeds. Therefore, "Let the words of my mouth, and the meditation of my heart, be acceptable in thy sight, O LORD," Psalms 19:14. Purify my heart from all carnal, worldly or evil intentions. Fill my heart with pure, holy, Godly intentions, "...as the servant of Christ, doing the will of God from the heart," Ephesians 6:6.

My Divine Destiny, My Life Work

Dear Lord Jesus, I pray that you will anoint and inspire me to identify and pursue my sacred life work. "The steps of a good man are ordered by the LORD," Psalms 37:23. "All things work together for good to them that love God, to them who are the called according to his purpose," Romans 8:28. My destiny is in your hands. You gave me your Word and your Spirit. Help me understand and fulfill every purpose for which I was born. Help me make my calling and election sure. "Looking diligently lest any man fail of the grace of God," Hebrews 12:15.

Called, Chosen, Faithful

God calls many, but He chooses few, Matthew 20:16. Only the faithful will be with Him forever. "They that are with him are called, and chosen, and faithful," Revelation 17:14. "Brethren, give diligence to make your calling and election sure: for if ye do these things, ye shall never fall," 2 Peter 1:10. "Be ye stedfast, unmoveable, always abounding in the work of the Lord," 1 Corinthians 15:58. "For we are made partakers of Christ, if we hold the beginning of our confidence stedfast unto the end," Hebrews 3:14. Lord, help me to be unwavering, steadfast and unmovable unto the end.

Temperance, Patience, Moderation

"Let your moderation be known unto all men. The Lord is at hand," Philippians 4:5. Lord, I pray that you will teach me to be temperate in all things; balanced, not extreme; moderate, not on a fringe. Help me "[add] to knowledge temperance; and to temperance patience; and to patience godliness," 2 Peter 1:6. Help me to "be patient toward all men," 1 Thessalonians 5:14. Deliver me from anxiety, panic and fear. "For God hath not given us the spirit of fear; but of power, and of love, and of a sound mind," 2 Timothy 1:7.

Supplication, Entreaty, Request

Lord, I want to be an intercessor, a master of effectual prayer. Grant that I may stand in the gap and make up the hedge between you and those who are in need of salvation and other miracles. "Praying always with all prayer and supplication in the Spirit, and watching thereunto with all perseverance and supplication for all saints," Ephesians 6:18. "In every thing by prayer and supplication with thanksgiving let your requests be made known unto God," Philippians 4:6. Lord, hear my cry as I seek you daily in behalf of myself, my loved ones, and all those you have given me.

Health and Healing for Sickness, Disease and Infirmities

"Is any among you afflicted? let him pray. ...Is any sick among you? let him call for the elders of the church; and let them pray over him, anointing him with oil in the name of the Lord: And the prayer of faith shall save the sick, and the Lord shall raise him up," James 5:13-15. Lord, I claim your promises to save the sick and raise them up. "I am the Lord that healeth thee," Exodus 15:26. Embolden me to anoint with oil, lay hands on the sick, and pray the prayer of faith. With your stripes, I am healed.

Prayer List #2 - My Life Work and Ministry

Making my Calling and Election sure - Things to do or accomplish.

Number My Days

"For what is your life? It is even a vapour, that appeareth for a little time, and then vanisheth away, For that ye ought to say, If the Lord will, we shall live, and do this, or that," James 4:14-15. "So teach us to number our days, that we may apply our hearts unto wisdom," Psalms 90:12. Lord, my life is in your hands and my days are numbered. "The time is at hand." Even Satan knows "he hath but a short time." Lord, help me to serve you fervently, bear much fruit, and convert many souls for your Kingdom.

Expectation, Faith, Confidence

Lord, you said, "What man is there of you, whom if his son ask bread, will he give him a stone? Or if he ask a fish, will he give him a serpent? If ye then, being evil, know how to give good gifts unto your children, how much more shall your Father which is in heaven give good things to them that ask him?" Matthew 7:9-11. You said, "Him that cometh to me I will in no wise cast out," John 6:37. "We have boldness and access with confidence by the faith of him," Ephesians 3:12. I fully expect my prayers to be fruitful.

Worry, Fear, Anxiety

"God hath not given us the spirit of fear; but of power, and of love, and of a sound mind," 2 Timothy 1:7. "Fear not them which kill the body, but are not able to kill the soul: but rather fear him which is able to destroy both soul and body in hell," Matthew 10:28. I have nothing to fear but God Himself. "If God be for us, who can be against us?" Romans 8:31. In the name of Jesus, I reject all worry, fear and anxiety. I will not fear men or devils, pain, sickness, death or disaster. I will trust in God.

Weariness, Weakness, Fatigue

Neither weakness nor weariness is cause to quit. "God hath chosen the weak things of the world to confound the things which are mighty," 1 Corinthians 1:27. God said, "My strength is made perfect in weakness." Paul replied, "Therefore I take pleasure in infirmities, in reproaches, in necessities, in persecutions, in distresses for Christ's sake: for when I am weak, then am I strong," 2 Corinthians 12:9-10. "Let us not be weary in well doing: for in due season we shall reap, if we faint not," Galatians 6:9. Lord, teach me to wait on you. I know you will renew my strength, Isaiah 40:31.

Rejoicing, Joy

"A woman when she is in travail hath sorrow, ...but as soon as she is delivered of the child, she remembereth no more the anguish, for joy that a man is born into the world," John 16:21-22. Lord, help me remember that all my trials on earth will soon be forgotten when I see your face in the resurrection. Then I will greatly rejoice. "For our light affliction, which is but for a moment, worketh for us a far more exceeding and eternal weight of glory," 2 Corinthians 4:17. "They that sow in tears shall reap in joy," Psalms 126:5.

What The Father Giveth

John the Baptist said, "A man can receive nothing, except it be GIVEN him from Heaven," John 3:27. I need not concern myself with anything YOU have not GIVEN me. Jesus said, "I pray not for the world, but for them which thou hast given me;" John 17:9. Lord, help me recognize the people and things you have GIVEN me among my own family, friends, and acquaintances. Help me make effectual prayerful intercession for all you have given me. "Of all which he hath given me I should lose nothing, but should raise it up again at the last day," John 6:39.

The Children God Has Given To Me

No one is more GIVEN to us than our own children. God GAVE Isaac to Abraham. God said, "I GAVE unto Isaac Jacob and Esau," Joshua 24:3-4. Our children are among our greatest responsibilities before God. Scriptures record many of the fathers blessing their children. Job made daily sacrifices and prayers for his children, and God called him a perfect and upright man. Lord, I commit myself now to being a lifelong intercessor for my children and all my descendants. I pray for saving grace, divine favor, guidance and providence for my children and descendants, in Jesus' name.

If My Children Have Sinned

Job made sacrifices and prayed for his children, saying, "It may be that my sons have sinned, and cursed God in their hearts," Job 1:5. "Thus did Job continually." Many people believe the Book of Job was the first book written in the Bible. If so, the first prayer in the Bible is that of a man praying that his children will not be condemned by sin. Lord, I pray today that none of my children or grandchildren will ever be condemned to Hell. Lead them not into temptation, but deliver them from evil. Lead them in the paths of righteousness, in Jesus' name.

Commanding Children, Keeping The Way Of The Lord

Both Israel and the Church trace their roots to the Covenant blessings God made with Abraham. The Children of Israel are his physical heirs, while true saints in the Church are Abraham's spiritual heirs by faith, Romans 4:12; Galatians 3:9. One reason God gave for blessing Abraham was, "I know him, that he will command his children and his household after him, and they shall keep the way of the LORD, to do justice and judgment," Genesis 18:19. Lord, I pray that my influence on my children will follow Abraham's example, to command them to keep the way of the Lord.

Teaching His Commandments

In Deuteronomy 6, God told Moses to teach His commandments, statutes and judgments to, "thy son, and thy son's son, all the days of thy life." "Hear, O Israel: The LORD our God is one LORD: And thou shalt love the LORD thy God with all thine heart, ...soul, ...might, ...These words ...shall be in thine heart: and thou shalt teach them diligently unto thy children, ...when thou sittest..., walkest..., liest down..., risest up." "Beware, lest thou forget the Lord." Lord, move me to teach the Oneness of God and all your commandments, statutes and judgments to my children continually.

Train Up A Child

Jesus taught, "The first of all the commandments is, Hear, O Israel; The Lord our God is one Lord: And thou shalt love the Lord thy God with all thy heart, ...soul, ...mind, ...strength: this is the first commandment," Mark 12:29-30. Moses said, "Ye shall not go after other gods, ...lest the anger of the LORD thy God be kindled against thee, and destroy thee from off the face of the earth," Deuteronomy 6:15. "Train up a child in the way he should go: and when he is old, he will not depart from it," Proverbs 22:6. Lord, help me train my children as you require.

The Blessings And Curses Of God

Moses told His people, "to fear the LORD, ...that He might preserve us alive," Deuteronomy 6:24-25. "...teach [your] children..., that it may go well with thee, and with thy children after thee," Deuteronomy 4:10,40. "If ye shall at all turn from following me, ...and will not keep my commandments and my statutes..., but go and serve other gods, and worship them: ...I cut off Israel out of the land which I have given them, ...because they forsook the LORD," 1 Kings 9:7,9. Lord, help me to teach my children about your blessings and curses, so they will fear, love and serve you.

For My Spouse And Our Marriage

"Whoso findeth a wife findeth a good thing, and obtaineth favour of the LORD," Proverbs 18:22. "Therefore shall a man leave his father and his mother, and shall cleave unto his wife: and they shall be one flesh," Genesis 2:24. "Marriage is honourable in all," Hebrews 13:4. "For a man ...is the image and glory of God: but the woman is the glory of the man. ..Neither was the man created for the woman; but the woman for the man," 1 Corinthians 11:7,9. Lord, bless our marriage, and make our relationship perfect between each other, and between us and you, and with all others.

For My Immediate Family

Lord, I pray that my spouse, children, grandchildren, parents, siblings, and all my family will find, know and do your perfect will all the days of their lives. Help every one of us to live by true Biblical standards of Godliness and holiness. Help us to know and hear your voice. Direct and guide us by your Word and by your Spirit. Deliver my family from sin and evil! I pray that you will meet all their needs daily, and bless them all with abundance for their spiritual, physical and financial well-being, in Jesus' name.

For All My Family and Dearest Friends

Lord, I pray for every member of my family and for my dearest and closest friends, that you will reveal yourself to them, and lead them every day in your perfect will. I pray that every one of them will be Born Again, filled with your Spirit, and live a holy, Godly life for your good pleasure. Bless them and meet all their needs, physically, mentally, spiritually, financially.

For My Extended Family

Lord, bless and have your way with my parents, grandparents, brothers, sisters, aunts, uncles, cousins, nieces, nephews, in-laws, step-family, and all other kinfolks. Help me to be a good and Godly influence in their lives, and help me to be a blessing to them in any way possible. Bless their marriages, their children. Provide for their well-being, their homes, their jobs, their educations, their health care. Help them to find a good Church where Truth, righteousness and holiness is preached and practiced.

My Friends

Friends can be good or bad. Job's friends became his worst tormentors. But, "the LORD turned the captivity of Job, when he prayed for his friends," Job 42:10. I may be the only intercessor between my friend and God. Lord, help me to stand in the gap and make up the hedge for my friends. Show them the ways of Truth, righteousness and holiness. Lead them by your Word and by your Spirit. Help them to do the will of God. Save their souls, and bless their homes, their lives and their families, in Jesus' name.

All My Relationships

"A man that hath friends must shew himself friendly: and there is a friend that sticketh closer than a brother," Proverbs 18:24. I pray that my life will be exemplary, and that the Spirit of the Lord will flow through me to all my family, friends and acquaintances. Help me to be kind, loving, Godly and excellent in all my ways with everyone. Use me as a vessel of Truth and righteousness. May everyone see Jesus living in me. Help me serve others, as unto the Lord. Help me daily lay down my life for my friends, John 15:13.

Offenses And Evil Influences

"Whoso shall offend one of these little ones which believe in me, it were better for him that a millstone were hanged about his neck, and that he were drowned in the depth of the sea," Matthew 18:6. "Let ...no man put a stumblingblock or an occasion to fall in his brother's way," Romans 14:13. Lord, if I have offended anyone, or put a stumblingblock or occasion to fall in my brother's way, please forgive me. Help me repair every bad relationship, and heal every injury I have caused to anyone, in Jesus' name.

Prayer List #3 - Immediate Family

Immediate Family and Closest Friends

Daily Provisions

"Give us this day our daily bread," Matthew 6:11. Lord, you taught us to trust you daily, giving no thought for the morrow; not to worry about clothes or what we eat or drink, because, as the lilies of the field, you array them in splendor. You will feed and clothe us. You said, "Seek ye first the kingdom of God, and his righteousness; and all these things shall be added unto you," Matthew 6:33. Lord, help us to see the error of laboring for earthly wealth, and give us instead, hearts to lay up true treasures in Heaven.

My Finances

"Remember the LORD thy God: for it is he that giveth thee power to get wealth," Deuteronomy 8:18. "Lay not up for yourselves treasures upon earth, where moth and rust doth corrupt, and where thieves break through and steal: But lay up for yourselves treasures in Heaven, ...for where your treasure is, there will your heart be also," Matthew 6:19-21. "Ye cannot serve God and mammon," Luke 16:13. "The love of money is the root of all evil," 1 Timothy 6:10. Lord, help me to be a good and faithful steward of all my talents and resources, and to pay my tithes, taxes, and other obligations.

My Role In The Church

"What doth the LORD thy God require of thee, but to fear the LORD thy God, to walk in all his ways, and to love him, and to serve the LORD thy God with all thy heart and with all thy soul," Deuteronomy 10:12. "...as for me and my house, we will serve the LORD," Joshua 24:15. Lord, give me a heart to serve you - to sing, to preach, to pray, to be helpful, or to work in any capacity that I may be needed. I covet your anointing and inspiration on all that I say and do, whether in public or private ministry.

For My Local Church

"Brethren, pray for us, that the word of the Lord may have free course, and be glorified, ...and that we may be delivered from unreasonable and wicked men: for all men have not faith," 2 Thessalonians 3:1-2. Lord, I pray our community will always have an Apostolic Pentecostal Church to stand for Truth, righteousness and holiness. Bless our Pastor, ministers, and saints, and provide all the needed resources. Help us to save many souls.

Prayer List #4 - Extended Family and Friends

Extended Family, Distant Friends, Friends from the Past

Fasting And Prayer

Fasting and prayer only reach maximum effectiveness through diligence, discipline, and force of habit. "When ye fast, be not, as the hypocrites, of a sad countenance: for they disfigure their faces, that they may appear unto men to fast. ...They have their reward. But thou, when thou fastest, anoint thine head, and wash thy face; That thou appear not unto men to fast, but unto thy Father which is in secret: and thy Father, which seeth in secret, shall reward thee openly," Matthew 6:16-18. Lord, help me to fast and pray faithfully and routinely, even if nobody but God is aware.

Spiritual Warfare

Lord, help me to be spiritually perceptive at all times, never deluded or deceived by my spiritual enemies. Remind me that I am not wrestling with flesh and blood, but with principalities, powers, rulers of darkness, and spiritual wickedness in high places. I hate every unclean spirit. Make me a stalwart man of war, taking dominion over Satan and his minions. Lord, I plead the blood of Jesus for my covering. I bind, resist, rebuke, and cast out devils who have come to steal, kill and destroy, breaking every yoke of bondage, oppression and possession, in Jesus' name.

Rebellion, Hardness Of Heart

Dear God, teach us the grave consequences of a rebellious, hard heart. "For rebellion is as the sin of witchcraft, and stubbornness is as iniquity and idolatry. Because thou hast rejected the word of the LORD, he hath also rejected thee," 1 Samuel 15:23. Jesus upbraided His own disciples for hardness of heart because they were slow to believe reports of His resurrection. Paul warned that a hard, impenitent heart "treasurest up unto [itself] wrath against the day of wrath and revelation of the righteous judgment of God," Romans 2:5. Lord, I give you a tender heart. Mold me.

Send Apostolic Ministers To Help

As Aquila and Priscilla took Apollos, and taught him the Apostolic Truth, "pray ye therefore the Lord of the harvest, that he will send forth labourers into his harvest," Matthew 9:38. Lord, send true Apostolic laborers to everyone on my prayer list. Teach them the whole Truth, in Jesus' name.

Prayer List #5 - For My Local Church

Ministers, Staff, Saints, Missionaries, others.

Send Angels To Help

"Are they not all ministering spirits, sent forth to minister for them who shall be heirs of salvation?" Hebrews 1:14. After Satan tempted Christ in the wilderness, "angels came and ministered unto him," Matthew 4:11. An angel delivered Peter from prison. An angel brought comfort to Paul during a storm at sea. Lord, I pray that the angels of the Lord will minister to me and my loved ones. Help us to live our lives to your glory. Send the angels to minister, help, strengthen, deliver and intervene in behalf of everyone on my prayer list, in Jesus' name.

Signs, Wonders, Miracles

"These signs shall follow them that believe; In my name shall they cast out devils; they shall speak with new tongues; they shall take up serpents; and if they drink any deadly thing, it shall not hurt them; they shall lay hands on the sick, and they shall recover," Mark 16:17-18. "By the hands of the apostles were many signs and wonders wrought among the people," Acts 5:12. Lord, perform signs, wonders and miracles in our lives and ministries. Heal every kind of sickness. Raise the dead. Deliver the oppressed. Baptize the hungry with the Holy Ghost.

For Preachers And Teachers

"And now, Lord, behold their threatenings: and grant unto thy servants, that with all boldness they may speak thy word, by stretching forth thine hand to heal; and that signs and wonders may be done by the name of thy holy child Jesus," Acts 4:29-30. Lord, I pray for every minister, preacher, and teacher of the Gospel, including myself. Use us mightily to deliver the Acts 2:38 message into every nook and cranny of the earth. Anoint, embolden, encourage, inspire, enable, empower us to convert multitudes to the Truth. Open a great and effectual door. Give us victory over all our adversaries.

For Soul Winners

"He that winneth souls is wise," Proverbs 11:30. Lord, lead us to a multitude of souls. "Of some have compassion, …and others save with fear, pulling them out of the fire;" Jude 1:22-23. Work with us, and confirm the Word with signs following, Mark 16:20. .Anoint our efforts, and save many, many people.

Prayer List #6 - Other Ministers, Churches and Saints

Pastors, Staff, Saints, others

Praying on Purpose

For Singers, Musicians, Songwriters, Producers

"Sing praises to God, sing praises; sing praises unto our King," Psalms 47:6. "Speaking to yourselves in psalms and spiritual songs, making melody in your heart to the Lord," Ephesians 5:19. Lord, I pray for everyone in music ministry - singers, musicians, songwriters and producers. I pray you will purge the music of the Church of all things carnal and vain, and restore authentic New Testament praise and worship. Enable our songwriters to produce the greatest songs ever written, and our singers to present them so that everyone may worship you in Spirit and in Truth, in Jesus' name.

For Writers, Publishers, Bloggers, Social Media, Audio-Video Publishers

"The Lord gave the word: great was the company of those that published it," Psalms 68:11. "Now go, write it before them..., and note it in a book, that it may be for the time to come for ever and ever," Isaiah 30:8. "The preacher sought to find out acceptable words: ...even words of truth. The words of the wise are as...nails fastened by the masters of assemblies," Ecclesiastes 12:10-11. I pray for Holy Ghost anointing on everyone who has any gift to write or publish the Gospel. Let the Word have free course and be glorified. Open countless publishing and broadcasting venues around the world.

For Missions, Evangelism, Church Planters

"And he said unto them, Go ye into all the world, and preach the gospel to every creature," Mark 16:15. Lord, I pray that you will prosper the efforts of every Apostolic, Pentecostal minister who stands for Truth, righteousness and holiness. Cause every attempt that is made to be fruitful. Provide open doors, meeting venues, financial resources, transportation, reliable travel, accommodations and many hungry souls to preach the Word to. "And this gospel of the kingdom shall be preached in all the world for a witness unto all nations; and then shall the end come," Matthew 24:14.

For All True Ministries And Churches

Jesus prayed for all future believers, "for them also which shall believe on me through **their** word," John 17:20. "That they all may be one." Apostles, Prophets, Evangelists, Pastors and Teachers, ministering, perfecting saints, edifying the body of Christ:," Ephesians 4:11-13. Lord, bless them all.

Prayer List #7 - Old Friends and Acquaintances

People I want God to Save and Bring into His Church

For Backsliders

Lord, I pray for backsliders everywhere. Where there is life, there is hope. I pray for every Child of God who is "falling away," 2 Thessalonians 2:2, has become a castaway, 1 Corinthians 9:27, who has made shipwreck, 1 Timothy 1:19, who has forsaken, having loved this present world, 2 Timothy 4:10, for every prodigal, Luke 15:16, whose lamp has gone out, Matthew 25:8, whose salt has lost its savor, Matthew 5:13, whose candlestick may be removed, Revelation 2:5, and whose name may be blotted out of the Book of Life, Revelation 3:5. SAVE THEM, OH, LORD. Revive their souls today, in Jesus' name!

For Those In Heresies, Deceived

"If our gospel be hid, it is hid to them that are lost: In whom the god of this world hath blinded the minds of them which believe not, lest the light of the glorious gospel of Christ, who is the image of God, should shine unto them," 2 Corinthians 4:3-4. Lord, multitudes are blinded by false doctrines and heresies; enslaved and condemned. But Jesus said, "The Spirit of the Lord is upon me, ...to preach deliverance to the captives, and recovering of sight to the blind," Luke 4:18. Open the eyes of the spiritually blind. Use us to preach the Truth that will deliver those in darkness.

For Those Who Have Rule

"I exhort therefore, that, first of all, supplications, prayers, intercessions, and giving of thanks, be made for all men; For kings, and for all that are in authority; that we may lead a quiet and peaceable life in all godliness and honesty," 1 Timothy 2:1-2. Grant wisdom, knowledge and understanding to our rulers, but stop the mouths and the works of evil men and despots in behalf of Godly men everywhere. "Thy Kingdom come, Thy will be done in earth, as it is in Heaven," Matthew 6:10. Grant that your Church may yet thrive in these evil times.

"But I say unto you, Love your enemies,
bless them that curse you, do good to them that hate you,
and pray for them which despitefully use you, and persecute you."
Matthew 5:44

Prayer List #8 - Those Who Have Rule

Public Officials - World, Nation, State, Local

Chapter 30

My Positive Confession

Read this confession out loud periodically, to renew your thought processes.

Lord, you made this day, and I rejoice and am glad in it. I am able to be glad because my hope is in you. I expect good things to happen today because you are watching over me and my loved ones, and you care for us.

Surely goodness and mercy will follow me all the days of my life, and I will dwell in the House of the Lord forever.

My "meat" is to do your will. You sent me to finish your work. None of my trials move me, neither do I count my life dear to myself, so that I may finish my course with joy.

I believe you, God. Whatever you say is true. Everything will be just as you promised to me. You are both the Author and the Finisher of my faith.

I have faith at least the size of a mustard seed, and you said that I can move mountains with that kind of faith. I will go up at once to possess my unclaimed possessions, because I am well able to overcome any and all obstacles.

According to your divine power that works in me, you have given unto me all things that pertain to life and godliness, and you have given to me exceeding great and precious promises, that I might be a partaker of your divine nature.

You have given me a divine measure of faith. I have words of faith in my mouth and in my heart. My faith does not stand in the wisdom of men, but in your power, God.

I am not justified by doing the works of the law, but I am justified by my faith in you. I have the victory that overcomes the world, because I have faith in you. My faith counts to you for righteousness. My faith in you saves me from every risk and danger, and makes me whole. I am comforted by the fact that you, Jesus, prayed for me that my faith will never fail.

You promised that you would never leave me nor forsake me; to be with me always - even to the end of the world. I know that ALL THINGS work together for good because I love you and I am called according to your purpose.

When the enemy comes in like a flood, your Spirit will raise up a divine standard against him. No weapon that is formed against me can prosper. This is my heritage in you.

By your power, I can run through an army or leap over a wall. You are for us, so who can be against us?

I do not stagger at your promises in unbelief, but I am strong in faith, giving glory to you. I believe, and you will help me with my unbelief. I seek first your Kingdom and your righteousness, so everything I need will be added to me.

Noah's rainbow is a sign to me that no flood of judgment will ever come to me again. Job's testimony is mine: "Though God slay me, I will trust Him. Though skin worms destroy this body, I will still see the glory of God."

I will not dwell with the "Egyptians" (unbelievers) of this world. I left my former life for a land that you promised to show me. You will make of me a great nation, and will bless me, and make my name great; and I will be a blessing: and you will bless them that bless me, and curse them that curse me: and in me, multitudes of families will be blessed.

I am willing and obedient, and I am eating of the good of the land. You love me partly because I love you. I find you because I seek you early.

You supply all my needs according to your vast riches in glory. I am content with the things I have, for you said, "I will never leave thee, nor forsake thee." I boldly say, "You are my helper, and I will not fear what man shall do unto me."

Praying for Results

I am not afraid, for you are with me. I am not dismayed, for you are my God. You strengthen me. You help me. You uphold me with your righteous right hand.

I know in whom I have believed, and I am persuaded that you are able to keep all I have committed unto you unto the Judgment Day.

I know that life and death are in the power of my tongue. I turn away wrath with a soft answer. I speak the same things that have been spoken by the greatest saints and believers from ancient times.

I count myself among the righteous saints of all the ages who through faith subdued kingdoms, wrought righteousness, obtained promises, stopped the mouths of lions, quenched the violence of fire, escaped the edge of the sword, out of weakness were made strong, waxed valiant in fight, and turned to flight the armies of aliens. Women received their dead raised to life again and others were tortured, not accepting deliverance that they might obtain a better resurrection. Others had trial of cruel mockings and scourgings, of bonds and imprisonment. They were stoned, they were sawn asunder, were tempted, and were slain with the sword. They wandered about in sheepskins and goatskins being destitute, afflicted, tormented (of whom the world was not worthy). They wandered in deserts and in mountains and in dens and caves of the earth. And these all, having obtained a good report through faith, received not the promise: God having provided some better thing for us, that they without us should not be made perfect.

Therefore, I know that after whatever tribulation I must endure, I will enter into your glorious Kingdom.

By my words I am justified, not condemned. I am the righteousness of God in Christ - a new creation in Him.

I do not confess "I can't" for "I can do all things through Christ which strengtheneth me," Philippians 4:13.

I will not confess lack, for "My God shall supply all of my needs according to His riches in glory by Christ Jesus," Philippians 4:19.

I will not confess fear, for "God hath not given us the spirit of fear; but of power, and of love, and of a sound mind," 2 Timothy 1:7.

I will not confess doubt or lack of faith, for "God hath dealt to every man the measure of faith," Romans 12:3.

I will not confess weakness, for "The Lord is the strength of my life," Psalm 27:1, and "The people that know their God shall be strong and do exploits," Daniel 11:32.

I will not confess that Satan has any dominion over my life, for "Greater is He that is within me than he that is in the world," 1 John 4:4.

I will not confess defeat, for "God always causes me to triumph in Christ Jesus," 2 Corinthians 2:14.

I will not confess lack of wisdom, for "Christ Jesus is made to me wisdom from God," 1 Corinthians 1:30.

I will not confess sickness, for "With His stripes I am healed," Isaiah 53:5, and Jesus "Himself took my infirmities and bare my sickness," Matthew 8:17.

I will not confess worries and frustrations, for I am "Casting all my cares upon Him who cares for me," 1 Peter 5:7.

I will not confess bondage, for "Where the Spirit of the Lord is, there is liberty," 2 Corinthians 3:17.

I will not confess condemnation, for "There is no condemnation to them which are in Christ Jesus," Romans 8:1.

I will not speak of loneliness, for I am never alone. Jesus said, "I am with you always, even unto the end of the world," Matthew 28:20, and "I will never leave you, nor forsake you," Hebrews 13:5.

I will not confess curses or bad luck, for "Christ has redeemed us from the curse of the law... that the blessing of Abraham might come on the Gentiles through Jesus Christ," Galatians 3:13-14. Abraham's blessing is on me!

Praying for Results

I will not confess discontent, because "I have learned, in whatsoever state I am, therewith to be content," Philippians 4:11.

I will not confess unworthiness, because "He hath made Him to be sin for us who knew no sin; that we might be made the righteousness of God in Him," 2 Corinthians 5:21.

I receive whatever I ask of Him because I keep His commandments and do those things that are pleasing in His sight. Jesus will give me whatever I ask the Father in His name.

I will be steadfast. Unmovable. Always abounding in the work of the Lord. I know that my labor is not in vain in the Lord.

Leaving the past behind me - and forgetting it - I press toward the mark for the prize of the high calling in Christ Jesus.

I love God's Word - my Bible. I will stand upon and live by the Word of God. I receive the incorruptible, indestructible, everlasting Seed of the Word of God into my soul.

I will abide in His Tabernacle because I walk uprightly, I work His righteousness, and I speak His Truth in my heart.

I agree in prayer and in faith with my brothers and sisters in the Lord for many wonderful things because Jesus said, "If two of you shall agree on earth as touching anything that they shall ask, it shall be done for them of my Father which is in heaven."

With JOY I draw water from the wells of salvation. The JOY of the LORD is my strength. I REJOICE because my trust is in Him. I shout for JOY because He defends me. I am JOYFUL because I love His name. I have fullness of JOY in His presence. I have pleasures forever more at His right hand.

I offer sacrifices of JOY in His tabernacle. I have wept, but JOY comes each morning. I have been sorrowful, but He turns my sorrow into JOY. I have sown in tears, but I will reap in JOY. My God wipes away all tears from my eyes. I am ransomed by the LORD, and I am going to Zion with songs and everlasting joy on my head: I obtain joy and gladness from Him, and sorrow and sighing flee away.

I go out with joy, and am led forth with peace: the mountains and the hills break forth before me into singing, and all the trees of the field clap their hands. Instead of the thorn comes up the fir tree, and instead of the brier comes up the myrtle tree.

He gives me beauty for ashes, the oil of joy for mourning, the garment of praise for the spirit of heaviness; that I am called a tree of righteousness, the planting of the LORD, that He might be glorified. And I build the old waste places, and raise up former desolations, and repair waste cities. Strangers stand and feed my flocks, and the sons of the alien are my plowmen and my vinedressers.

Although the fig tree shall not blossom, neither shall fruit be in the vines; the labor of the olive shall fail, and the fields shall yield no meat; the flock shall be cut off from the fold, and there shall be no herd in the stalls: yet I will rejoice in the LORD, I will joy in the God of my salvation. The LORD God is my strength, and He makes my feet like hinds' feet, and He makes me to walk upon my high places.

The LORD God in our midst is mighty; He will save, He will rejoice over me with joy; I will rest in His love, He will joy over me with singing. I smell like the sweet savor of Jesus unto God.

I know that He favors me, because my enemies do not triumph over me. I am good ground for the seed of God's word. I hear it, I understand it, and bear much fruit by it.

I have found God's treasure as it were hid in a field, and I will joyfully sell whatever I have to sell to have it. Living in His Kingdom is righteousness and peace and joy in the Holy Ghost.

I am striving to hear Him say, WELL DONE, so that I may enter into the JOY of the LORD forever. My eyes will one day behold Him as He is, and my heart will rejoice, and no one will ever take away that JOY again.

AMEN.

Chapter 31

Basic Principles Of Prayer

A Simple Outline Summarizing Prayer

1. A Godly Life Begins With Prayer

    a. The Premise
        i. Prayer is the living connection between your heart and God's.
        ii. A relationship with God cannot exist apart from prayer.
        iii. Prayerlessness is Godlessness.

    b. The Promise
        i. Prayer is God's preferred and favored contact with people.
        ii. Correct prayer moves God to response.
        iii. Incorrect prayer is ineffective.

    c. The Process
        i. Earnest prayer, not heartless prayer
        ii. Consistent prayer, not inconsistent prayer
        iii. Thorough prayer, not thoughtless prayer

2. Prayer will get you into trouble, but prayer will get you out of trouble again.

    a. First results may not appear to be the desired results.
        i. God may have to take away an old thing before He gives you a new thing.
        ii. Satan may deal you one more blow before he goes down defeated.
        iii. Victory is often preceded by temporary defeat.

    b. Faith is the key
        i. All faithlessness is sin, whether in prayer or in other areas of life.
        ii. Prayer without positive expectation is powerless.

          iii. Truth is greater than facts.

   c.   Results that sometimes seem negative may actually be positive.

          i. We sometimes fail to know or understand the will of God in a matter.

          ii. His ways are higher than our ways.

          iii. Not my will, but Thy will be done.

3.   Dramatic victories are dependent on effectual fervent prayer.

   a.   Many losses can be attributed to lack of proper prayer.

          i. We fail to give proper weight to the urgency of many circumstances.

          ii. God must be consulted and His intervention must be earnestly sought.

          iii. Lack of petition renders God unmoved and inactive.

   b.   Presumption is a formidable enemy.

          i. We wrongly assume God will work if we have done little or nothing to invite His intervention.

          ii. Presuming we are in right standing when sin stands between us and God yields undesirable results.

          iii. Problems in our relationship with God renders us deficient and powerless in His presence.

   c.   Prayer remedies our relationship and subsequently our effectiveness and fruitfulness.

Chapter 32

Notable Prayers in the Bible

I want to take one last look at several other Biblical examples of prayer before I finish. There are so many aspects of prayer that it is like viewing a beautiful **diamond that has been cut with many facets**.

You will never really be able to see or appreciate all the **countless lessons and benefits of prayer**. Every aspect of prayer has a different lesson in it.

In this final overview, I am hoping that you will be able to glean a few more important lessons. Here is a PARTIAL list of notable prayers of men and women of God in the Bible.

The mother of James and John asked Jesus for special favors for her sons - namely a special place in the Kingdom of Christ. His reply?

> "You know not what you ask."
> *Matthew 20:22*

Sometimes we ask for things we should not ask for. Paul said, "We know not what we should pray for as we ought," Romans 8:26.

> "Ye ask, and receive not, because ye ask amiss,
> that ye may consume it upon Your lusts."
> *James 4:2-3*

One of the first recorded prayers in the Bible was Abraham's intercession for Lot's family in Sodom and Gomorrah. Abraham asked God about saving the cities of Sodom and Gomorrah.

> "Peradventure there be fifty righteous within the city:
> wilt thou also destroy and not spare the place
> for the fifty righteous that are therein?"
> *Genesis 18:24*

Praying on Purpose

You remember how he negotiated down to forty, then thirty, then twenty, then ten. God agreed to save them at every negotiating point. But then Abraham stopped praying.

Ultimately, Abraham's prayers did NOT save the city, BUT God delivered his family from the destruction of the twin cities.

I personally think that Abraham might have saved the entire city if he had not stopped praying. Who can know? Many of us have stopped praying too soon. And most of us have at some time been tempted to give up because a prayer was not answered as quickly as we had wanted.

Even Jesus' disciples needed help with their prayers. Obviously, they did not feel like they knew how to pray very well.

They said, "Lord, teach us to pray." That is when He gave them what we call the "Lord's Prayer." It is actually not the Lord's prayer. It is OUR prayer, a model - a template - for our own prayers.

> "Our Father which art in heaven,
> Hallowed be thy name.
> Thy kingdom come.
> Thy will be done in earth,
> as it is in heaven.
> Give us this day our daily bread.
> And forgive us our debts,
> as we forgive our debtors.
> And lead us not into temptation,
> but deliver us from evil:
> For thine is the kingdom,
> and the power,
> and the glory,
> for ever.
> Amen."
> *Jesus*
> *Matthew 6:9-13*

Jesus was a master of prayer. His own praying was impressive.

Praying for Results

In Gethsemane, He sweat "as it were great drops of blood falling to the ground," as He prayed earnestly. In the end, He submitted to the answer that He really did not want. "Nevertheless, not my will but Thine," Luke 22:42.

He had wanted the disciples to pray with Him, but they failed Him.

What might have happened differently if the disciples had done their duty, and joined Him in intercession that night?

Perhaps Peter would not have cut off Malchus' ear. Perhaps he would not have denied the Lord only hours later. We will never know.

One thing we know. There is POWER in prayer. And to fail to pray is to abdicate or displace the power of God that might have worked miraculously in any given situation.

The scriptures show us that Jesus prayed regularly. He took time to pray, both alone and in public. It was apparently a vital part of his daily manner, to the extent that he often went aside far from the crowd. He disciplined Himself to pray regularly.

If you want to do the will of God, you HAVE to pray. There is no other option.

English Missionary Florence Allshorn spoke of "The Prayer Test."

"There is only one test of our prayer life. Do we want God? Do we want Him so much that we will go on if it takes 5, 6, 10 years to find Him? There is only on test really… do we want God?"

If you really want to know God, you will HAVE to pray. You will have to TAKE TIME to pray.

Anything worthwhile in life takes time. Ask any artist, musician, or athlete. Ask any doctor, lawyer, minister, engineer, or builder. Progress and excellence in any endeavor takes time. Likewise, the pursuit and development of a right relationship with God takes time - TIME IN PRAYER.

Sometimes, God will respond to your prayer quickly. But at other times, He will take more time than you may want Him to. We must be willing to wait on His will to be done.

It is not wise to attempt by prayer to force our will over His will.

Jesus prayed with the will of God in mind. Many people are praying for things that are the exact opposite of God's will. Go ahead and pray, but let God decide. **"Thy will be done**," should be the disclaimer and footnote to every prayer we pray.

Praying in the Spirit also helps assure that you are praying the will of God. "The **Spirit also helpeth our infirmities**: for we know not what we should pray for as we ought: but **the Spirit itself maketh intercession** for us with groanings which cannot be uttered," Romans 8:26.

We hardly know how great an answer may come when we pray.

The thief on the cross next to Jesus said, "Lord, remember me when you come into your Kingdom." He did not know the Bible. He did not know how to be saved. His approach was not even scriptural. Jesus overruled Old Testament teachings to save the man. The New Covenant was not even in effect yet, since He had not yet died and resurrected. So, against all odds, Jesus took that thief to paradise with Him that very day.

HOW MUCH WOULD YOU PRAY...

- if God gave you any and every request?
- if God saved, healed or delivered everyone you prayed for?
- if your life would be made infinitely better for it?

You can never know exactly how God will respond until you toss aside all your inhibitions, bypass all your doubts and fears, and PRAY! Then and only then will you find out how glorious God can show Himself to be.

Moses could not imagine himself being the man for the job God was calling him to. **"Who am I**, that I should go unto Pharaoh, and that I should bring forth the children of Israel out of Egypt?"

And God said, "Certainly **I will be with thee**; and this shall be a token unto thee, that I have sent thee: When thou hast brought forth the people out of Egypt, **ye shall serve God upon this mountain**," Exodus 3:11-12.

Moses had been in the wilderness forty years. He had almost lost his own identity. But when he saw the burning bush on the back side of the desert, God told him that all Israel would one day worship with him there.

You see, God already had plans long before Moses prayed. God was already planning to bring the children of Israel out of bondage in Egypt.

The next time you feel like God has abandoned you on the back side of a desert somewhere, remember that you will not always be alone. Someday, God will bring to pass the Heavenly vision that you did not even see at the time. In the very stressful, discouraging place where you now are, you may one day minister to many others who have been the beneficiary of your hard trial.

Moses could never have dreamed that one day ALL his Jewish brethren would be with him in that wilderness.

And **YOU may not be able to imagine** how God will ever make good things come out of the hard trial that you are now going through, but you just keep on praying and asking God to have His way in your life.

It may be family who will be the beneficiaries of your hard trial. It may be friends. It may be someone entirely new in your life. But whoever it is, you will know in that day that God had a reason for doing what He did in you.

Moses still had more questions for God.

He said to God,

> "When I come unto the children of Israel, and shall say unto them,
> The God of your fathers hath sent me unto you; and they shall say to me,
> What is his name? what shall I say unto them?"

God said, "I AM THAT I AM." He told Moses to tell them, "I AM hath sent me unto you," Exodus 3:13-14.

Moses was eighty years old by this time. All his dreams had probably died by then. But he did not realize that **God had to do what he did** with Moses. God did not want Moses to spend those eighty years in Egypt.

Who knows whether Moses would even have been WILLING to leave Pharaoh's palace if he had spent his whole life living in luxury?

Instead, God chose to break him in the desert. Moses came to the end of himself there. He had nothing but God. And that is the best place that a man can be in.

Those forty years in Midian probably did not seem like blessed years, but they were. God had chosen him before he was ever born. His mother, Jochebed, had no idea how God was working when she made the little ark and put baby Moses into the Nile River. But God WAS working. And He was answering Jochebed's prayers, no doubt.

It is good for us to **be patient, and continue to pray** and trust God with our future. **Trust God in your exile**. Trust God in your wilderness. Tomorrow you may begin to see a long parade of miracles that will astonish you beyond your wildest dreams, and it may begin in the very same place where you had your terrible trial.

All prayers are meaningful. Some prayers are for big things. Some prayers are for small things. But all prayers are important.

God works every kind of miracle in response to every kind of prayer.

"And the people murmured against Moses, saying, What shall we drink?
And **he cried unto the LORD; and the LORD shewed him a tree**,
which when he had cast into the waters, **the waters were made sweet**."
Exodus 15:24-25.

Abimelech's entire household was barren until Moses prayed. **Then children were born**.

Fiery serpents bit the children of Israel until Moses prayed. Then **the pestilence ceased**.

Praying for Results

God would have destroyed all of Israel for worshipping the Golden Calf, but Moses prayed, and **God spared His harsh Judgment**.

Hannah would have remained barren, but she prayed, and **gave birth to Samuel**, who became one of the greatest of all prophets.

"The children of Israel said to Samuel,
Cease not to cry unto the LORD our God for us,
that he will save us out of the hand of the Philistines.
And Samuel took a sucking lamb,
and offered it for a burnt offering wholly unto the LORD:
and Samuel cried unto the LORD for Israel; and the LORD heard him.
...the LORD thundered with a great thunder on that day upon the
Philistines, and discomfited them; and they were smitten before Israel."
1 Samuel 7:8-10

And then there was Gideon...

"**Gideon said unto God**, If thou wilt save Israel by mine hand,
...**I will put a fleece of wool in the floor**;
and if the dew be on the fleece only, and it be dry upon all the earth beside,
then shall I know that thou wilt save Israel by mine hand,
...he rose up early on the morrow,
...and wringed the dew out of the fleece, a bowl full of water.
And **Gideon said unto God**, Let not thine anger be hot against me,
...**let it now be dry only upon the fleece**,
and upon all the ground let there be dew.
And God did so that night: for it was dry upon the fleece only,
and there was dew on all the ground."
Judges 6:36-40

David was a great man of much prayer. He said,

"My voice shalt thou hear in the morning, O Lord;
in the morning will I direct my prayer unto thee, and will look up."
Psalms 5:3

"When they were sick, my clothing was sackcloth:
I humbled my soul with fasting

and my prayer returned into mine own bosom.
I behaved myself as though he had been my friend or brother;
I bowed down heavily as one that mourneth for his mother."
Psalms 35:13-14

"He will regard the prayer of the destitute,
he will not despise their prayer."
Psalms 102:17

Solomon prayed and dedicated the Holy Temple that he had built unto the LORD.

"And the LORD appeared to Solomon by night, and said unto him,
I have heard thy prayer, and have chosen this place
to myself for an house of sacrifice.
If I shut up heaven that there be no rain,
or if I command the locusts to devour the land,
or if I send pestilence among my people;
If my people, which are called by my name, shall humble themselves,
and pray, and seek my face, and turn from their wicked ways;
then will I hear from heaven, and will forgive their sin,
and will heal their land.

Now mine eyes shall be open, and mine ears attent
unto the prayer that is made in this place.
For now have I chosen and sanctified this house,
that my name may be there for ever:
and mine eyes and mine heart shall be there perpetually."
2 Chronicles 7:12-22

Following Solomon's excellent prayer, God replied generously, but clearly stated His terms of acceptance. He warned of what would happen if the people failed to meet His terms. History confirms its fulfillment following their failure to meet the terms.

Elijah prayed against the prophets of Baal, and the **Lord sent fire** down from Heaven. The altar was destroyed, and the false prophets died.

Praying for Results

"Elijah the prophet came near, and said,
...Hear me, O LORD, hear me,
that this people may know that thou art the LORD God,
and that thou hast turned their heart back again.
**Then the fire of the LORD fell, and consumed the burnt sacrifice,
and the wood, and the stones, and the dust,
and licked up the water that was in the trench.**
And when all the people saw it, they fell on their faces: and they said,
The LORD, he is the God; the LORD, he is the God."
1 Kings 18:36-39

Later, Elijah prayed, and **God sent a drought** and a famine in the land for three and a half years. Then he prayed again, and **it rained**.

Elisha prayed when Syrian armies came to kill, and **God's angels appeared in Heavenly chariots** all along the hills. Prayer can bring help from Heaven.

Under Hezekiah, revival came to the kingdom of Judah.

"Then the priests the Levites arose and blessed the people:
and their voice was heard and
their prayer came up to his holy dwelling place, even unto heaven."
II Chronicles 30:27

Hezekiah prayed when surrounded by evil armies, and **the angel of the Lord killed 185,000 in one night**. Prayer can defeat our enemies. Again, Hezekiah prayed, and **his terminal illness was cured**. God gave him fifteen more years. Prayer can bring miraculous healings.

Daniel prayed, and **God shut the mouth of the hungry lions**. Prayer can deliver you from a lions' den, or whatever prison you are in. Daniel prayed, and **God revealed the meaning of the handwriting on the wall**. God will reveal His secrets to us if we pray.

Nehemiah prayed, and King Cyrus donated enough **money to rebuild Jerusalem**, which lay in ruins. God will supply all your need according to His riches in glory.

Praying on Purpose

Ezra prayed that God would restore Jerusalem, and God moved on a Persian king to sponsor the entire project.

"We had spoken unto the king, saying,
The hand of our God is upon all them for good that seek him;
but his power and his wrath is against all them that forsake him.
So we fasted and besought our God for this: and he was intreated of us.
...And [I] weighed unto them the silver, and the gold, and the vessels,
even the offering of the house of our God, which the king,
and his counsellors, and his lords, and all Israel there present, had offered:
...So took the priests and the Levites the weight of **the silver, and the gold,
and the vessels, to bring them to Jerusalem unto the house of our God.**"
Ezra 8:22-25,30

Job prayed for his friends, and **God healed his awful disease, and restored double all that he had lost.** God will revive us from the brink of death or destruction.

Jonah prayed, and **the whale vomited him onto the beach**, and immediately went back into the ministry.

Zacharias prayed for a child in his old age, and God gave him and Elisabeth a son named John the Baptist.

"According to the custom of the priest's office,
his lot was to burn incense when he went into the temple of the Lord.
And the whole multitude of the people were praying
without at the time of incense.
And there appeared unto him an angel of the Lord
standing on the right side of the altar of incense.
And when Zacharias saw him, he was troubled, and fear fell upon him.
But the angel said unto him, Fear not, Zacharias: **for thy prayer is heard;
and thy wife Elisabeth shall bear thee a son,
and thou shalt call his name John.**
And thou shalt have joy and gladness; and many shall rejoice at his birth."
Luke 1:9-14

Jesus often went apart from the crowd to spend time alone praying.

Praying for Results

"When he had sent the multitudes away,
he went up into a mountain apart to pray:
and when the evening was come, he was there alone."
Matthew 14:23

"He went out into a mountain to pray,
and continued all night in prayer to God."
Luke 6:12

"He took Peter and John and James,
and went up into a mountain to pray.
And as he prayed, the fashion of his countenance was altered,
and his raiment was white and glistering.
And, behold, there talked with him two men, which were Moses and Elias:
Who appeared in glory, and spake of his decease
which he should accomplish at Jerusalem."
Luke 9:28-31

Jesus prayed often, and taught His disciples to pray often.

"If ye abide in me, and my words abide in you,
ye shall ask what ye will, and it shall be done unto you."
John 15:7

"All things, whatsoever ye shall ask in prayer, believing, ye shall receive."
Matthew 21:22

"Whatsoever ye shall ask in my name, that will I do,
that the Father may be glorified in the Son.
If ye shall ask any thing in my name, I will do it."
John 14:13-14

One hundred and twenty believers prayed for days, and God shook Jerusalem with an outpouring of the Holy Ghost. Within days, **8,120 people had received the baptism of the Holy Ghost**.

"When they were come in, they went up into an upper room…,
And suddenly there came a sound from heaven
as of a rushing mighty wind,

and it filled all the house where they were sitting.
And there appeared unto them cloven tongues like as of fire,
and it sat upon each of them. And they were all filled with the Holy Ghost,
and began to speak with other tongues, as the Spirit gave them utterance,
...then they that gladly received [Peter's] word were baptized: and
the same day there were added unto them about three thousand souls."
Acts 1:13; 2:2-4,41

The Apostles knew that prayer was the key to everything. They said,

"We will give ourselves continually to prayer
and to the ministry of the word."
Acts 6:4

A group of saints called a house prayer meeting, and **an angel rescued Peter from prison** and impending execution.

The Apostles prayed, and God anointed them **to go all over the world** and preach the gospel, with power to do signs, wonders and miracles.

Peter and John prayed, and **many in Samaria received the Holy Ghost**.

Peter prayed over the dead body of Dorcas, and **she came to life**.

Cornelius prayed, and God sent Peter to preach the Gospel. **His entire household was filled with the Holy Ghost and baptized in Jesus' name**.

A man in Macedonia prayed for God to send help, and **God showed him to Paul in a vision.** Paul changed his plans to go to Bythinia, and went to Macedonia instead, where many souls were converted.

Paul and Silas prayed, and **God opened the Philippian jail** with an earthquake. Afterward, the jailer and his family were converted.

Paul was a radical advocate of prayer, who prayed continually, and taught extensively on prayer.

"Husbands and wives: "Defraud ye not one the other
except it be with consent for a time,

that ye may give yourselves to fasting and prayer."
I Corinthians 7:5

"Praying always with all prayer and supplication in the Spirit,
and watching thereunto with all perseverance and supplication
for all saints; and for me that utterance may be given unto me,
that I may open my mouth boldly
to make known the mystery of the Gospel."
Ephesians 6:18

"In everything by prayer and supplication with all thanksgiving
let Your requests be made known unto God."
Philippians 4:6

Peter taught on prayer.

[Husbands honor your wives] "…that Your prayers be not hindered.
For the eyes of the Lord are over the righteous,
and his ears are open unto their prayers,
but the face of the Lord is against them that do evil."
I Peter 3:7.

"The end of all things is at hand:
be ye therefore sober and watch unto prayer."
I Peter 4:7.

John taught that the prayers of the saints ascend continually before the Throne of God in Heaven.

"The four beasts and four and twenty elders fell down before the Lamb,
having every one of them harps, and golden vials full of odours,
which are the prayers of saints."
Revelation 5:8.

"And the smoke of the incense, which came with the prayers of the saints,
ascended up before God out of the angel's hand."
Revelation 8:4

Praying on Purpose

"Pray without ceasing."
1 Thessalonians 5:17

"The great people of the earth today are the people who pray!
I do not mean those who talk about prayer;
nor those who say they believe in prayer;
nor those who explain prayer;
but I mean those who actually take the time to pray.
They have not time. It must be taken from something else.
That something else is important, very important and pressing,
but still, less important and pressing than prayer.
There are people who put prayer first,
and group the other items in life's schedule around and after prayer.
These are the people today who are doing the most for God
in winning souls, in solving problems, in awakening churches,
in supplying both men and money for mission posts,
in keeping fresh and strong their lives far off in sacrificial service
on the foreign field, where the thickest fighting is going on,
and in keeping the old earth sweet a little while longer."

S. D. Gordon
1859-1936

Chapter 33

Valuable Quotes On Prayer

"As is the business of tailors to make clothes
and cobblers to make shoes,
so it is the business of Christians to pray."
Martin Luther
1483-1546

"Whenever God determines to do a great work,
he first sets His people to pray."
Charles H. Spurgeon
1834-1892

"Do not have your concert first,
and then tune your instrument afterwards.
Begin the day with the Word of God and prayer,
and get first of all into harmony with Him."
J. Hudson Taylor
1832-1905

"He who runs from God in the morning
will scarcely find Him the rest of the day."
John Bunyan
1628-1688

"I will try and remember always to approach God in secret with as much
reverence in speech, posture, and behavior as in public."
David Livingstone
1813-1873

Praying on Purpose

"Prayer itself is an art which only the Holy Ghost can teach us.
He is the giver of all prayer.
Pray for prayer - pray till you can pray."
Charles H. Spurgeon
1834-1892

"Prayer is not learned in a classroom but in the closet."
E. M. Bounds
1835-1913

"Closet communion needs time for the revelation of God's presence.
It is vain to say, 'I have too much work to do to find time.'
You must find time or forfeit blessing.
God knows how to save for you the time you sacredly keep
for communion with Him."
A. T. Pierson
1837-1911

"This morning about nine I withdrew to the woods for prayer.
I was in such anguish that when I arose from my knees
I felt extremely weak and overcome.
...I cared not how or where I lived,
or what hardships I went through,
so that I could but gain souls for Christ."
David Brainerd
1718-1747

"I must secure more time for private devotions.
I have been living far too public for me.
The shortening of devotions starves the soul,
it grows lean and faint.
I have been keeping too late hours."
William Wilberforce
1759-1833

Praying for Results

"Always respond to every impulse to pray.
The impulse to pray may come when you are reading
or when you are battling with a text.
I would make an absolute law of this – always obey such an impulse."
Martyn Lloyd-Jones
1899-1981

"Time spent in prayer will yield more than that given to work.
Prayer alone gives work its worth and its success.
Prayer opens the way for God Himself
to do His work in us and through us.
Let our chief work as God's messengers be intercession;
in it we secure the presence and power of God..."
Andrew Murray
1828-1917

"None can believe how powerful prayer is, and what it is able to effect,
but those who have learned it by experience.
It is a great matter when in extreme need to take hold on prayer.
I know, whenever I have prayed earnestly, that I have been amply heard,
and have obtained more than I prayed for.
God indeed sometimes delayed, but at last He came."
Martin Luther
1483-1546

"Those who know God best are the richest and most powerful in prayer.
Little acquaintance with God, and strangeness and coldness to Him,
make prayer a rare and feeble thing."
E. M. Bounds
1835-1913

"History is silent about revivals that did not begin with prayer."
Edwin Orr
1912-1987

Praying on Purpose

"The men who have done the most for God in this world
have been early on their knees.
He who fritters away the early morning, its opportunity and freshness,
in other pursuits than seeking God will make poor headway
seeking Him the rest of the day.
If God is not first in our thoughts and efforts in the morning,
He will be in the last place the remainder of the day."
E. M. Bounds
1835-1913

"Prayer is the greatest power God has put into our hands for service —
praying is harder than doing, at least I find it so,
but the dynamic lies that way to advance the Kingdom."
Mary Slessor
1848-1915

"When I am praying the most eloquently,
I am getting the least accomplished in my prayer life.
But when I stop getting eloquent and give God less theology
and shut up and just gaze upward and wait for God to speak to my heart
He speaks with such power that I have to grab a pencil and a notebook
and take notes on what God is saying to my heart."
A. W. Tozer
1897-1963

"The price of prayerlessness far exceeds the price of prayer.
It is always too soon to quit praying,
even when praying is the last thing we seem to be able to do."
Harold Lindsell
1913-1998

"True prayer is a lonely business."
Samuel Chadwick
1860-1932

Praying for Results

"The trouble with nearly everybody who prays is that
he says 'Amen' and runs away before God has a chance to reply.
Listening to God is far more important than giving Him our ideas."
Frank Laubach
1884-1970

"I would rather train twenty men to pray, than a thousand to preach;
A minister's highest mission ought to be to teach his people to pray."
H. MacGregor

"Nothing tends more to cement the hearts of Christians
than praying together. Never do they love one another so well
as when they witness the outpouring of each other's hearts in prayer."
Charles Finney
1792-1875

"Do not pray for easy lives. Pray to be stronger men.
Do not pray for tasks equal to your powers,
pray for powers equal to your task."
Phillips Brooks
1835-1893

"Prayerlessness is disobedience, for God's command
is that men ought always to pray and not faint.
To be prayerless is to fail God, for He says, 'Ask of me.'"
Leonard Ravenhill
1907-1994

"Those persons who know the deep peace of God,
the unfathomable peace that passeth all understanding,
are always men and women of much prayer."
R. A. Torrey
1856-1928

Praying on Purpose

"Prayer must carry on our work as much as preaching;
he preacheth not heartily to his people that will not pray for them."
Richard Baxter
1615 – 1691

"Prayer is not only asking, but an attitude of mind which
produces the atmosphere in which asking is perfectly natural."
Oswald Chambers
1874-1917

"If your faith does not make you pray, have nothing to do with it:
get rid of it, and God help thee to begin again."
C. H. Spurgeon
1834-1892

"Notice, we never pray for folks we gossip about,
and we never gossip about the folk for whom we pray!
Prayer is a great deterrent."
Leonard Ravenhill
1907-1994

"Beware in your prayers, above everything else, of limiting God,
not only by unbelief, but by fancying that you know what He can do.
Expect unexpected things 'above all that we ask or think.'"
Andrew Murray
1828-1917

"If I could hear Christ praying for me in the next room,
I would not fear a million enemies.
Yet distance makes no difference.
He is praying for me."
Robert Murray McCheyne
1813-1843

Afterword

Select Prayer Topics

*The following 102 mini-lessons are selected Prayer Topics
from more than 4800 Bible lessons contained in
Ken Raggio's "**My Daily Bible Companion**."*

Enoch Walked With God

What does it mean, "Enoch walked with God..."? Presumably, Enoch lived in continual fellowship with God. Continual communication. Constant contact. Daily devotions. You and I can walk with God, too. "That I may know him, and the power of his resurrection, and the fellowship of his sufferings," Philippians 3:10. Paul instructed us to "Pray without ceasing," I Thessalonians 5:17. "For our conversation is in heaven," Philippians 3:20. Walk with Him. Talk with Him. Have sweet communion with Him daily.

Genesis 5:22 - "And Enoch walked with God after he begat Methuselah three hundred years."

You Must Hear And Obey The Voice Of God

If you think it is important that GOD hears YOUR voice when you pray, how much more important is it that YOU hear GOD's voice when He speaks? Some people do all the talking, but rarely, if ever, hear God's voice. Noah would not have survived if he had not both heard AND obeyed God's voice. "The LORD said unto Noah, Come thou and all thy house into the ark; for thee have I seen righteous before me in this generation."

Genesis 7:5,16 - "And Noah did according unto all that the LORD commanded him. ...and the LORD shut him in."

Receiving Instructions

Prayer is a two-way street. We pray today. God may speak tomorrow. After Jacob spent twenty years in Laban's household, things went sour.

Laban became adversarial. God spoke to Jacob and instructed him to leave. It was a defining moment of Jacob's life. If we want to receive instructions of that kind, we need a heart that desires to hear His voice. We need God's point of view.

Genesis 31:3 - "And the LORD said unto Jacob, Return unto the land of thy fathers, and to thy kindred; and I will be with thee."

An Altar And Offerings At Bethel

After being displaced from Shechem, Jacob returned to the "the house of God," Bethel. He built an altar and made offerings to the Lord. Shortly thereafter, his precious wife, Rachel, died giving birth to Benjamin, and soon his father, Isaac, died. Our inevitable tragedies are much easier to bear when we have already been to the altar beforehand. Why not consecrate today?

Genesis 35:14 - "And Jacob set up a pillar in the place where he talked with him, even a pillar of stone: and he poured a drink offering thereon, and he poured oil thereon."

Joseph's Gift

From his childhood, God spoke to Joseph in dreams and supernatural revelations. God revealed that he would be exalted above his own family. Years later, God interpreted the dreams of Pharaoh's butler and baker to Joseph, and eventually, the dreams of Pharaoh himself. Joseph denied that it was a human ability. Joseph's insights came from his personal and intimate communion with God. We, too, may discover amazing insights in prayerful, contemplative times with Him.

Genesis 41:16 - "And Joseph answered Pharaoh, saying, It is not in me: God shall give Pharaoh an answer of peace."

Going Up To God

Moses met God in Mount Sinai. That is when and where he received the Ten Commandments. Nothing is said about prayer, but in fact, the entire event was about Moses and God in conversation. Sometimes our conversations with God seem more like business as usual than like prayers, but that is the stuff of relationships. You do not have to be on your knees, or speaking in a sanctimonious tone of voice to have priceless communion with God.

Exodus 19:3 - "And Moses went up unto God, and the LORD called unto him out of the mountain."

The Premise Of Prayer

Prayer is the living connection between you and God. Dialogue, not monologue, is the stuff of relationships. How do you know and bond with others without conversation? Can a husband and wife spend happy years together without meaningful conversations? Can parents and children truly bond without frank and honest discussions? Even so, the bilateral exchanges of my words with God's bind me to Him. I pour out my heart to Him, and He responds compassionately. Prayers are the terms of endearment.

Exodus 19:19 - "Moses spake, and God answered him by a voice."

Confessing Sins

This is the first occurrence in the Bible of any requirement for confession. After Moses listed several sins, he called for the guilty party to confess his sin. A precedent for all time was set. As a general rule, the priests confessed all Israel's sins when they offered sacrifices. God requires that we acknowledge our wrong-doing. He is more interested in producing righteousness in us than in punishing our wrongs.

Leviticus 5:5 - "And it shall be, when he shall be guilty in one of these things, that he shall confess that he hath sinned in that thing."

God Hears It All

God hears more than just the prayers we pray. He hears everything we say. It is possible to say all the right things in prayer, and then nullify them with negative talk. Let your words be "Yes, Yes," or "No, No." Make your everyday conversation support your prayers. Otherwise, your prayers will be rendered worthless.

Deuteronomy 1:34-35 - "And the LORD heard the voice of your words, and was wroth, and sware, saying, Surely there shall not one of these men of this evil generation see that good land, which I sware to give unto your fathers."

What Does Your Heart Say?

We usually think of prayer as the way we communicate our requests to God. In reality, God is influenced by all our words, spoken or not. He discerns our thoughts and intentions, and acts accordingly. That is why we must be extremely careful of all our thoughts and words. God knows when our hearts are not pure. You do not have to say evil things out loud. God reads you like a book.

Deuteronomy 8:17,20 - "And thou say in thine heart, My power and the might of mine hand hath gotten me this wealth, ...so shall ye perish."

Seeking Counsel From Men Of God

Sometimes, God wants us to consult with those men He has ordained as ministers. They walk with God. They study His ways. They know His will. You can pray and search all over the place, but the answer may be in the house of God. They are only men, but God uses men. Men of God certainly know better than laymen. God made it that way.

Deuteronomy 17:9 - "And thou shalt come unto the priests the Levites, and unto the judge that shall be in those days, and enquire; and they shall shew thee the sentence of judgment."

Prayers That Backfire

God is never going to answer a prayer that contradicts His Word, His will, or His promises. If you ask God to do something that is evil in His sight, do not be surprised if He does exactly the opposite of what you ask. God may turn your blessing into a curse, or your curse into a blessing. Sanctify your prayers by understanding and seeking His will.

Deuteronomy 23:5 - "Nevertheless the LORD thy God would not hearken unto Balaam; but the LORD thy God turned the curse into a blessing unto thee, because the LORD thy God loved thee."

The Word Is In Thy Mouth

Moses prophesied lavish blessings on the people if they obeyed God's commandments, but cruel curses if they rebelled. Our divine purpose can only be realized through faithful obedience to God. Disobedience wrecks that. But obedience is entirely possible by believing and speaking the Word of God. Speak the Word daily. Life and blessing is in it.

Deuteronomy 30:11 - "For this commandment which I command thee this day, it is not hidden from thee, neither is it far off, ...But the word is very nigh unto thee, in thy mouth, and in thy heart, that thou mayest do it."

A Lamp For David's Sake

David said, "For thou art my lamp, O LORD: and the LORD will lighten my darkness," 2 Samuel 22:29. Many of David's descendants were evil: Solomon, then Rehoboam, then Abijam. The northern tribes never had another righteous king, but for David's sake, God preserved two tribes at Jerusalem. What if David had never prayed? Your descendants may become completely godless if you neglect to pray.

1 Kings 15:4 - "For David's sake did the LORD his God give him a lamp in Jerusalem, to set up his son after him, and to establish Jerusalem."

Give Your Problem To God

King Hezekiah received a vicious letter from the Assyrian king threatening to take control of Israel. Hezekiah had no might against Assyria, so he took the letter into the house of God and asked God to read the letter. That night, the angel of the Lord killed 185,000 Assyrian soldiers. God has solutions we can't even imagine.

2 Kings 19:14 - "And Hezekiah received the letter of the hand of the messengers, and read it: and Hezekiah went up into the house of the LORD, and spread it before the LORD."

Hezekiah Prayed And Was Healed

King Hezekiah was dying, and Isaiah came to tell him to set his house in order. But Hezekiah turned his face to the wall and prayed to the LORD, weeping sorely. The word of the LORD told Isaiah to turn back and tell Hezekiah, "I have heard thy prayers. ...I will add unto thy days fifteen years." Isaiah said, "This sign shalt thou have." The shadow would go backwards ten degrees. Isaiah cried unto the LORD: and he brought the shadow ten degrees backward. Never accept defeat without a prayer of faith.

2 Kings 20:7 - "And he recovered."

They Enquired Not In The Days Of Saul

Here is a conspicuous Biblical phenomenon. Most stories about righteous men include some account of prayer. Stories of evil men almost never mention prayer. It is a warning signal, like a canary in a coal mine. If the canary dies, miners know that oxygen levels are low and evacuate the mine. When prayer levels get too low, it is time to pray or evacuate. That was Saul's weakness. David immediately rectified that problem.

1 Chronicles 13:3 - "Let us bring again the ark of our God to us: for we enquired not at it in the days of Saul."

Dedicatory Prayer

When Solomon dedicated the new Temple, his prayer was an awe-inspiring communion with God - a model template for all time. Acknowledging God's infinite sovereignty, his words flowed with truest worship, heartfelt contrition, and earnest intercession for God's best blessings upon the people. God's response was mind-blowing. Want to see God move like that? Pray like that!

2 Chronicles 7:1 - "...when Solomon had made an end of praying, the fire came down from heaven, and consumed the burnt offering and the sacrifices; and the glory of the LORD filled the house."

Praying for Results

The Lord Hears

Our Creator listens. The Spirit who made the worlds is attentive to our voices and hears every word we speak. We all have times when it seems "the heavens are brass," but don't you believe it! Not a word escapes Him. He who knows the number of the stars and calls them all by name, who sees every sparrow fall, and knows the number of the hairs of your head - He hears you!

2 Chronicles 7:12 - "The LORD appeared to Solomon by night, and said unto him, I have heard thy prayer."

The Promise Of Prayer

Abraham Lincoln said, "I have been driven many times to my knees by the overwhelming conviction that I had nowhere else to go." God promises faithfully to hear the prayers of His people. Who else in the world guarantees to care and intervene? Abandon all others, but seek the Lord!

2 Chronicles 7:14 - "If my people, which are called by my name, shall humble themselves, and pray, and seek my face, and turn from their wicked ways; then will I hear from heaven, and will forgive their sin, and will heal their land."

Repenting for Someone Else

Who would you pray for if you knew YOUR prayers would prevent harsh judgment for sins? Hezekiah repented for the people's failures, and God showed mercy.

2 Chronicles 30:18-20 - "...had not cleansed themselves, yet did they eat the passover otherwise than it was written. But Hezekiah prayed for them, saying, The good LORD pardon every one that prepareth his heart to seek God, the LORD God of his fathers, though he be not cleansed according to the purification of the sanctuary. And the LORD hearkened to Hezekiah, and healed the people."

God Put It In My Heart

Twice, Nehemiah said, "God put it in my heart." First, it was to rebuild the walls of Jerusalem. Second, it was to gather the nobles, rulers and others to verify their genealogy. Certainly, the future of Jerusalem ultimately depended much more on the integrity of the people than with the integrity of the walls. If Nehemiah had only prayed, and not listened to God, Jerusalem's fate might have been vastly different. God IS speaking. Are you hearing?

Nehemiah 7:5 - "My God put into mine heart to gather together the nobles, and the rulers, and the people."

Job Offers Sacrifices To Sanctify His Children

The book of Job was probably written by Moses before the book of Genesis, making it the oldest book in the Bible. It tells the trials of Job, "perfect and upright, one that feared God, and eschewed evil." The first specific behavior mentioned of Job was that he made intercession for his children every day. Therefore, the first godly behavior ever identified in the Bible was INTERCESSION for children!

Job 1:5 "Job ...rose up early in the morning, and offered burnt offerings ...for Job said, It may be that my sons have sinned, and cursed God in their hearts."

Pure Prayer

Unless you live isolated in a cave, somebody will eventually accuse you of impure motives. Job's friends stared at his suffering for seven days before commenting, but when they started talking, they were vicious. In times like those, only you and God know the whole truth. Job knew his own heart. "My prayer is pure," he said. It doesn't matter what other people think about you or your prayer life. You and God know the truth. Pray on.

Job 16:17 - "Not for any injustice in mine hands: also my prayer is pure."

Struggling With Unanswered Prayer

Job pleaded with his friends to stop attacking him. He was overwhelmed and struggling to make sense of his trials. He rehearsed all the prayers he had prayed and all the efforts he had made to correct his mistakes and persuade God to deliver him from his plight. Sooner or later, we all get the feeling that God does not care or is not listening. But God IS listening. Just hold on a little longer, and you will see.

Job 19:7 - "Behold, I cry out of wrong, but I am not heard: I cry aloud, but there is no judgment."

Clapping, Shouting, Singing, Praising

It is unthinkable that God, in all His glorious majesty, might not be praised by His creation. "The LORD most high is terrible; He is a great King over all the earth." He will subdue all people and all nations. He will give His people their promised inheritance. So let us all exalt Him - with a shout, with a trumpet, singing praises to the King of all the earth! Applaud Him! Cheer Him! Lift your voice in songs and praise the LORD!

Psalms 47:1 - "O clap your hands, all ye people; shout unto God with the voice of triumph."

Lead Me To The Rock

When you are overwhelmed, go to the Rock. When enemies encroach, run to the strong tower. The psalmist trusted in the covert of God's wings. He said he would abide in His Tabernacle forever. He believed that God would preserve him and prolong his life. Nobody is safe alone. I call Him Jesus, My Rock.

Psalms 61:2 - "From the end of the earth will I cry unto thee, when my heart is overwhelmed: lead me to the rock that is higher than I. For thou hast been a shelter for me, and a strong tower from the enemy."

Repetitious Prayers

Jesus said, "When ye pray, use not vain repetitions." Saying forty "Our Fathers" or twenty "Hail, Marys" is vain repetition. Worthless. Yet repetitious prayer is perfectly in order. Five times in the Psalms, David asked God to "make haste" to help him. Twenty-six times he prayed, "Deliver me." Eight times he prayed "Let them be ashamed," over his enemies. Literally dozens of phrases are oft repeated throughout the book of Psalms. Every time you have a need, pray about it, even if it is the one-hundredth time.

Psalms 70:1 - "Make haste, O God, to deliver me."

Dark Trials Inspire Us To Pray

People who "sit in darkness and in the shadow of death, being bound in affliction and iron, ...cried unto the LORD in their trouble, and He saved them out of their distresses." Again, "They that go down to the sea in ships, that do business in great waters; These see the works of the LORD, and his wonders in the deep. ...they cry unto the LORD in their trouble, ...he bringeth them unto their desired haven." Affliction compels men to search out God.

Psalms 107:20 - "He sent his word, and healed them, and delivered them from their destructions."

The Prayer Of The Upright Is His Delight

Does God love to hear your voice? Judge your tongue. Soft answers turn away wrath. Grievous words stir up anger. The tongue of the righteous uses knowledge rightly, but the mouth of fools pours out foolishness. A wholesome tongue is a tree of life, but a perverse tongue is a breach in the spirit. The words of the pure are pleasant words, but the mouth of the wicked pours out evil things. The prayer of the upright is God's delight.

Proverbs 15:29 - "The LORD is far from the wicked: but he heareth the prayer of the righteous."

Praying for Results

They That Seek The LORD Understand All Things

The surest way to get wisdom and understanding is to seek the LORD. We must not merely ask for His blessings, but conscientiously hear and obey His instructions, whether they are ancient or current directives. "He that turneth away his ear from hearing the law, even his prayer shall be abomination." We must empty ourselves if we hope to be filled with His treasures. "He that covereth his sins shall not prosper: but whoso confesseth and forsaketh them shall have mercy."

Proverbs 28:5 - "Evil men understand not judgment: but they that seek the LORD understand all things."

Ye Shall Have A Song

Sometimes, we grow silent as we wait for a much-desired victory. Like the saints in Babylon, who hung their harps on willow trees, our songs are sometimes silenced because of our hard trials. But when Jesus comes, we will suffer no more defeats. We will have victory forever. Instantly, our songs will return - to stay!

Isaiah 30:29 - "Ye shall have a song, as in the night when a holy solemnity is kept; and gladness of heart, as when one goeth with a pipe to come into the mountain of the LORD, to the mighty One of Israel."

Terminal Illness Can Be Cured Through Prayer

King Hezekiah was sick and dying, and Isaiah warned him to set his house in order. But Hezekiah turned his face toward the wall and prayed, weeping sorely. Mercifully, God sent word again by Isaiah that He would add fifteen years to Hezekiah's life. God gave him a sign to confirm His promise. The shadow on the sundial went backwards. You never know how God may answer your prayers. Just PRAY, expecting a miracle!

Isaiah 38:8 - "I will bring again the shadow of the degrees, which is gone down in the sun dial of Ahaz, ten degrees backward."

Seek Ye The LORD While He May Be Found

God invites the thirsty to come drink, and those with no money to buy and eat without money or price. "Seek ye the LORD while he may be found, call ye upon him while he is near." Today, you have a glorious opportunity to find favor and blessings from God. Tomorrow may be too late. No one is guaranteed another heartbeat.

Isaiah 55:7 - "Let the wicked forsake his way, and the unrighteous man his thoughts: and let him return unto the LORD, and he will have mercy upon him; and to our God, for he will abundantly pardon."

I Will Make Them Joyful In My House Of Prayer

God is always mindful of those who are righteous unto Him, regardless of their significance in the eyes of others. He remembers those who keep His judgments and do justice. He tells even the eunuchs and the strangers who are faithful not to say that they are cut off from the congregation. God promises joy to His people who come into His house to pray.

Isaiah 56:7 - "Even them will I bring to my holy mountain, and make them joyful in my house of prayer: ...for mine house shall be called an house of prayer for all people."

Travail In Prayer, Or Travail In Judgment

Many people disdain the seemingly unsavory task of travailing in prayer. In over forty years of ministry, I have known precious few people who relish true, travailing prayer. But it is a divinely-ordained occupation. If we fail to agonize in prayer for victory over the world, the flesh and the devil, we will someday agonize because we did not.

Jeremiah 4:30 - "When thou art spoiled, what wilt thou do? ...For I have heard a voice as of a woman in travail, and the anguish as of her that bringeth forth her first child, ...saying, Woe is me now!"

I Know The Thoughts I Think Toward You

NEVER think that God does not want to hear your prayers. Even while in Babylonian captivity, God told His people that He WANTED a right relationship with them! He WANTED them to pray!

Jeremiah 29:11-13 - "I know the thoughts that I think toward you, saith the LORD, thoughts of peace, and not of evil, to give you an expected end. Then shall ye call upon me, and ye shall go and pray unto me, and I will hearken unto you. And ye shall seek me, and find me, when ye shall search for me with all your heart."

Nebuchadnezzar Blesses God

When Shadrach, Meshach and Abednego walked out of the fiery furnace without even the smell of smoke on them, Nebuchadnezzar realized that he and all his officials had witnessed an astonishing miracle. When God-fearing people take a stand, God is glorified, and the world takes note.

Daniel 3:28-30 - "Nebuchadnezzar spake, and said, Blessed be the God of Shadrach, Meshach, and Abednego, who hath sent his angel, and delivered his servants that trusted in him, ...there is no other God that can deliver after this sort. Then the king promoted Shadrach, Meshach, and Abednego, in the province of Babylon."

Communion With God In Prayer Is Worth Every Risk

I would rather be in a lion's den if God is there, than to live in a luxurious castle without God. Obviously, Daniel felt that way, too. Never let anybody interfere with your relationship with God.

Daniel 6:10-11 - "Now when Daniel knew that the writing was signed, he went into his house; and his windows being open in his chamber toward Jerusalem, he kneeled upon his knees three times a day, and prayed, and gave thanks before his God, as he did aforetime. Then these men assembled, and found Daniel praying and making supplication before his God."

It Is Time To Seek The LORD

Just a little earlier, the prophet had denounced the people for their sins and concluded that they would seek the LORD and would not find Him, because "He hath withdrawn Himself from them," Hosea 5:6. Then, in a sudden about-face, he said, "It is time to seek the LORD." God may sometimes withdraw from you because you provoked His anger, but that is all the more reason why you should seek Him until He responds.

Hosea 10:12 - "Break up your fallow ground: for it is time to seek the LORD, till he come and rain righteousness upon you."

Effectual Prayer Requires Right Relationship With God

The foremost important factor in effectual prayer is not faith. It is right relationship with God. It is possible to have faith without right relationship. Prayer will not work, no matter how much faith you have, if you are not in right standing with God. Malachi rebuked Israel for dishonoring God, having no fear of God, and offering polluted and blemished sacrifices.

Malachi 1:8-10 - "Will he be pleased with thee, or accept thy person? ...will he regard your persons? ...I have no pleasure in you, saith the LORD of hosts, neither will I accept an offering at your hand."

The Message Of Repentance

Did John preach Jesus' message, or did Jesus preach John's message? Neither. Repentance is the first word in the New Covenant. Jesus said, "Except ye repent, ye shall all likewise perish." Sin separates men from God. Just ask Adam and Eve. If you want to see the Kingdom of God, you have to get rid of your sins. That begins with recognizing your sins, admitting and confessing them, and asking God to forgive you for committing them.

Matthew 4:17 - "From that time Jesus began to preach, and to say, Repent: for the kingdom of heaven is at hand."

Forgive Us Our Debts As We Forgive Our Debtors

Most people do not seem to realize that if they refuse to forgive someone, they cannot be forgiven of their own sins. You have to set others free if you want to be set free. Otherwise, you will never be released from your own sins. That should be enough reason for anybody to forgive anybody else. "If ye forgive men their trespasses, your heavenly Father will also forgive you: But if ye forgive not men their trespasses, neither will your Father forgive your trespasses," 6:14-15. Remember that when you pray.

Matthew 6:12 - "Forgive us our debts, as we forgive our debtors."

Steal Away And Pray

All in one day, Jesus learned that John had been beheaded; He took a ship to a desert place, but multitudes followed; He healed their sick; He fed over 10,000 with five loaves and two fishes; the people tried to make Him a king (John 6:15); He went into a mountain to pray alone; a storm arose; He walked on the waters back to His ship. When days are hectic, follow Jesus' example. Steal away and pray.

Matthew 14:23 - "He went up into a mountain apart to pray: and when the evening was come, he was there alone."

How Oft Shall I Forgive My Brother?

Your act of forgiving those who have trespassed against you can have more influence with God than any prayer you pray. Your forgiveness, or lack thereof, is God's criteria for forgiving you. Forgive not; be not forgiven. Forgive; be forgiven. I never met anybody who actually believed that Jesus only wanted Peter to forgive 490 times. You must forgive EVERY TIME.

Matthew 18:21-22 - "[Peter] said, Lord, how oft shall my brother sin against me, and I forgive him? till seven times? Jesus saith unto him, I say not unto thee, Until seven times: but, Until seventy times seven."

Prayers Not Prayed

I have often wondered how history might have been different if Jesus' disciples had prayed with Him in Gethsemane. He told them, "Watch and pray, that ye enter not into temptation." But they didn't. Maybe Peter would not have cut off the man's ear if he had prayed first. Maybe he would not have denied the Lord thrice if he had prayed. Maybe astonishing miracles would have happened. What miracle will you never receive because you didn't pray when you should have?

Matthew 26:45 - "...and saith unto them, Sleep on now."

Morning Prayer

Why start your day with prayer? In the quest for spiritual mastery, we should remember that we are protégés of the great King. We are not self-enlightened. We desperately need divine guidance. Early morning consultation with the Master sets the tone for the entire day. Without time in His presence, we are destined to pursue a carnal path. Morning prayer establishes a spiritual focus that affects the whole day.

Mark 1:35 - "And in the morning, rising up a great while before day, he went out, and departed into a solitary place, and there prayed."

Get What You Need, When You Need It

The disciples went through the corn fields plucking corn on the Sabbath. Pharisees swarmed in like a posse on a crime scene, demanding an explanation from Jesus. He reminded them that David went into the House of God and ate shewbread, which was also unlawful. God has rules, but He sometimes allows exceptions to His rules in extenuating circumstances to meet His people's needs. Never hesitate to ask, no matter what time it is.

Mark 2:27-28 - "The sabbath was made for man, and not man for the sabbath: Therefore the Son of man is Lord also of the sabbath."

Praying for Results

Spiritual Inquiries Have Priority Over Temporal Matters

We are not told why Jesus' mother and brothers stood outside a house while He ministered to a crowd inside. "Thy mother and thy brethren without seek for thee," someone told Jesus. Jesus looked at the crowd and said, "Behold, my mother and my brethren!" Men and women who earnestly seek the LORD are very dear to Him. Your family is important, but saving eternal souls is a higher priority than tending to temporal matters.

Mark 3:31-35 - "For whosoever shall do the will of God, the same is my brother, and my sister, and mother."

Repentance Initiates Interactivity With God

Nowadays, computer software engineers are pressing the envelope to enable men and computers to be more "interactive." That indicates increasing engagement between man and machine - both becoming increasingly dependent upon each other. When Jesus charged His disciples to go out, two by two, to preach a call to repentance, they were compelling men to interact with God. The act of repentance pushes you into the arms of your merciful Creator who yearns to have perpetual communion with you. Repent. Engage. Discover God. Discover your purpose.

Mark 6:12 - "And they went out, and preached that men should repent."

Get Alone And Pray

After Jesus performed the miracle of feeding the multitudes with five loaves and two fishes, He instructed the disciples to get into their ship and go to Bethsaida. He also sent the multitudes away. Then He went ALONE into a mountain to pray. Later that night, He would be walking on the waters of the Sea of Galilee to save His disciples from a storm. You never know what crisis may arise within the next few hours. Do your praying now, while you can.

Mark 6:46 - "When he had sent them away, he departed into a mountain to pray."

If God Refuses, You Can Ask Again

A Syrophenician woman begged Jesus to cast the devil out of her daughter. Jesus said, "Let the children [Jews] first be filled: for it is not meet to take the children's bread, and to cast it unto the dogs [Gentiles]." She argued, "Yet the dogs under the table eat of the children's crumbs." Jesus was impressed. "For this saying go thy way; the devil is gone out of thy daughter." Do not be reluctant with your prayers. Come BOLDLY before His Throne of grace.

Mark 7:30 - "When she was come to her house, she found the devil gone out."

Are You Praying Like The Devil's Advocate?

When Jesus informed the disciples how He must suffer many things and be killed, Peter took Him and began to rebuke Him. Peter acted like too many of us. We dislike pain and suffering, and do not believe it is the will of God. But sometimes it is. To fight against the will of God is to play the devil's advocate. Just hold your peace and let God have His way.

Mark 8:33 - "He rebuked Peter, saying, Get thee behind me, Satan: for thou savourest not the things that be of God, but the things that be of men."

Some Things Require Prayer And Fasting

When Jesus cast out the deaf and dumb spirit from the young boy, the disciples wanted to know why they could not. They asked Him privately, "Why could not we cast him out?" "Prayer and fasting," He said. From the days of Eden, man's appetite has caused him to sin against God. Satan never stops tempting men. Fasting breaks that yoke. It crucifies the appetite and deals a blow to Satan. Prayer calls down the power of God.

Mark 9:29 - "And he said unto them, This kind can come forth by nothing, but by prayer and fasting."

Praying for Results

Sometimes, A Delayed Answer Is Better

Zacharias and Elisabeth prayed for a child for many years, but finally grew old and childless. One day, as Zacharias burned incense in the Temple of the Lord, an angel of the Lord stood by him and said, "Fear not, for thy prayer is heard; and thy wife Elisabeth shall bear thee a son." God always sees the long-term, but we cannot. We think He failed to answer, but divine delay brings a more wonderful fulfillment.

Luke 1:13 - "Thou shalt call his name John. And thou shalt have joy and gladness; and many shall rejoice at his birth."

The Amazing Power And Authority Of The Word

In most cases, Jesus healed and delivered the people with nothing more than His spoken Word. When Jesus spoke, sicknesses, maladies and devils all vanished. The spoken Word of God miraculously penetrates atoms, molecules, living cells, and more. It restructures broken things and purifies evil things, leaving them well, and whole and free. You can have similar results by speaking the Word of God in faith.

Luke 4:36 - "And they were all amazed, and spake among themselves, saying, What a word is this! for with authority and power he commandeth the unclean spirits, and they come out."

Pray For Them Which Despitefully Use You

If you really believe that all things work together for the good to them who love God, and are the called according to His purpose (Romans 8:28), then you have to come to terms with the reality that even your enemies are doing you good. Since that IS the case, you have every reason to pray for your enemies. They are blessing you! My friend, the enemy.

Luke 6:27-28 - "But I say unto you which hear, Love your enemies, do good to them which hate you, Bless them that curse you, and pray for them which despitefully use you."

Praying on Purpose

Prayer Changes the Supplicant

It is easy enough to understand that prayer is a powerful agent for change, but there is a perspective you may not have considered. Prayer changes YOU. It is a side-effect of prayer. The more time you spend in communion with God through prayer, the more you consider His will, His ways and your relationship with Him. Prayer causes you to be introspective, heart-searching and responsive. Surely, prayer changes things. But prayer also changes people who pray.

Luke 9:29 - "And as he prayed, the fashion of his countenance was altered."

Why Sleep Ye? Rise And Pray

Jesus tried to get His three best friends to strengthen themselves in prayer, because He knew what tragic circumstances they would face in the next few hours. But they sensed the impending drama, and they were overwhelmed. After Jesus prayed alone for a while, He checked on them, and "he found them sleeping for sorrow." If the Lord prompts you to pray, there must be a worthwhile reason. Take care never to miss your cue when His Spirit prompts you to pray.

Luke 22:46 - "And said unto them, Why sleep ye? rise and pray, lest ye enter into temptation."

Fasting And Prayer

Not enough people practice consecrated fasting anymore. Fasting means you stop eating for a while. Jesus told the disciples that they failed to cast out certain devils because they had not fasted and prayed first. A carnally-minded person is no match for devils. Fasting and prayer corrects the balance of our two natures. Fasting weakens our flesh and our doubtful carnal mind. Prayer enables God's Spirit to work in believers. Fasting weakens and decreases the old man, and prayer strengthens and gives victory to the new man.

John 3:30 - "He must increase, but I must decrease."

True Worshipers Have Favor With God

"It was that Mary which anointed the Lord with ointment, and wiped his feet with her hair, whose brother Lazarus was sick." When the greatest crisis of your life comes around, it will be comforting to know that you have recently been worshiping the Lord from a sincere heart. True worshipers have favor with God.

John 11:5,11,23 - "Now Jesus loved Martha, and her sister, and Lazarus. ...and after that he saith unto them, Our friend Lazarus sleepeth; but I go, that I may awake him out of sleep. ...Jesus saith unto her, Thy brother shall rise again."

If You Ask Anything In My Name, I Will Do It

Jesus made an extraordinary promise to those who believe that He is God incarnate. "He that believeth on me, the works that I do shall he do also; and greater works than these shall he do; because I go unto my Father." He raised the dead, healed all kinds of diseases, delivered the oppressed, and more. WE can do GREATER? YES! Ask in His name!

John 14:13-14 - "Whatsoever ye shall ask in my name, that will I do, that the Father may be glorified in the Son. If ye shall ask any thing in my name, I will do it."

Afraid Of The Answer? Pray Anyway

Jesus told His disciples that He was going away. Curiously, nobody asked Him where He was going. "None of you asketh me, Whither goest thou?" Apparently, they sensed His impending death and were afraid to discuss it. "Because I have said these things unto you, sorrow hath filled your heart." Later, He confronted their fears. Sometimes, we are afraid to pray because we are afraid of what the answer will be. Pray anyway. It is the right thing to do.

John 16:20 - "Ye shall weep and lament, but the world shall rejoice: and ye shall be sorrowful, but your sorrow shall be turned into joy."

The Hour Of Prayer

The very next day after Pentecost, "Peter and John went up together into the temple at the hour of prayer, being the ninth hour [3PM]." There they met and healed a man who had been born lame. That miracle drew an enormous crowd on Solomon's Porch. That great miracle tends to overshadow the fact that it happened because Peter and John went to pray at "The Hour of Prayer." We would certainly see far more miracles if we daily attended the hour of prayer.

Acts 3:1 - "Now Peter and John went up together into the temple at the hour of prayer."

Prayerful People Are Best Suited For Sacred Divine Destiny

God took special note of Cornelius' prayerfulness and chose him to be the first Gentile to receive the Holy Ghost. An angel told him to send for Simon Peter. "He lodgeth with one Simon a tanner, whose house is by the sea side: he shall tell thee what thou oughtest to do." Cornelius sent servants to Joppa and found Peter in prayer. Prayerful people are prime candidates for sacred divine destiny.

Acts 10:9 - "On the morrow, as they went on their journey, and drew nigh unto the city, Peter went up upon the housetop to pray about the sixth hour."

They Heard Them Speak With Tongues

Cornelius and his family and friends were filled with the Holy Ghost while Peter was preaching to them. Peter's brethren were astonished to see the Holy Ghost fall on the Gentiles, but could not deny it, "for they heard them speak with tongues." Speaking in tongues is the very first evidence. Next? Peter immediately commanded them to be baptized in Jesus' name! THAT is the Apostolic way.

Acts 10:47-48 - "Can any man forbid water, that these should not be baptized, which have received the Holy Ghost as well as we? And he commanded them to be baptized in the name of the Lord."

Praying for Results

If God Speaks To You, Stop Everything And Answer

Paul told the crowd how Jesus arrested him on his murderous rampage against Christians in Damascus. "Suddenly there shone from heaven a great light round about me. And I fell unto the ground, and heard a voice saying unto me, Saul, Saul, why persecutest thou me?" If God speaks to you, it is time to stop everything else and listen. Nothing takes precedence over conversation with God.

Acts 22:8,10 - "I answered, Who art thou, Lord? And he said unto me, I am Jesus of Nazareth, whom thou persecutest. ...And I said, What shall I do, Lord?"

Overcoming The Flesh In Jesus' Name

The flesh and the Spirit are always at war. Our carnal mind is enmity against the Spirit of Christ. Paul confessed exasperation: "The good that I would I do not: but the evil which I would not, that I do. ...O wretched man that I am! who shall deliver me from the body of this death?" Crucify the carnally-minded old man and nurture the Spirit-minded new man by prayer and meditation in the Word, to daily overcome the world, the flesh and the devil, in Jesus' name.

Romans 7:25 - "I thank God through Jesus Christ our Lord."

Call Upon The Name Of The Lord

"If thou shalt confess with thy mouth the Lord Jesus, and shalt believe in thine heart that God hath raised him from the dead, thou shalt be saved. For with the heart man believeth unto righteousness; and with the mouth confession is made unto salvation." That verse CANNOT override Jesus' requirements. "Except a man be born of water and of the Spirit, he cannot enter into the kingdom of God," John 3:5. Both verses must work together. Repent (Luke 13:3). Be baptized (Acts 2:38), calling upon the name of the Lord. Receive the Holy Ghost (John 7:39).

Romans 10:13 - "Whosoever shall call upon the name of the Lord shall be saved."

Pray Continually Without Ceasing

Paul listed over two dozen admonitions to the saints in Rome. At the heart of them came this: "Continuing instant in prayer." Similarly, he charged the Thessalonians to "pray without ceasing," I Thessalonians 5:17. Combining both admonitions, they say of prayer, "Continue... without ceasing." Is that really possible? Can a person actually pray "continually" and "without ceasing"? Try it! EVERY time you find yourself idle, start praying! Pray every possible moment. You will be amazed at the results.

Romans 12:11-12 - "...fervent in spirit; serving the Lord; Rejoicing in hope; patient in tribulation; continuing instant in prayer."

Three Worthy Prayer Requests

In his epistle to the Romans, Paul begged them to join together in prayer for him. He had three special prayer requests. 1. That he would be delivered from those who do not believe. 2. That his ministry would be accepted by the saints. 3. That God would allow him to rejoin them and that they all would be revived. We would do well to pray for the same things, namely: 1. Deliverance from enemies. 2. Success in the ministry according to the will of God. 3. Daily renewal.

Romans 15:32-33 - "That I may... with you be refreshed."

Periodically Separate Yourselves To Fasting And Prayer

In lecturing husbands and wives, Paul instructed both the man and woman to give themselves freely to the other, and not defraud (or withhold from) the other. An exception was made for fasting and prayer, by mutual consent. Prayer and fasting holds a higher priority than even the responsibilities of marriage.

1 Corinthians 7:5-6 - "Defraud ye not one the other, except it be with consent for a time, that ye may give yourselves to fasting and prayer; and come together again, that Satan tempt you not for your incontinency. But I speak this by permission, and not of commandment."

It Is A Shame And Dishonor For A Man To Have Long Hair

Long, uncut hair is called a covering. "If a woman have long hair, ...her hair is given her for a covering." This "covering" of uncut hair typologically represents that the woman has a covering - the man.

1 Corinthians 11:4,7,14 - "Every man praying or prophesying, having his head covered, dishonoureth his head. ...For a man indeed ought not to cover his head, forasmuch as he is the image and glory of God: but the woman is the glory of the man. ...Doth not even nature itself teach you, that, if a man have long hair, it is a shame unto him?"

Her Hair Is Given Her For A Covering When She Prays

God covers Christ. The man covers the woman. She must wear uncut hair, representing that she is covered by the man. "Her hair is given her for a covering." Paul says here that SHORN hair is the SAME as SHAVEN - not covered at all. Paul calls shorn (cut) hair on a woman a SHAME and DISHONORABLE.

1 Corinthians 11:5-6 - "Every woman that prayeth or prophesieth with her head uncovered dishonoureth her head: for that is even all one as if she were shaven. For if the woman be not covered, let her also be shorn: but if it be a shame for a woman to be shorn or shaven, let her be covered."

To Prophesy, Men Must Have Short Hair, And Women Have Uncut Hair

Paul makes it perfectly clear that a man with long-hair, or a woman with shorn (cut) hair brings dishonor and shame into the Church. "Every man praying or prophesying, having his head covered, dishonoureth his head." "But every woman that prayeth or prophesieth with her head uncovered dishonoureth her head: for that is even all one as if she were shaven." DISHONOR. SHAME. Hair is the only subject, not hats or veils. Modern Christian men proudly wear long hair and women proudly cut their hair. How can that not be disobedient to these instructions?

1 Corinthians 11:6-7 - "Let her be covered. For a man indeed ought not to cover his head."

I Would That Ye All Spake With Tongues

From the Day of Pentecost, the early Church was full of the Holy Ghost and spoke in unknown tongues. Praying in tongues was the most rudimentary and fundamental part of being a Christian. That should still be the case today.

1 Corinthians 14:2,4-5,18 - "For he that speaketh in an unknown tongue speaketh not unto men, but unto God: for no man understandeth him; howbeit in the spirit he speaketh mysteries. ...He that speaketh in an unknown tongue edifieth himself; ...I would that ye all spake with tongues. ...I thank my God, I speak with tongues more than ye all."

Pray With The Spirit

Paul prayed in unknown tongues and happily admitted it. He taught that we should pray as best we can understand in our native tongue. But he also acknowledged that sometimes our prayer needs exceed our understanding. That is when we should enter into the Spirit and pray as God gives the utterance. The Spirit makes intercession in ways we cannot know how to do, even though we earnestly groan or cry.

1 Corinthians 14:15 - "What is it then? I will pray with the spirit, and I will pray with the understanding also."

Consulting Prognosticators Instead Of God?

It is appalling to see professing Christians consulting horoscopes and astrological prognosticators. Those things come from superstitious soothsayers, fortune-tellers, and other deceivers. God rules the stars! The stars rule nothing. Seek the Lord.

Galatians 4:8-10 - "When ye knew not God, ye did service unto them which by nature are no gods. But now, after that ye have known God, ...how turn ye again to the weak and beggarly elements, whereunto ye desire again to be in bondage? Ye observe days, and months, and times, and years. I am afraid of you, lest I have bestowed upon you labour in vain."

Trusting Idols, Consulting Witches Ends In Damnation

Among the works of the flesh that Paul listed, are these two: "idolatry, witchcraft." Both are increasingly pervasive in modern society, from Europe, to North America, Africa, and many other hot-beds around the world. Vast segments of society engage in idolatry because of Roman Catholicism, Hinduism, occultism and more. Witchcraft is almost universally accepted in "Harry Potter" books and movies, Disney themes, video gaming, blockbuster movies, voodoo, and so many other forms and venues. God utterly hates those who consult or trust in false gods and unclean spirits. Reject and denounce idols and witchcraft.

Galatians 5:21 - "They which do such things shall not inherit the kingdom of God."

Let Us Not Desire Things We Should Not Desire

Throughout the scriptures, you will find a certain amount of similarity of these keywords: prayer, wish, desire, would God, yearn, covet (good things). You do not always have to speak a prayer, because God knows the desires of your heart. A good desire is a good prayer. An evil desire is an evil wish or an evil prayer. From the heart, the mouth speaks. If you desire wrong things, God knows before you ask, whether or not you ever say it.

Galatians 5:26 - "Let us not be desirous of vain glory, provoking one another, envying one another."

We Have Access By One Spirit

Some people ask, "Who should I pray to? The Father? The Son? The Holy Ghost?" "There is one God, and one mediator between God and men, the man Christ Jesus," 1 Timothy 2:5. It is the MAN, Jesus Christ, who revealed the invisible God to us. How? He is the INCARNATION of God - all the fullness of God is in Christ. He is the Image of the Invisible. When you pray to Jesus, you are speaking to the fullness of God – the Holy Spirit Father, who is embodied in the human Son.

Ephesians 2:18 - "For through him we both have access by one Spirit unto the Father."

Exceeding Abundantly Above All That We Ask Or Think

We are forever underestimating the power of God, to our shame. We go to doctors, lawyers, bankers and other men expecting them to solve our problems. But we neglect to pray for the same solutions because we cannot imagine how God can help. We expect doctors to heal us and lawyers to solve our legal problems, but we cannot imagine how God can do the same. God created the universe. He can CREATE solutions you cannot imagine!

Ephesians 3:20-21 - "Unto him that is able to do exceeding abundantly above all that we ask or think, ...Unto him be glory in the church."

Put Away Evil Speaking, Bitterness, Wrath, Malice

You do not have to pray to be talking to God. God hears even your daily conversations, so if your conversation betrays your prayers, be warned. "Every idle word that men shall speak, they shall give account thereof in the day of judgment," Matthew 12:36. Our future is, in large part, determined by the things we say. Bad attitudes corrupt our speech. Bitterness, wrath, anger, clamor, and malice poison our words. "The mouth of the righteous speaketh wisdom," Psalm 37:30. Sanctified hearts sanctify words.

Ephesians 4:31 - "Let all bitterness, and wrath, and anger, and clamour, and evil speaking, be put away from you, with all malice."

Speaking Psalms And Singing Songs

When the river of the Holy Ghost flows through your life, your entire lifestyle will exude Holy Spirit. You will talk about things of God. You will quote scriptures, recite poems, sing songs about your experiences and relationship with God, and you will be thankful. Have you done a reality check lately? Do you sing and praise God enough?

Ephesians 5:19-20 - "Speaking to yourselves in psalms and hymns and spiritual songs, singing and making melody in your heart to the Lord; Giving thanks always for all things unto God ...in the name of our Lord Jesus Christ."

Praying for Results

I Thank My God For Your Fellowship In The Gospel

So many everyday sayings bear a similar message. "Count your blessings." "Stop and smell the roses." "You don't appreciate what you had until you lose it." "In every thing, give thanks." What on earth is more precious than a good and godly friend? If you have fellowship with even a few saints of God, you possess one of earth's most precious treasures. Every time you think of them, thank God for blessed spiritual brothers and sisters.

Philippians 1:3-5 - "I thank my God upon every remembrance of you, ...For your fellowship in the gospel from the first day until now."

Always Praying For You Because I Have You In My Heart

"Always in every prayer of mine for you all making request with joy, ...because I have you in my heart." Paul, with Timothy, wrote this to the Philippian saints. The secret to being able to pray faithfully and consistently for someone is to have them in your heart. We do not normally pray for those who mean little. But when you love someone, you pray often for them.

Philippians 1:3,7 - "I thank my God upon every remembrance of you, ...it is meet for me to think this of you all, because I have you in my heart."

Pray For Someone To Have A Change Of Heart

How explicit can your prayers be? Does it help to pray about extensive details? How far will God go to do what you ask? Paul prayed for the Philippians to have abounding love, knowledge, and judgment. He prayed that they would "approve things that are excellent." Can we expect that kind of prayer to be effectual? Will God actually cause someone's attitude to improve, or cause them to have better values? YES! Pray for everything you wish.

Philippians 1:10 - "That ye may be sincere and without offence till the day of Christ; Being filled with the fruits of righteousness."

Rejoice In The Lord Alway: And Again I Say, Rejoice

Eleven times in only four chapters, Paul used the words "rejoice" and "rejoicing." Obviously, he sensed that the Philippians were not enjoying the goodness and blessings of God. That is probably true about us, too. Our problems and difficulties weigh heavily on us, and we squander precious time being down-trodden, discouraged or depressed. We must deliberately focus our attention away from our problems and toward God and His countless blessings. Stop wasting your life on negative cogitations. Start celebrating everything that God has done for you.

Philippians 4:4 - "Rejoice in the Lord alway: and again I say, Rejoice."

Do Everything In The Name Of Jesus

"The name of the LORD is a strong tower: the righteous runneth into it, and is safe," Proverbs 18:10. "Neither is there salvation in any other: for there is none other name under heaven given among men, whereby we must be saved," Acts 4:12. Pray in Jesus' name. Preach in Jesus' name. Baptize in Jesus' name. Receive the Holy Ghost in Jesus' name. Heal the sick in Jesus' name. Cast out devils in Jesus' name. Do EVERYTHING in Jesus' name.

Colossians 3:17 - "And whatsoever ye do in word or deed, do all in the name of the Lord Jesus."

Always Making Mention Of You In Our Prayers

Before you ever hesitate to pray the second, or third, or fourth time for a thing, just remember that the Bible is full of repeated prayers. I suspect that there are more prayers in the Bible that occurred more than once, than otherwise. Virtually every man of God was known to ask God more than once for a thing. There are many things and many people who deserve to be prayed for daily.

1 Thessalonians 1:1-2 - "Unto the church of the Thessalonians... We give thanks to God always for you all, making mention of you in our prayers."

How Shall We Escape If We Neglect So Great Salvation?

If you want to be saved, you must initiate the redemptive process, which begins by no other means than repentance. Unless and until you have confessed your sins before God and asked His forgiveness, you cannot be saved. That is the very first step. If you neglect repentance, there will be no escape. The New Birth requires Death, Burial, and Resurrection: Repentance, Water Baptism, and Spirit Baptism.

Hebrews 2:3 - "How shall we escape, if we neglect so great salvation; which at the first began to be spoken by the Lord, and was confirmed unto us by them that heard him?"

Strong Crying And Tears

Sometimes, God ordains you to a particular trial, and no amount of prayer will change that fact (i.e., Job, Noah, Joseph, Jesus). In Gethsemane, Jesus prayed "with strong crying and tears," saying, "Father, if it be possible, let this cup pass from me: nevertheless not as I will, but as thou wilt," Matthew 26:39. You must learn to "count it not strange concerning your fiery trial," 1 Peter 4:12.

Hebrews 5:7-8 - "When he had offered up prayers and supplications with strong crying and tears ...yet learned he obedience by the things which he suffered."

Put Your Sacrifice On The Altar With Faith In God

The Spirit of God tugs at your heart, telling you to give up something very dear on an altar of sacrifice. God called Abraham to offer his only son, Isaac. By faith, Abraham gave God what He wanted. As you obey, believe that the outcome will be good. It will be.

Hebrews 11:17-19 - "He that had received the promises offered up his only begotten son, Of whom it was said, That in Isaac shall thy seed be called: Accounting that God was able to raise him up, even from the dead; from whence also he received him in a figure."

Doubtful Prayers

Every request we make of God has to be made with genuine expectation that He will grant it. Prayer without faith is little more than a pointless monologue. If you want something from God, believe He will give it or don't bother asking. God is infinitely capable and abundantly willing to grant our petitions.

James 1:6-7 - "...ask in faith, nothing wavering. For he that wavereth is like a wave of the sea driven with the wind and tossed. For let not that man think that he shall receive any thing of the Lord."

Stop Laughing. Start Weeping.

Stop laughing and get serious about making prayerful intercession for those who are bound by sin and Satan. Why do we require constant comedy and entertainment? Why must everything be funny? The ancients showed us that it is WEEPING between the porch and the altar that leads to revival. God blesses those who "sigh and cry" for the abominations of the people, (See Ezekiel 9:4).

James 4:9-10 - "Be afflicted, and mourn, and weep: let your laughter be turned to mourning, and your joy to heaviness. Humble yourselves in the sight of the Lord, and he shall lift you up."

The Prayer Of Faith

Do you know what the prayer of faith is? It certainly is NOT doubting prayer! When, from your heart of hearts, you genuinely cast your cares upon Him, expecting His intervention, all the healing balm of Heaven comes to save and heal. The prayer of faith elicits amazing responses from God. Every time Jesus discerned great faith in someone, a great miracle occurred. Nothing excites Him more. Pray the prayer of faith.

James 5:15 - "The prayer of faith shall save the sick, and the Lord shall raise him up; and if he have committed sins, they shall be forgiven him."

Effectual Fervent Prayer

Effective prayer produces the intended result. So how does it work? A hammer rarely drives a nail in a single blow. We must strike at the need again and again until prayer works its miracle. The Syrophenician woman asked Jesus to heal her daughter. Because His ministry was to Israel, and she was a Gentile, He refused her request. But she argued with God and won! She impressed Him with her great faith, so He healed her daughter. Strike another blow with prayer!

James 5:16 - "The effectual fervent prayer of a righteous man availeth much."

Speaking In Tongues Shows That He Is In Us

Jesus commanded His disciples to receive the Holy Ghost (John 20:22). He said, "Ye shall receive power, after that the Holy Ghost is come upon you," Acts 1:8. In Acts 2:4, "they were all filled with the Holy Ghost, and began to speak with other tongues, as the Spirit gave them utterance." "On the Gentiles also was poured out the gift of the Holy Ghost. For they heard them speak with tongues," Acts 10:45-46. The Holy Ghost baptism is Christ in you.

1 John 4:13 - "Hereby know we that we dwell in him, and he in us, because he hath given us of his Spirit."

Building Up Yourselves, Praying In The Holy Ghost

Jesus' Apostles "told you there should be mockers in the last time, who should walk after their own ungodly lusts. These be they who separate themselves, sensual, having not the Spirit." These days, mockers lay siege upon the Church. Scoffers and mockers with foaming rabid atheism blaspheme God, rip the Bible to shreds, and castigate Christians and ministers of the Gospel. But true believers can survive the onslaught, building up themselves by praying in the Holy Ghost. Yes. Speaking in tongues.

Jude 1:20 - "But ye, beloved, building up yourselves on your most holy faith, praying in the Holy Ghost."

He That Hath An Ear, Hear What The Spirit Is Saying

Every one of the seven Churches of Asia received this identical message from the Lord: "He that hath an ear, let him hear what the Spirit saith unto the churches." At first glance, this seems like such an elementary instruction. But in a world of incessant distractions, when televisions, computers and countless other devices scream for our attention, the call of God is being drowned out. You have an ear. Do you hear the voice of God speaking to you? Be quiet. Be prayerful. Listen carefully. It is a still, small voice.

Revelation 2:7,11,17,29; 3:6,13,22 - "He that hath an ear, let him hear what the Spirit saith unto the churches."

I Wept Much Because No Man Was Worthy

In Heaven, a great, mysterious Book sealed with Seven Seals was waiting to be opened. No man knew its contents. A strong angel called, "Who is worthy to open the book, and to loose the seals thereof?" No man in Heaven or earth was worthy to even look upon it. John wept profusely. Where is the man or woman who will weep today for the Book of God to be opened to this generation? Will you?

Revelation 5:4 - "And I wept much, because no man was found worthy to open and to read the book, neither to look thereon."

The Angel Offers Incense With Our Prayers

Why is it significant that the prayers of the saints ascend before God with the smoke of the incense? May I speculate that our prayers do not always smell savory to God? We ask so many things amiss. We pray for things that are contrary to His will. Our prayers are often misguided, or faithless, or prayed with wrong intentions. Could that possibly be why the angel perpetually offers incense with our prayers?

Revelation 8:4 - "And the smoke of the incense, which came with the prayers of the saints, ascended up before God out of the angel's hand."

Praying for Results

"What should we think of a petitioner, if,
while having an audience with a prince,
he should be playing with a feather or catching a fly?

Continuance and perseverance are intended in the expression of our text.
David did not cry once, and then relapse into silence;
his holy clamour was continued
till it brought down the blessing.

Prayer must not be our chance work,
but our daily business, our habit and vocation.
As artists give themselves to their models,
and poets to their classical pursuits,
so must we addict ourselves to prayer.

We must be immersed in prayer as in our element,
and so pray without ceasing.
Lord, teach us so to pray that we may be
more and more prevalent in supplication."
Charles Spurgeon
1834-1892

The last word…

Jesus prayed specifically for you and me while He was on earth.

"Neither pray I for these alone,
but for **them also which shall believe on me through their word**."
John 17:20

Praying for Results

Dear Friend,

For almost six years, I worked feverishly, researching and writing in excess of 50 hours every week to produce, first of all, my major life-work, a 1438-page Bible Commentary entitled **MY DAILY BIBLE COMPANION.**

It is the compilation of over 4,800 100-word mini-Bible lessons, written for **"TODAY'S BIBLE STUDY,"** most of which have already been read in every nation on earth. My subscribers are in 215 nations at this writing. Having written step-by-step, point-by-point Bible lessons from Genesis to Revelation, virtually every topic in the Bible has been dealt with. I have already received literally thousands of testimonial letters from around the world expressing thanks and appreciation for these daily lessons. Letters continue to arrive daily. I hope and pray that you will enjoy them, too.

Because it is quite comprehensive in going point-by-point through the entire Bible, it became necessary to publish the work in two volumes.

Volume 1 contains lessons from the **Old Testament**.

Volume 2 contains lessons from the **New Testament**.

The **Kindle e-Book** edition contains the **entire book in ONE volume**.

I urge you to get **MY DAILY BIBLE COMPANION**. You won't be sorry.

In addition, I just released, **PRAYING ON PURPOSE, PRAYING FOR RESULTS**, one of the most powerful and inspirational books on PRAYER that you will ever read. **LONG WINDING ROAD, A Very Personal Story** is also now available.

Several more books are soon to follow, including **GREATEST DOCTRINES, DANIEL, HOW THE WORLD WILL END**, and at least three other inspirational books in the coming year or so.

Thank you for purchasing this book. I pray that God will bless the teaching of His Word to you. Please visit my website (**kenraggio.com**) and enjoy the vast FREE Bible resources that you will find there.

God bless you.
Sincerely,

Ken Raggio

Over 4,800 Point-by-Point Mini-Lessons through the entire Bible!

KEEP THIS AWESOME 1200+ PAGE BOOK BY YOUR FAVORITE
EASY CHAIR, OR ON YOUR NIGHTSTAND.

It is a unique Daily Reader that is packed with
amazing Genesis-to-Revelation Bible lessons.

Read as many as you want each day: 2, 3, 4 or more.
Presented in easily understandable 100-Word topics
in four general categories:

- **PRAYER**   **Illustrations, Examples, Lessons about Prayer**
- **PRINCIPALS**   **People, Places and Things in the Bible**
- **PRINCIPLES**   **Virtues, Vices, Values in the Bible, Great Precepts**
- **PROPHECIES**   **1200+ Prophecies (Fulfilled and Unfulfilled) Explained**

Order Vol. 1 Old Testament – 650 pgs: **https://www.createspace.com/3839857**
Order Vol. 2 New Testament – 788 pgs: **https://www.createspace.com/3856644**

Order KINDLE e-Book (Entire Bible): **http://amzn.com/** Search "Ken Raggio"

Coming soon in PRINT & Amazon KINDLE

HOW THE WORLD WILL END – What The Bible Says

Here is God's Revealed Plan for our future!

Bible Prophecy foretells key major, even epic events all the way to Armageddon, the Millennial Kingdom of Jesus Christ, and beyond - to the eternal Kingdom of God. This book covers so much exciting material that most people have never seen, heard or studied. It is a must-read - showing absolutely amazing revelations of many rarely discussed events to come. You will never again think of the future in the same terms.

This is one of the most comprehensive books on Last Days Prophecies you will find anywhere. In-depth studies of Daniel, Revelation, and scores of other major prophecies.

TO ORDER, VISIT http://kenraggio.com

Coming soon in PRINT & Amazon KINDLE

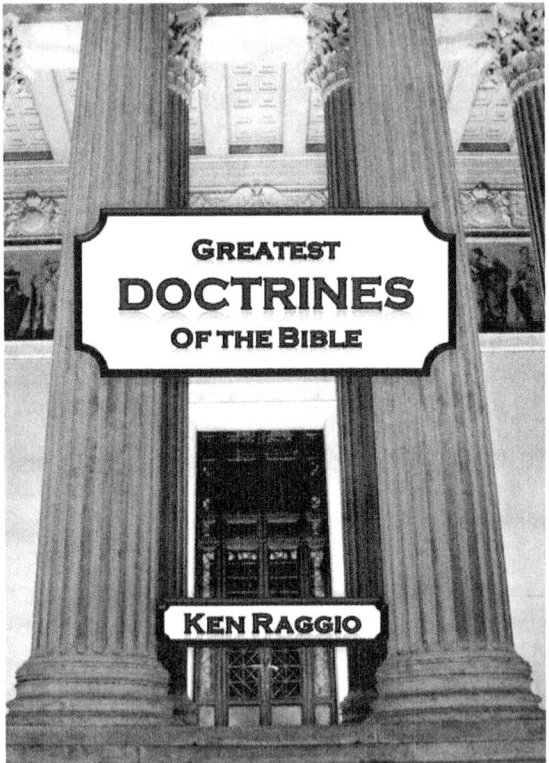

GREATEST DOCTRINES OF THE BIBLE

This is not a theological textbook, but an electrifying look at some of the most primordial of all divine precepts – an extraordinary, provocative look at the most fundamental, foundational and universal truths of the Bible. For some, it will be a revelation of never-before-seen glories of God, as well as an awesome faith builder!

Christianity is suffering the blight of multitudes of false teachers, false preachers, charlatans, pseudo-Christians and worse. Ken Raggio will take you back to the original New Testament doctrines that the Apostles fervently believed and preached. You will sense the authenticity of these great and core doctrines of the Early Church – the faith that was once delivered to the saints. You need this book. Every believer needs it.

TO ORDER, VISIT **http://kenraggio.com**

Coming soon in PRINT & Amazon KINDLE

TREASURES OF DARKNESS

How to see the glory of God in the darkest trials of your life.

This book was born in the furnace of a great personal trial, and is nothing short of a revelation of how God works behind the scenes during your greatest difficulties. God wants you to be able to see clearly in the dark. This book is a fascinating journey into the world of the Spirit, and will definitely enhance your night vision, and show you how to see the Treasures of Darkness!

Chapters include:

Blinded By The Light | God Plays Hide-And-Seek | Let There Be Light | Dark Matter | String Theories and Spin | and much, much more.

TO ORDER, VISIT http://kenraggio.com

Coming soon in PRINT & Amazon Kindle

A DIVINELY ORDERED LIFE

What appears to be chaos in the eyes of a true Christian is quite the opposite in the eyes of God. It is possible to analyze your own situation intellectually without ever understanding how things will ever work out.

But this book explores a broad spectrum of Biblical analogies and metaphors that demonstrate the exact processes by which God orders your life, even when it seems like everything is falling apart.

The steps of a man are ordered by the Lord. This book will help you identify, understand and appreciate many of the principles that God uses to meticulously order your Divine Destiny.

TO ORDER, VISIT http://kenraggio.com

Coming soon in PRINT & Amazon KINDLE

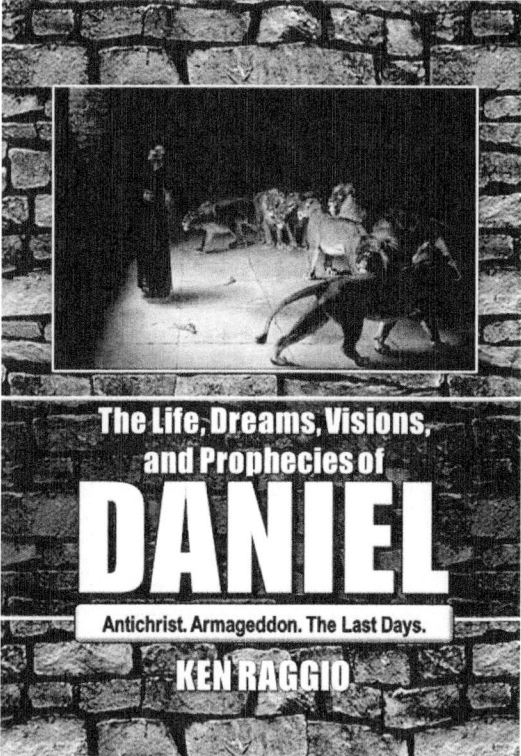

THE LIFE, DREAMS, VISIONS AND PROPHECIES OF DANIEL

A rich, in-depth look at the life and prophetic essence of the prophet Daniel. It includes a close-up character study of Daniel's life, followed by a point-by-point examination of each dream, vision and prophecy.

Includes MAJOR Last-Days Prophecies you need to understand.

Nebuchadnezzar's Image | The Four Beasts Of Daniel | The Iron and Clay Feet and the Four-Headed Leopard | Daniel's Dreadful Beast | Daniel's Seventy Weeks Prophecy | Daniel Chapter 11 (Revelation of the coming Man of Sin), and much more. This is a very powerful book.

TO ORDER, VISIT http://kenraggio.com

Now Available in PRINT $14.99 - also in KINDLE e-Book

LONG WINDING ROAD

...a very personal story about forty years in the ministry.

Chapters Include:

The Groves | The Call | Facing the Music | Apprenticeship | The Work of an Evangelist | A Word, A Dream, A Miracle | Planting A Church | A Major Paradigm Shift | Which Way From Here? | Catch the Spirit of Love | Holy Ghost or Nothing | Crash and Burn | Separation Time | and more…

TO ORDER IN PRINT, VISIT: https://www.createspace.com/3862073

TO ORDER KINDLE e-Book: Visit http://amzn.com/ Search "Ken Raggio"

Praying on Purpose

"FRIEND" ME on FACEBOOK!

Read my Daily Inspirational Posts!

ALSO…

JOIN the KEN RAGGIO FACEBOOK "FANPAGE"

Ken Raggio – Bible Resources – Lessons – Sermons - Prophecy

Read the daily PROPHECY MINI-LESSONS on my FB Fanpage!

Click "LIKE" at this site.

Praying for Results

"FOLLOW ME" on TWITTER!

Daily Power Quotes, Mini-Lessons, and Prophecy Updates

Twitter ID:

http://twitter.com/kenraggiocom

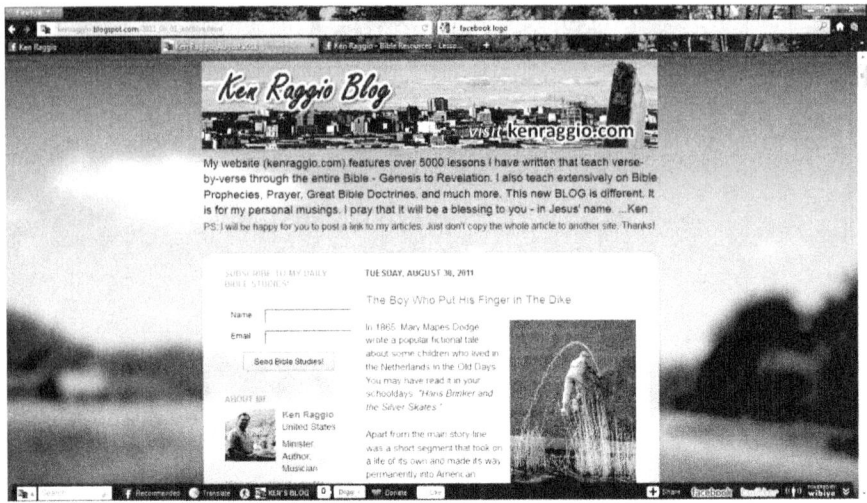

VISIT MY BLOG!

Personal Musings On God, Religion, and Daily Christian Living

kenraggio.blogspot.com

SUBSCRIBE to "Today's Bible Study"
FREE! - BY E-MAIL

Four 100-Word Mini-Bible Lessons Each Day in your Email Box
Subscribe here: kenraggio.com

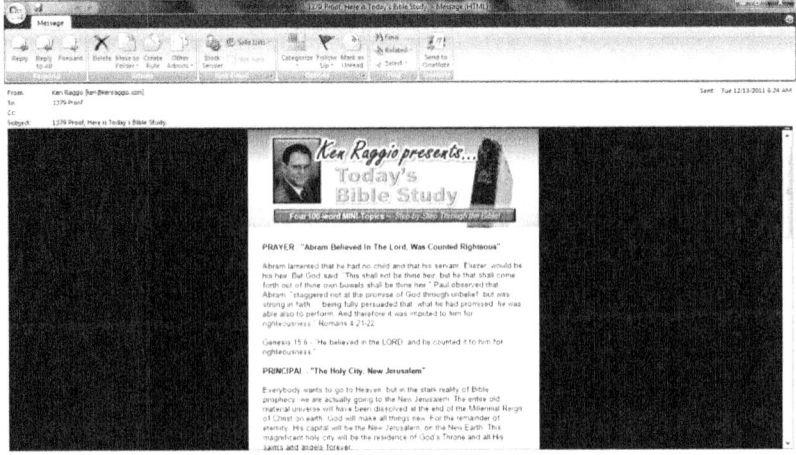

VISIT KENRAGGIO.COM

Thousands of pages of

Bible Studies – Sermons – Lessons – Prophecy Articles

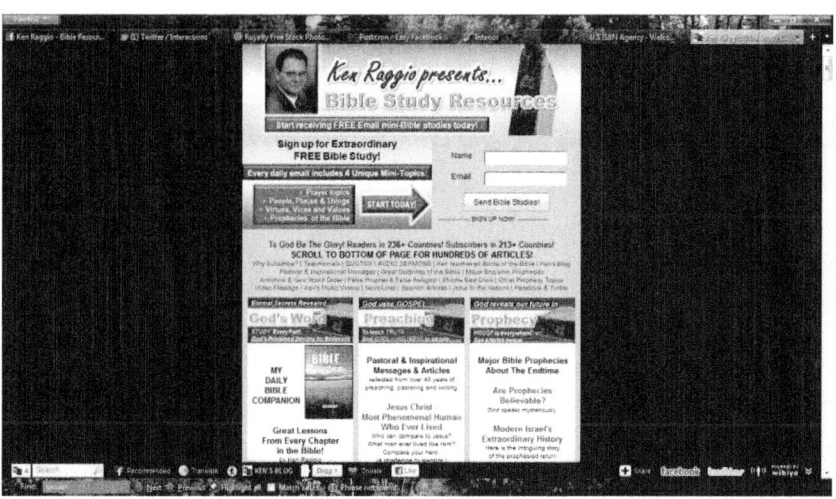

ABOUT THE AUTHOR

A Pentecostal minister since 1966, Ken Raggio has been a Pastor, Evangelist, Singer, Songwriter, Musician, Broadcaster, Journalist, Editor and Author. Ken has maintained a major Internet presence since 1996 at kenraggio.com and has many thousands of subscribers in 215 nations to "Today's Bible Study," a daily email containing four 100-word mini-Bible-lessons. He is now focused on writing and producing video teaching series.

Printed in Great Britain
by Amazon